Irish Preaching, 700-1700

IRISH PREACHING
700-1700

Alan J. Fletcher and Raymond Gillespie
EDITORS

FOUR COURTS PRESS

Set in 10.5 on 12.5 point Ehrhardt for
FOUR COURTS PRESS LTD
Fumbally Lane, Dublin 8, Ireland
e-mail: info@four-courts-press.ie
http://www.four-courts-press.ie
and in North America for
FOUR COURTS PRESS
c/o ISBS, 5804 N.E. Hassalo Street, Portland, OR 97213.

© the various authors 2001

A catalogue record for this title
is available from the British Library.

ISBN 1–85182–550–9

All rights reserved. No part of this publication
may be reproduced, stored in or introduced into
a retrieval system, or transmitted, in any form or by
any means (electronic, mechanical, photocopying,
recording or otherwise), without the prior
written permission of both the copyright
owner and publisher of this book.

Printed in Great Britain
by MPG Books, Bodmin, Cornwall.

Contents

7
PREFACE

9
LIST OF CONTRIBUTORS

11
INTRODUCTION

18
Irish preaching before the end of the ninth century:
assessing the extent of our evidence
Thomas O'Loughlin

40
Preaching in medieval Ireland: the Irish tradition
Brian Murdoch

56
Preaching in late-medieval Ireland: the English and the Latin tradition
Alan J. Fletcher

81
Preaching in late-medieval Ireland: the Franciscan contribution
Colmán N. Ó Clabaigh, OSB

94
The vocacyon of Johan Bale (1553): a retrospective sermon from Ireland
J.-A. George

108
'Zeal for God and for souls': Counter-Reformation
preaching in early seventeenth-century Ireland
Bernadette Cunningham

127
The reformed preacher: Irish Protestant preaching, 1660–1700
Raymond Gillespie

145
INDEX

153
INDEX OF MANUSCRIPTS

Illustrations

59
Figure 1: T.C.D., MS 677, p. 178.

79
Figure 2: The moralised hand (T.C.D., MS 677, p. 252).

96
Figure 3: Title page from *The vocacyon of Johan Bale* ([Wesel], 1553).

115
Figure 4: The Counter-Reformation preacher (from Anthony Gearnon, *Parrathas an anma* [Louvain, 1645], p. 335).

Preface

Books, like people, have their own histories and this one is no exception. It is not the result of a conference or a programmatic approach to the study of preaching in Ireland. Rather it grew out of the happy conjunction of the interests of the contributors and it has all the strengths and weaknesses inherent in such a project. Despite the fact that from the earliest days of Christianity preaching has been one of the main ways of conveying the faith, its study has been largely neglected in the Irish context. Such studies as there have been have dealt with sermon texts as items of linguistic curiosity or have tended to be confined to rather specialised areas. This book is an attempt to draw together some of the evidence of preaching activity in Ireland across linguistic and confessional divisions. As befits an initial exploration of a large subject this is a short work which can only begin to examine the potential offered by the study of preaching but we have been cognisant of the words of the Old Testament preacher that 'a fool's voice is known by multitude of words' (Ecclesiastes 5:3). Even this preliminary exploration would not have been possible without the co-operation of a number of people. Most important in this regard are the contributors who have borne with remarkable good grace the trials of editorial foibles and waited patiently for the appearance of this work. The book itself would never have appeared without a generous grant from the National University of Ireland Publication Fund and the enthusiasm of Michael Adams and all those at Four Courts Press.

A.J.F.
R.G.

Contributors

Bernadette Cunningham is deputy Librarian in the Royal Irish Academy. Her book on *The world of Geoffrey Keating: history, myth and religion in seventeenth-century Ireland* was published in 2000.

Alan J. Fletcher lectures in the Department of Old and Middle English, University College, Dublin. His study of performance in Ireland before 1650, *Drama, performance, and polity in pre-Cromwellian Ireland*, was published in 2000.

Jodi-Anne George lectures in the Department of English in the University of Dundee. She is the author of a recent book on *The Canterbury Tales* of Geoffrey Chaucer.

Raymond Gillespie teaches in the Department of Modern History, NUI Maynooth. He has written extensively on social and religious change in early modern Ireland including *Devoted people: religion and belief in early modern Ireland* (Manchester, 1997).

Brian Murdoch is Professor of German in the University of Stirling. He has published widely on aspects of Celtic literature, including a recent book on the early literature and drama of Cornwall.

Colmán Ó Clabaigh OSB is a monk of Glenstal Abbey. His study of the Observantine reform in fifteenth-century Ireland, based on his doctoral thesis in NUI Galway, will be published in 2001.

Thomas O'Loughlin teaches in the Department of Theology and Religious Studies, University of Wales, Lampeter. He has written widely on the early Irish church and its theology, most recently in his book *Celtic theology: humanity, world and God in early Irish writers* (London, 2000).

Introduction

Students of history and of literature have seldom been drawn to sermons or been known to take them seriously. For historians, sermons have often been regarded as stock expressions, and tedious ones, of the piety of their age, short on the kind of historically pertinent detail that otherwise might justify their study and make them interesting. This view is understandable, though one suspects that it has proceeded more often from an assumption of what sermons are likely to contain than from much actual first-hand acquaintance with their content. Students of literature, similarly, have been inclined to dismiss sermons, if for rather different reasons. Before a sermon might hope to catch a littérateur's attention, it had first to sparkle with rhetorical fireworks. In literary studies, interest shown in sermons such as John Donne's tour de force, 'Death's duel', to cite one salient example, has been the conspicuous exception to prove the rule – necessarily, since bravura performances like those that the witty dean of St Paul's managed are few and far between. While it is true that sermons from any period are rarely devoid of artifice, as some of the chapters of this book will illustrate, the primary aim of preaching is to inform, exhort and move its hearers to Christian living. Artifice might well assist each of these ends, but it was not meant to stand in for them or be an end in itself. Whenever it was, the sermon's moral intent was in danger of collapsing under the weight of its rhetorical cleverness. So for historians and literary critics alike, as measured by the lack of secondary analytical work on the subject the study of sermons, has tended to remain with Cinderella in the ashes.

To sketch the state of sermon studies in these terms, however, is also to sketch a receding scholarly landscape. This is how things looked in the recent past. Seismic shifts in the institutional practice of both historiography and literary criticism have since made the traditional boundaries between these (and other) disciplines seem increasingly tenuous. The shock waves resulting from the academic re-think have also taken sermon studies in their wake. Literary critics have now begun applying various subtle strategies for interpreting and interrogating texts to the sorts of document that their predecessors of less than a generation ago would have shunned. Equally, some historians have started taking more account of imaginative works of literature that not so very long ago would have been ruled out as reliable quarries of forensic historical evidence. Another important consequence of the general procedural and disciplinary shake-up has been to place at the centre of attention things once viewed as peripheral. Former margins have now become fashionable sites for exploration. In this climate, sermons need no longer expect to languish quite as they did a few years ago. Their study is currently being revisited and redefined.[1]

It therefore seems timely to ventilate the study of preaching in Ireland, hence this book, offered as a prolegomenon to further research. Anyone who already has some knowledge of the subject will know that several 'microstudies' have been written, especially of this preaching in its earliest phases, but the late medieval and early modern periods have been largely ignored. Certainly, no attempt has been made to track developments in preaching throughout the period which this book spans, that is, from approximately 700 to 1700, nor has any general survey been undertaken of the traces that this period of preaching in Ireland has left behind.[2]

The fact alone that during this period preaching never ceased to be a potent cultural force flags its importance as an object of study. At the start of our chronology, preaching was instrumental in evangelizing Ireland. Thereafter, it continued to help consolidate the confessional and social identity of individuals and groups. Although the crucial role played by preaching in the original evangelization cannot be overemphasized, surprisingly few specimens of sermons composed in Ireland between the early and the late medieval period are to be found (though doubtless future research will add further items). This is a burden under which each of the first three chapters of this book labours. There are various reasons why the dearth should have come about, in addition to the obvious one that the older and the more thumbed a sermon manuscript became, the less likely would be its chances of survival. Some sermon manuscripts were no doubt simply read to bits; others would have been discarded as times and requirements changed. To be sure, neglect of preaching would also necessarily have contributed to the relative manuscript scarcity: a church's failure to supply baptism, communion, Mass, prayer for the dead, and *preaching*, declared the Old Irish law text *Bretha Nemed toísech*, would redound to its disgrace.[3] The fact that this and other secular law texts like *Córus Béscnai*, as well as Church law as codified, for example, in the *Ríagal Phátraic*, all stressed the necessity of preaching, suggests that sometimes preaching was going by default.[4] But a

---

1 For a recent outstanding example of a history of medieval English preaching written by a scholar whose initial training was in literary studies, see H.L. Spencer, *English preaching in the late middle ages* (Oxford, 1993). Also, Larissa Taylor, *Soldiers of Christ* (Oxford, 1992). 2 This book takes preliminary steps; a comprehensive and systematic handlist of primary sources remains a desideratum. 3 D.A. Binchy (ed.), *Corpus Iuris Hibernici* (6 vols, Dublin, 1978), vi, p. 2211, lines 27-8: 'Cadead mifolai daortha eclasa? Ní hannsa: beth gan bathais, cin comna, cen oifrenn, cin imond anma, *cin precept* ...'. 4 The law texts *Córus Béscnai* and *Bretha Nemed toísech* belong to the earlier part of the Old Irish period (either to the seventh or eighth centuries) and the *Ríagal Phátraic* to the eighth century. For a general introduction to *Córus Béscnai*, *Bretha Nemed toísech* and the laws generally, see F. Kelly, *A guide to early Irish law* (Dublin, 1988), and for the *Ríagal Phátraic*, see J.G. O'Keeffe, 'The rule of Patrick' in *Ériu* i (1904), pp 216-24.

more important explanation of the relative scarcity of manuscripts than either the vagaries of time or preaching's neglect is probably the fact that, because during the Middle Ages the oral was as formative of culture as the literary, a preacher with a well stocked brain may simply not have needed to commit his sermon to parchment at all, nor need he have relied on a written copy of it when preaching. After all, since preaching was an oral art, its practice was supported by the memory techniques that oral culture had evolved. Committal of preachable matter to memory may be another reason why the number of manuscripts on which the first three chapters of this book are able to focus is not large.

In the first essay, Thomas O'Loughlin faces an additional difficulty: since most of the early medieval texts that he is concerned with are in Latin, the *lingua franca* of medieval Europe, he has to try to establish which ones originated in Ireland. Coming at the start of this book, it also falls to him to address the equally radical question of what actually constitutes a sermon, since 'sermon' is not always a self-evident category. To clinch a text's use in preaching, he relies on stylistic criteria similar to those also invoked in Brian Murdoch's and Alan Fletcher's essays. The putative sermon text may feature direct forms of address to an audience; may assume in the way it is written that it is being read to an audience; or may presuppose some particular liturgical moment as the occasion of its delivery. As for the authors of early sermons originating in Ireland, only two, Columbanus and Eriugena, are known by name before the end of the ninth century. Moreover, since their work seems to have been destined for specialized audiences, it is by the same token less representative of the kind of preaching that one imagines was more commonly available to the laity. Before we can hope to distinguish what texts may have served the purposes of more ordinary preaching, we have first to recognize and then banish a modern prejudice. A nationalist politics has been active in certain studies of early preaching in Ireland. It betrays itself in an overeagerness to claim Irish paternity for some early medieval Latin sermons on insufficiently secure grounds. As yet, the nearest we can come to glimpsing ordinary preaching in Ireland in the early period is in some of the sermons of the homiliary known as 'In nomine Dei summi'. To say 'glimpsing' is appropriate because, while their substance may originally have been delivered in the vernacular, it was nevertheless preserved in Latin and therefore at a linguistic and literary remove from the words actually preached. Characteristic of the style of preaching that features in 'In nomine Dei summi' is a formulation of the Christian faith as straightforward sets of injunctions and instructions. Early medieval preaching in Ireland was, moreover, 'neither trail-blazing nor backwaterish', but in touch with a pan-European preaching tradition.

Of course, once sermons start appearing in Irish, the answers to certain questions, like that of where they originated, are virtually assured. Brian

Murdoch's sources, in contrast to those considered by O'Loughlin, are mainly in Irish, and the bulk dates from the High Middle Ages. Here, the Middle Irish homilies of the manuscript known as the *Leabhar Breac* constitute Murdoch's principal corpus. Some feed off earlier texts (an unusual Irish example of *ad status* preaching, the *Leabhar Breac*'s *sermo ad reges*, for instance, recruits the famous, mid-seventh century Hiberno-Latin tract *De duodecim abusivis seculi*). Many favour eschatological themes, a preoccupation similarly shared by some contemporary (and earlier) sermons recorded in Latin. Also conspicuous is the relatively workmanlike cobbling to which the compilers of the sermons in the *Leabhar Breac* subjected their source texts in the process of converting them to sermon use. Not only do some sermon compilers show an appetite for texts of other genres (like the *De duodecim abusivis seculi* tract), they also bite off more than they can chew: for example, Irish saints lives may have been filleted to provide some of the *Leabhar Breac*'s Sanctorale preaching but have not been fully digested and remain with traces of the genre of their origin clinging to them.

By the time of the late Middle Ages in Ireland, the period with which Alan Fletcher's essay deals, rules about what constituted good sermon construction were being widely observed, both in theory and in practice. Familiar late medieval rules of sermon form structure many of the sermons circulating in late medieval Ireland, especially sermons in English and in Latin. Several sermons in these languages were imported. In fact, relatively little indigenous English and Latin sermon writing during this period is identifiable and, as in the earlier medieval period so also now in the later, there was no evident reluctance to use material of British and Continental origin. Late medieval Ireland was not disconnected from Europe in its preaching any more than it was in many other areas of cultural endeavour, and this predictably, given that the four international Orders of friars, soon after their founding in the thirteenth century, took up Irish residence.

In fact, so outstanding was the Franciscan contribution to preaching that it has merited a chapter to itself. Colmán Ó Clabaigh's study of the Franciscan preaching missions in Ireland also bridges the late medieval and early modern periods, and begins to introduce far more names and personalities than were encountered in the first three chapters. It is fair to say that, from a modern vantage point, medieval preaching in Ireland is usually faceless. In this regard, the contrast as we move from the late medieval to the early modern periods could hardly be crisper. Personalities begin to register in the early modern period with greater frequency, as the anonymity characteristic of earlier centuries is increasingly replaced by named individuals and by the observation of their personal idiosyncracies. Thus it has been possible in this period to speak of the sermon not only as a text but as a performance. Formal rhetorical training, gesture and intonation, become effectively clear for the first time and help us to gauge the reaction of listeners to preachers.

In addition, more plentiful evidence, some of which is qualitatively different from anything going before, now begins to make the writing of a different kind of history possible.

The advent of the Reformation gave considerable impetus to preaching both as a way of communicating the ideas of reform and as a propaganda machine.[5] The rise of printing, rather than reducing the importance of the oral transmission of ideas, complemented it. However the rise of printing did have the effect of blurring genres. By the sixteenth century, where 'sermon' ends and other genres begin is revealed as an interestingly complex question. A striking personality on the preaching scene at this time was John Bale, short-tenured bishop of Ossory from 1552 to 1553. As J.-A. George shows, Bale was more than happy to recycle his very life experiences as preachable matter; indeed, he seems to have made this habit a point of principle. The sheer amount of self-involvement and the industry of self-fashioning that show in his 1553 work, *The vocacyon of Johan Bale to the bishoprick of Ossorie in Irelande*, are precisely what distinguish it from most other pre-Reformation religious writing. Granted, George rightly draws attention to moments of continuity and comparison between *The book of Margery Kempe*, a spiritual biography of the fifteenth century, and *The vocacyon*. Yet distinctive of *The vocacyon* is the way in which Bale turned himself into his own sermon text, as it were, and his life narrative into a novel sort of *exemplum* from which (Protestant) morals could be derived and offered to a congregation of readers. Kempe likewise may have sought to negotiate an identity for herself in her *Book*, but not ostensibly in terms of preaching. On the contrary, as a good Catholic woman, she knew that orthodoxy forbade her that particular vocation: 'I preche not, ser, I come in no pulpytt', she asserted to one of her detractors.[6] *The vocacyon* makes it clear both implicitly and explicitly that Bale held preaching in the highest esteem. While his preaching proper in Ireland does not survive, *The vocacyon* reports the reformed gist of some of it: for example, he announced to Kilkenny congregations (which, for the most part, seem either to have been unreceptive or downright hostile), that priests should marry, not fornicate and sodomise. But as intimated, *The vocacyon* refracts preaching in a more sophisticated guise both in the manner of its conception and composition. The degree to which Bale had taken to heart the evangelical imperative to preach is also gauged by the way preaching concerns spill over into other written endeavours apart from *The vocacyon*. His plays, some of which had their first known airing in Kilkenny, often employ formulas of address characteristic of sermon style; indeed,

---

5 Robert Scribner, 'Preachers and people in the German towns', reprinted in his *Popular culture and popular movements in Reformation Germany* (London, 1987), pp 123-44. 6 S.B. Meech and H.E. Allen (eds), *The book of Margery Kempe* (Early English Text Society, OS 212, Oxford, 1940; rept 1961), p. 126, lines 18-19.

playwriting seems for Bale to have been a means whereby the concerns of the pulpit could be redimensioned on the stage.[7]

If preaching, over and above the sacred office that it was for his medieval predecessors, was also now for Bale the lodestar around which his very acts of self-representation and his dramas might be oriented, then the preaching of the counter-reformers, by contrast, that Bernadette Cunningham studies in her essay, was less self-conscious. This it was to the extent that it reconnected, doubtless in a pointedly revivalist way, with the faceless, universal spirit of medieval Catholicism. The indebtedness of Counter-Reformation preaching to the traditions and values that medieval preaching cherished is repeatedly apparent in the seventeenth century. To cite but one example from Cunningham's survey (and there are many): when in 1649 the Cistercian monk Malachy Hartry eulogized his confrère Thomas Lombard, he commended Lombard for the way in which he had preached by word and example. On the face of it, Hartry's commendation seems ordinary enough, but the point is that the consonance of a preacher's word and example had anciently been celebrated as an ideal, and ran like a refrain from the beginning to the end of the Middle Ages. True, the sober demeanour of dissenting preachers was also favourably mentioned as being appropriate to their message, but the terms chosen by the rhetoric of dissent for couching this idea were inflected very differently.

The reformed preaching against which the counter-reformers might define their own reactionary efforts provides a valuable point of access to the social construction of the faith communities for whom it was intended. Raymond Gillespie's account of Irish Protestant preaching in the last decades of the seventeenth century also shows, in marked contrast to the early chapters, what kind of historiography the comparatively richer sources of this later period permit.[8] Bible exegesis in preaching had always served as a way of curbing the various (potentially volatile) senses of Scripture and disciplining them in accordance with the aspirations, social as much as spiritual, of the body of believers. Protestant preaching was no different, and both in its temperament and content acted as a vector of cohesive social values. Furthermore, during this period different modes of preaching can be distinguished within Protestantism which register different denominational allegiances (one might say, denominational 'lifestyles'). There was, on the one hand, a 'plain and practical' preaching favoured by the established Church, with its fear of 'enthusiasm'; on the other, an emotional,

---

7 On Bale's dramatic activity in Kilkenny, see A.J. Fletcher, *Drama, performance, and polity in pre-Cromwellian Ireland* (Toronto, 2000), pp 166-74. 8 Also important here is Katherine P. Meyer, '"The last day I sate at this board ...": sermons recorded at Youghal, Bandon and Mallow, 1676-1688' in Kevin Herlihy (ed.), *Propagating the word of Irish dissent, 1650-1800* (Dublin, 1998), pp 63-73.

theatricalized preaching characteristic of the dissenters. Gillespie shows the extent to which sermons generated by the different denominations within Protestantism were socially performative. Indeed, voluntary religion had the most to gain from such performance. Without it, dissenting communities would have been even harder pressed to survive, deprived as they were of many of the advantages enjoyed by members of the established Church.

Thus this volume, in sum, maps a changing social landscape from a neglected perspective. Work on the diachronic history of preaching in Ireland is in its infancy, and its growth has not been encouraged by the fact that relatively few of the primary source texts are available in modern editions. Nevertheless, we hope that these essays will suggest some paths for future exploration, and that they may extend to the historiography of preaching in Ireland an initial welcome in from out of the cold.

Irish preaching before the end of the ninth century: assessing the extent of our evidence

Thomas O'Loughlin

One of the surprises awaiting the historian of theology who turns his or her attention to Christianity in early medieval Ireland is the paucity of homiletic materials.[1] While the Cambrai Homily – especially its colour-coded distinctions in martyrdom – is widely cited,[2] it is amazing how few other homilies in the vernacular have survived. Indeed, from the period before the eleventh century we have the 'Old Irish homily'[3] and the instruction on the symbolism of the Eucharistic liturgy from the *Stowe Missal* (Royal Irish Academy, Dublin, MS D.II.3).[4] Whether or not the latter should be considered a homily or a catechetical text depends on where one wishes to draw the line between these categories; they overlap in many ways in the pre-ninth century period. In favour of considering it as a text that was for homiletic use (that is, at the actual liturgy) is the fact that it assumes that its audience 'read' the liturgy not from a text but from its actions. This implies that it was to be read by the user of the missal to those who themselves could not use a book. It is this homiletic situation that is decisive in determining that the 'tract', as it has become known, should be considered a homily.

When we turn to homilies in Latin from the ninth century and earlier, the situation is better with regard to the quantity of material. However, 'the

---

1 See J.F. Kenney, *The sources for the early history of Ireland: I, ecclesiastical* (New York, 1929), pp 732-44, who noted that '[t]he great bulk of this literature ... is later than the ninth century' (p. 732). 2 Kenney, *Sources*, item 111, p. 283; the text was edited in Whitley Stokes and John Strachan (eds), *Thesaurus palaeohibernicus* (2 vols, Cambridge, 1901-3, rept Dublin, 1975), ii, pp 244-7; and see P. Ní Chatháin, 'A reading in the Cambrai Homily' in *Celtica* xxi (1990), p. 417. This homily has received much scholarly attention over the years, the most notable contributions being: L. Gougaud, 'Les conceptions du martyre chez les Irlandais' in *Revue Bénédictine* xxiv (1907), pp 360-73; P. Ó Néill, 'The background to the Cambrai Homily' in *Ériu* xxxii (1981), pp 137-48; and C. Stancliffe, 'Red, while and blue martyrdom' in D. Whitelock, R. McKitterick and D. Dumville (eds), *Ireland in early medieval Europe* (Cambridge, 1982), pp 21-46. 3 Compare Kenney, *Sources*, item 603, p. 734. 4 The 'Tract on the Mass' was edited in Stokes and Strachan, *Thesaurus*, ii, pp 252-5, and re-printed from there in G.F. Warner in his edition of *The Stowe Missal* (Henry Bradshaw Society 32, London,

amount of homiletical literature coming from Irish circles at this early time is not very great.'[5] Assessing how much material we have is problematic in that many short texts, for example the three texts entitled *Dies Dominica* listing the wonders of Sunday,[6] were probably used in instructing the laity as sermons, yet they do not have the form of homilies. Equally, many items in collections of 'useful information', for example the Ps-Bedan *Collectanea*,[7] are best understood if they are thought of as *memoranda* for use in popular instruction.[8] However, while acknowledging that there cannot be a firm demarcation between catechetics and homiletics (and throughout the study of early Irish homiletics scholars have noted overlaps between these texts and the homilies which are their primary interest) it is better to exclude such simple instructional materials from the category of 'homily' lest its catchment area become so diffuse as to be useless. So we must first propose a working description of the category of 'homily.'[9] In those cases where the author is known, a homily can be described as a text which tries to persuade as well as to instruct the reader and, consequently, the reader is addressed directly. Anonymous texts can be considered homilies if the reader is not the target addressee, but rather the medium through which the text's message will be conveyed orally to another group. A clear example of this can be found in Sermon II in a small collection of homilies edited by Robert McNally, where the opening line assumes that the reader of the text is reading it to an audience or congregation: *Ad eclesiam* [sic] *frequenter conuenite!*[10] Another useful descriptive element, applying to both named-author and anonymous works (but of more significance in the latter case), is where the text assumes some actual liturgical context, appearing to have been written for use at the Eucharist or some other office. This third element is crucial in classifying the 'Tract' from the *Stowe Missal* as a homily, and is equally useful as a rule-of-thumb in the case of Sermon III and Sermon VII in the McNally collection.[11]

1915, rept 1989), pp 37-42. For a survey of scholarly comment on this text, cf. T. O'Loughlin, *Celtic theology: humanity, world and God in early Irish writers* (London, 2000), ch. 8. **5** This was the judgement, with which I concur, of R.E. McNally, shortly before his death in 1977, in '"In nomine Dei summi", seven Hiberno-Latin sermons' in *Traditio* xxxv (1979), pp 121-43 at p. 121. **6** R.E. McNally (ed.), *Scriptores Hiberniae Minores* i (CCSL 108B, Turnhout, 1973), pp 175-86; for bibliography see M. Lapidge and R. Sharpe, *A bibliography of Celtic-Latin literature, 400-1200* (Dublin 1985), items 903, 904, and 905 and cf. T. O'Loughlin, 'The significance of Sunday: three ninth-century catecheses' in *Worship* lxiv (1990), pp 533-44. **7** M. Bayless and M. Lapidge (eds), *Collectanea Pseudo-Bedae* (SLH 14, Dublin, 1998); see Lapidge and Sharpe, *Bibliography*, item 1257. **8** Compare T. O'Loughlin, 'The list of illustrious writers in the Pseudo-Bedan Collectanea,' in H. Conrad O'Briain, A.M. D'Arcy, and J. Scattergood (eds), *Text and gloss: studies in insular learning and literature presented to Joseph Donovan Pheiffer* (Dublin, 1999), pp 34-48. **9** The distinction of *homilia / homelia* and *sermo* which is often stressed by liturgists, is of little relevance in describing the materials from the early medieval period. **10** McNally 'Seven Hiberno-Latin sermons', p. 136 (I shall have much more to say about this collection later). **11** McNally, 'Seven Hiberno-Latin sermons', pp 139-40 and 143.

From the period before the end of the ninth century there are only two authors whose homilies we possess: Columbanus (d. 615) and John Scottus Eriugena (d. 877?). Let us first consider Eriugena since we have just one homily of his: the *Homily on the prologue to the Gospel of John*.[12] Because of the intellectual stature of Eriugena, and since the homily provides an insight into his conception of the relationship between the modes of human understanding and the revelation of divine Wisdom in Christ, it has received wider scholarly attention than any other homily written by an Irishman.[13] However, while the *Homily* is truly a theological gem,[14] its style and content place it outside the normal course of preaching. Unless preached to a specialist and well-trained congregation, it is questionable if it was a successful piece of preaching. In 1977 Peter Dronke argued convincingly that the text, while prose, has a profoundly poetic character;[15] and it is clear that Eriugena was as skilled in rhetoric as in theology. But these very qualities put the *Homily* in a category apart: Melchizedek-like, it had neither predecessors nor imitators in Irish preaching from the early Middle Ages.

Turning to Columbanus, we encounter the work of an earlier *peregrinus* who made his name on the continent, but so far as his homilies are concerned twentieth-century attention has focused on the question of their authenticity. Traditionally, seventeen sermons (labelled *Instructiones*) were attributed to Columbanus. But by the time of the most recent edition, the party in favour of Columbanian authorship (then a minority) considered thirteen to be the work of the abbot of Bobbio.[16] More than a century ago, Albert Hauck[17] questioned whether any of these sermons was by Columbanus, and his doubts were later supported when Otto Seebass criticized their putative authorship in more detail.[18] The question has been contentious in Columbanus

12 E. Jeauneau (ed.), *Jean Scot, Homélie sur le prologue de Jean* (SC 151, Paris, 1969); there is an English translation by J.J. O'Meara in *Eriugena* (Oxford, 1988), pp 158-76. The homily is in Lapidge and Sharpe, *Bibliography*, item 702, and compare Kenney, *Sources*, item 394, pp 585-6. 13 There are twenty-four references to it in M. Brennan, *Guide des etudes Érigéniennes – a guide to Eriugenian studies* (Fribourg – Paris, 1989). That bibliography has been up-dated by G. van Riel, 'A bibliographical survey of Eriugenian studies 1987-1995' in G. van Riel, C. Steel, and J. McEvoy (eds), *Iohannes Scottus Eriugena: the Bible and hermeneutics* (Leuven, 1996), pp 367-400. The most recent article known to me devoted specifically to the *Homily* is K. Ruh, 'Die Homelie über den Prolog des Johannes-Evangeliums des Johannes Eriugena' in K. Wittstadt (ed.), *St. Kilian: 1300 Jahre Martyrium des Frankenapostel* (Würzburg, 1989), pp 491-500. 14 I know of no better introduction to the thought of Eriugena than the *Homily* – his other works intimidate students, provoking them to read books about Eriugena rather than by him. However, the *Homily*'s length, and beauty, make it attractive to those meeting Eriugena for the first time, and whets the appetite for other works by him. 15 'Theologia veluti quaedam poetria: quelques observations sur la fonction des images poétiques chez Jean Scot' in R. Roques (ed.), *Jean Scot Érigéne et l'histoire de la philosophie* (Paris, 1977), pp 243-52. 16 G.S.M. Walker (ed.), *Sancti Columbani opera* (Dublin, 1957, rept. 1970), pp 60-121. 17 'Ueber di sogenannte *Instuctiones Columbani*' in *Zeitschrift für kirchliche Wissenschaft und kirchliches Leben* vi (1885), pp 357-64. 18 'Über die sogenannte Instructiones Columbani' in *Zeitschrift für*

scholarship. By 1929 Kenney was able to observe: 'No less than seventeen texts of sermons or homilies exist which have been attributed to Columbanus. It is quite certain, however, that the majority of these do not belong to him.'[19] By 1985, the position had hardened against attributing any sermon to Columbanus, for in that year Lapidge and Sharpe excluded the *Instructiones*, as a group, from the list of works attributed to Columbanus, and dated them to the fifth century.[20]

Recently the situation has been dramatically reversed. Clare Stancliffe has reviewed the entire debate from Hauck's time and, on the basis of a fresh study of the contents, style (in particular the use of rhythmical *clausulae*), and likely contexts for their composition, has concluded that the thirteen sermons in Walker's edition are the work of one man, and that their author and Columbanus are identical.[21] She concludes:

> ... it is difficult to see how the thirteen sermons could display their Columbanian authorship more convincingly than they have in the course of this study. Each different angle that we have tried gives the same result: that of the manuscripts, of the sources, of the Latinity, and of parallels, both verbal and in content, with other genuine works by Columbanus.[22]

> Columbanus himself was the author of all thirteen sermons ... he composed them, as a series, for his monks in northern Italy towards the end of his life, between his arrival in Lombardy late in 612 and his death in 615. Once correctly attributed, these sermons take their place as the only coherent exposition of Irish ascetic spirituality to have come down to us from the formative period of early Irish monasticism. They also provide us with an insight into the religious inspiration of one of Ireland's greatest and most forceful *peregrini*.[23]

The significance of Stancliffe's conclusion for our view of early Irish homiletics can hardly be overstated. For those who accept her conclusions there is now a sermon corpus from a single Irish author whose quality of theological engagement and compositional skills we can investigate. Yet, the thirteen homilies of Columbanus, to an extent like the Eriugena homily, are in a

---

Kirchengeschichte xiii (1892), pp 513-34.   19 Kenney, *Sources*, item 44, pp 196-7 at 196.   20 See Lapidge and Sharpe, *Bibliography*, item 1251. Their date of the fifth century is based on one of Hauck's objections, and the central objection of Seebass, that the *Instructiones* make use of the work of Faustus of Riez (c. 408 - c. 490) and were the work of one of the immediate pupils of Faustus.   21 Clare Stancliffe, 'The thirteen sermons attributed to Columbanus and the question of their authorship' in M. Lapidge (ed.), *Columbanus: studies in the Latin writings* (Woodbridge, 1997), pp 93-202.   22 Stancliffe, 'Thirteen sermons', pp 193-4.   23 Stancliffe, 'Thirteen sermons', p. 199.

category apart and do not tell us much about ordinary preaching to congregations in Ireland. First, the *Instructiones* represent the preaching of one outstanding religious leader and thinker – that is why the thirteen sermons survived and why other homilies were attributed to Columbanus. Secondly, they were aimed at a monastic audience – the instructions of an abbot to his disciples;[24] and thirdly, they assume a range of religious questions, for instance the relationship between Arianism and orthodoxy, that pertain to contemporary northern Italy and which would have been out of place in more standard preaching whose purpose was the instruction, edification, and exhortation of the laity. As they exist in written form they seem analogous to the *Enarrationes in Psalmos* of Augustine: although once delivered viva voce in an assembly, from the time they were written down they were consulted as a book is studied rather than as prompts to new homiletic action.

For evidence of the ordinary preaching of the period we must turn to the homily collections with Irish connections. Let us begin with their discovery, and then proceed to the questions they pose when considered as evidence for Irish preaching before the end of the ninth century. The first collection identified was that contained in a Breton manuscript of the late ninth or early tenth century, Biblioteca Apostolica Vaticana, Reg. lat. 49, by André Wilmart.[25] The first fifty-three folios of this manuscript contained 'with some exceptions, commentaries and homilies, mainly on parts of the gospels.'[26] Wilmart saw these as forming a unified catechetical collection which he proposed as having been in use in Brittany in the ninth century, and on this basis he produced a partial edition, naming the collection the *Catechesis Celtica*.[27] Since then it has become the cornerstone of many studies of 'Celtic' homiletics.[28] Although Wilmart never gave any serious consideration to connections between his collection and Ireland, many have subsequently studied 'links' and suggested that it may be representative of contemporary Irish preaching.[29] This working assumption has underlain many studies.[30] Whatever light the collection may throw upon insular, or Celtic, theology, the claim that it shows us anything which is *specific* to Irish

---

24 On the significance of this relationship, see T. O'Loughlin, 'Master and pupil: Christian perspectives' in William Johnston (ed.), *The encyclopedia of monasticism*, (Chicago, 2000), pp 835-7.   25 *Codices Reginenses Latini* i (Vatican City, 1937), pp 112-17.   26 *Codices Reginenses Latini* i, p. 112.   27 A. Wilmart, 'Catéchéses celtiques' in his *Analecta Reginensia* (SeT 59, Vatican City, 1933), pp 29-112; Lapidge and Sharpe, *Bibliography*, item 974.   28 See the bibliography cited in Lapidge and Sharpe, *Bibliography*; and M. McNamara, 'The affiliations and origins of the *Catechesis Celtica*: an ongoing quest' in T. O'Loughlin (ed.), *The scriptures and early medieval Ireland* (Turnhout, 1999), pp 179-98   29 See, for example, D. Ó Laoghaire, 'Irish elements in the *Catechesis Celtica*,' in P. Ní Chatháin and M. Richter (eds), *Irland und die Christenheit / Ireland and Christendom: Bibelstudien und Mission / The Bible and the missions* (Stuttgart, 1987), pp 146-64.   30 For example B. Grogan, 'Eschatological teaching in the early Irish Church' in M. McNamara (ed.), *Biblical studies: the medieval Irish contribution* (Dublin 1976), pp 46-58 at 49-50.

preaching must be approached with great caution. However, the range of homilies does reflect the interests of the Church in northern, mainly rural, Europe at the time, and since we have no reason to suggest that Ireland stood outside those more general concerns, we can infer that the interests of many Irish preachers would have been similar.

This list of its sermons, taken from Wilmart', gives an indication of the homiletic interests of the compiler of the collection. It is a mixture of exegetical homilies devoted to pericopes from the gospels, homilies for the major feasts, and a few other assortments.

Item Content
1   Mt 4:1-11[31] [The opening verse of this piece of text corresponds to a division in the Eusebian apparatus].[32]
2   Mt 19:16-30 [Pericope opens at Eusebian division].
3   Mt 21:16-30 [Whole Eusebian section].
4   Mt 20:1-16 The text opens with the numeral CCX. [This is a relic from a text with the Eusebian apparatus for this pericope corresponds to a whole Eusebian section which is CC/X and would have been expressed in the margin as:

$$\frac{CC}{X}$$

or, with less likelihood, as CC.X. The sermon itself is taken, in the main, from a homily by Gregory the Great.]

5   Mt 20:1-16. Another homily on the same pericope.
6   Ps 1:1-6.
7   On the Lord's Prayer.
8   – not a homily.
9   – not a homily.
10   Mt 4:23-5:12 [Pericope opens at Eusebian division].
11   Mt 20:17-21:17. Palm Sunday [Pericope opens at Eusebian division].
12   Another homily on this pericope.
13   Jn 13:4-15. For Holy Thursday [Pericope opens at Eusebian division].

---

31 Where a scriptural reference occurs in this list, it is to be assumed that the homily is a commentary on that pericope. 32 For an account of how the Eusebian sections were used as dividers within the text – a purpose for which they were not intended – see T. O'Loughlin, 'The Biblical text of the Book of Deer (C.U.L. Ii.6.32): evidence for the remains of a division system from its manuscript ancestry,' in K. Forsyth (ed.), *Studies in the Book of Deer*, forthcoming; and idem, 'The Eusebian apparatus in some Vulgate Gospel Books' in *Peritia*, xiii (1999), pp 1-92. Observations by the present author are placed within square brackets.

14 Mt 26:20-30. For Holy Thursday [Pericope opens at Eusebian division].
15 – not a homily.
16 Gen 1:1-25. Easter Vigil.
17 – collection of snippets including parts of a homily by Caesarius of Arles.³³
18 Mt 27:1-15. This is preceded by the numeral CCCLIII. [This is probably a relic, garbled by the time it was copied into this manuscript, of a Eusebian number. The pericope opens at Eusebian division which is CCCXVII/II and this could have been corrupted to the numeral CCCLIII by someone who did not appreciate its significance].
19 Another homily on the same pericope.
20 Homily for Easter Day.
21 Jn 20:26-31 [Pericope opens at Eusebian division].
22 – not a homily but an explanation of the Easter Octave.
23 Mt 26:24 [Pericope does *not* open at Eusebian division].
24 Mt 10:16 / Lk 10:3. These texts are identified as a doublet within the Eusebian apparatus.³⁴
25 Mt 6:33 / Lk 12:31. These texts are identified as a doublet within the Eusebian apparatus.
26 Apoc 5:13.
27 Lk 13:6-9 [Pericope opens at Eusebian division].
28 Mt 9:10-13 [Pericope opens at Eusebian division].
29 Jn 14:1-2. [Pericope opens at Eusebian division].
30 Apoc 4:5.
31 Jn 2:1-11. [Pericope does *not* open at Eusebian division, nor it this a Eusebian Section; however, it is a narrative unit within the text as the story of the marriage at Cana].
32 Lk 2:21. On the circumcision. [Pericope does *not* open at Eusebian division].
33 Mt 20:29-34 [Pericope corresponds to a Eusebian section].
34 Lk 11:27-28 [Pericope corresponds to a Eusebian section].
35 Mt 7:12 [Pericope corresponds to a Eusebian section].
36 Mt 13:45-6 [Pericope does *not* open at Eusebian division].
37 Mt 21:11-12 [Pericope does *not* open at Eusebian division].³⁵

---

[33] Since my concern here is not the *Catechesis* as such, it would take me to far afield to examine this selection of short texts, however, they are not out of place in the collection as they are bits of useful knowledge for a preacher.   [34] Here, and on several subsequent occasions, Wilmart recognised that the link between two texts which form the basis of the homily was to be found in the Eusebian apparatus.   [35] Wilmart believed that this unit of text was in some way related to the Eusebian apparatus (he says '*relato canone*'), however, there is no relationship between this pericope's boundaries and the divisions of the text into Eusebian sections.

38   Mt 12:42 [Pericope does *not* open at Eusebian division].[36]
39   Mt 21:1-9 [Pericope opens at a Eusebian section].
40   Lk 2:1-2, 6-20. Christmas Day [Pericope does *not* open at Eusebian division].
41   Job 40:10. Behemoth.
42   – collection of snippets.[37]
43   Mt 19:16-30. On the second coming [Pericope opens at a Eusebian section].
44   On fasting.
45   Mt 5:5.[38] The gift of tears [Pericope corresponds to a Eusebian section].
46   On Sunday as the Lord's Day.

This list shows that the great feasts apart, this collection is devoted to the exegesis of Scripture (twenty-nine homilies); 'theme homilies' play a very small part in it. There is cumulative evidence that the compiler thought of the text in small units through imagining that the Eusebian sections formed the genuine structural divisions within the text. If we accept that there was such a use of a text divided into Eusebian sections, this would explain the preponderance of Matthew (twenty-one homilies), then Luke and John (four each, but two of the Lucan pericopes are related to feasts), and why there is no reference to Mark. Such a filtering of the four gospels into a more synoptic format was exactly how the Eusebian apparatus worked. Why bother with Mark, and to a lesser extent this also applied to Luke and John, when the material was covered in Matthew?[39]

While today it is attractive to suppose that the emphasis of the *Catechesis* on exposition of Scripture, in a fairly ordered manner, represented preaching as a whole, it must be remembered that this is the only collection extant with such a concentration. Moreover, with regards to its relevance to Ireland, this rests only on an assumption that forces similar to those which produced the work in Brittany operated also in Ireland (although it should be noted that this assumed communality is based on the fact of the interchange of ideas in Latin among clergy, not on some supposed pan-Celtic unity).

In recent years these two collections, each of which survives in only a single manuscript, have been referred to by several writers as the *Catechesis Cracoviensis* and the *Catechesis Veronensis*.[40] The first was intended for a

---

36 See previous note, again there is no basis for Wilmart's judgement.   37 See note on item 17 above.   38 Wilmart states, in error, that it is based on Mt 5:4.   39 Compare T. O'Loughlin, 'Tyconius' use of the Canonical Gospels' in *Revue Bénédictine* cvi (1996), pp 229-33.   40 These titles were suggested by Prof. Martin McNamara by analogy with Wilmart's title of the *Catechesis Celtica*, and have now gained some currency among scholars working on Hiberno-Latin. However, it should be noted that (1) they are not *catecheses* but *homiliaria*; and (2) while the designation '*Celtica*' made sense for Wilmart as he saw the collection as having an intimate link with Brittany, the designations '*Cracoviensis*' and '*Veronensis*' merely tell us the present

monastic audience, while the second, focusing on the liturgical year, contains eleven homilies covering the period from Christmas to Pentecost. The Cracow manuscript, Cathedral Library 140 Kp (43), was produced in Italy in the late eighth or early ninth centuries, according to the current critical consensus.[41] David, who produced a partial edition in 1937, argued that Continental monastic instructions presupposed a Continental monastic setting before the impact of the Carolingian reforms, and he believed certain features of 'Irish monasticism' was detectable in that monastic environment. This led him to conclude that these conferences were composed by an Irish monk in France in the eighth century. However, in 1954, Bernhard Bischoff, while generally accepting David's argument, maintained that the work (and not just the manuscript) was produced in Italy after 800.[42] Bischoff was convinced of its Irish credentials and referred to it as an 'Irish Monastic Collection', agreeing with David that 'Irish elements' and parallels 'can be traced in it' but noted that 'the language is, to a considerable degree, romanised'.[43] However, Bischoff's judgement as to its origin appears to be principally based upon the palaeography of the manuscript, and his dating of 'after 800' is almost certainly based exclusively on the manuscript's date. Since the collection of conferences focused on the various prescribed fasts and draws almost exclusively from Matthew, it has been called *Fragmenta in Matthaeum de ieiunio e cod[ice] Cracouiensi 43* in *Clauis Patrum Latinorum*, and it was this aspect that Edmondo Coccia highlighted when he pointed out that while the collection was a series of homilies for the various fasts following, in rough sequence, the liturgical year, they were not for use at Mass but for the formal instruction of monks.[44] This was a point made by David when he chose the word *conferences* as their title but which has been lost from sight in many discussions through the use of 'sermon' or 'homily' as generic terms.[45] Coccia, in support of his general thesis that the role of the

locations of the manuscripts, by analogy Wilmart would have had to name that in Reg. lat. 49 as the '*Catechesis Vaticana*.' 41 P. David, 'Un receuil de conférences monastiques irlandaises du VIIIe siècle' in *Revue Bénédictine* xlix (1937), pp 62-89. The manuscript has been described by E.A. Lowe in *Codices Latini Antiquiores*, xi, 1593; it has been listed by Lapidge and Sharpe, *Bibliography*, as item 802, and by E. Dekkers, *Clauis Patrum Latinorum* (3rd ed., Steenbrugge, 1995) as item 1122. 42 B. Bischoff, 'Turning-points in the history of Latin exegesis in the early Irish Church: A.D. 650-800' in McNamara (ed.), *Biblical studies*, pp 74-160 at 159, n. 124 [= 'Wendepunkte in der Geschichte der lateinischen Exegese im Frühmittelalter', *Mittelalterliche Studien. Aufsätze zur Schriftkunde und Literaturgeschichte* (Stuttgart 1966), pp 189-279 at 229 (first published in *Sacris Erudiri* vi (1954), pp 189-279 at 221)]. 43 Bischoff, 'Turning-points', pp 95 and 159, n. 124. 44 E. Coccia, 'La cultura irlandese precarolingia: Miracolo o Mito?' in *Studi Medievali* viii (1967), pp 257-42 at 347. 45 This was a point that Coccia noted (p. 348, n. 458) from Jean Leclercq's *L'amour des lettres et le désir de Dieu* (Paris, 1957), p. 160. In that work – without any reference to Ireland – Leclercq took the conferences as edited by David as typical of a general monastic development of the eighth century: 'From the eighth century on, we have examples of sermons written to be read to the community [cites David's

Irish in pre-Carolingian Europe had been massively exaggerated, also highlighted the non-Irish aspects of David's argument such as the French qualities of the Latin.[46]

The project to edit the Verona homilies preserved in Verona, Biblioteca Capitolare LXVII (64), has passed to Lawrence Martin and an edition from him is expected in the near future.[47] As with the Cracow collection the links with Ireland are based on three kinds of evidence. First, certain palaeographical traces possibly indicate insular influence. Martin says on this 'there is nothing in the general appearance of [the first scribe's] hand that would not fit northern Italy, although he uses a few abbreviations which might suggest insular influence'; while the second scribe used 'a flat-headed "insular g"'.[48] The second kind of evidence is the presence of 'traces' of 'the insular biblical text' in the collection, on the assumption that if biblical lemmata found in these homilies could be shown to be exclusive to biblical manuscripts from the insular region, then this would be an indicator of the area of origin. Thirdly, a provenance might be suggested by the presence in the work of parallels with other insular works or works circulating in the insular area. Sometimes these 'links' are based on specific common portions of text, while at other times they are based upon more general perceptions. McNally in a preface which he wrote for the collection said that it contained 'expressions and ways of writing and thinking that reflect the early Irish tradition.'[49]

While all these arguments when mustered have a cumulative force, their criteriology is open to question. It is as if, once anyone has suggested an Irish connection, the next investigator proceeds to find confirmation of the hypothesis. When 'Irish provenance' has been supported by two investigators, a third proceeds on that basis until 'Irish provenance' gradually becomes 'common knowledge'. However, a few comments should be made about the practice of treating works labelled 'Irish' in the mid-twentieth century as 'Irish unless proven otherwise.' First, most of these claims are based on partial evidence. We do not have editions of the works themselves, nor comparative studies of these works. Until we do, conclusions based on 'symptoms' are not only inherently weak, but very likely to promote the interests of the investigator. The arguments of David for his collection's 'Irish' origins against the evidence of the Latinity is a case in point: he was obliged to explain apparent monastic 'irregularities': since Ireland was considered both orthodox

---

1937 article], although they were often intended for a larger public. In this case they are more markedly doctrinal in nature.' (*The love of learning and the desire for God: a study in monastic culture* (New York 1961), p. 170.) **46** Coccia citing David, p. 70. **47** The most complete account of the collection is to be found in L.T. Martin, 'The Catechesis Veronensis' in O'Loughlin (ed.), *The scriptures and early medieval Ireland*, pp 151-61. It is item 804 in Lapidge and Sharpe, *Bibliography*. **48** Martin, 'The Catechesis Veronensis', p. 152. **49** Martin, 'The Catechesis Veronensis', p. 157.

theologically and 'irregular' in discipline, his dilemma was solved. So he relied on evidence inherently weak – traces of a specifically Irish monasticism, however that might be defined – while down-playing evidence inherently strong – similarities in Latinity between the conferences and continental charters. Equally, Martin noted the paucity of insular abbreviations in the manuscript, but rather than suggesting that one scribe in the history of the copying of the text had an irregularity in his abbreviations resulting from contact with someone with insular features in his hand, he uses it to support the insular origin of the text. One swallow may not make a summer, but, it seems, one insular trace in script not only can tell us something about the manuscript as an artefact, but about the origin of the author being copied!

Secondly, many of these designations originated using the 'Ireland is exceptional' thesis: a text 'fits' nowhere else, or has 'peculiarities', so where can it come from? The answer usually lies along the Atlantic seaboard, Brittany, Cornwall, Wales, and Ireland. 'Out there' they did things differently! Leave alone the cultural politics of this as a criterion of Irish origins,[50] we should note its internal contradiction. If these works are so peculiar that they are egregious from their surroundings, why then were they copied and used in so alien an environment? Surely, when one meets works with wholly Continental manuscript histories – for example, all the manuscripts from northern Italy in which Bischoff detected Irish symptoms – it is more logical to revise one's perceptions of what were the acceptable ranges in monastic thought and practice, than to seek an 'alien' source. Indeed, the problem becomes a circular conundrum: how can a northern Italian monastic book of a particular time be alien to the monasticism of that place at that time? Conversely, if a work were Irish, and consequently 'distinctive,' why was it given any value at that time?[51]

Thirdly, while a distinctive biblical text and distinctive palaeographical features have been used as key indicators of insular origins, they can rarely provide more than supporting evidence. Such symptoms are not so exclusively insular that their random presence elsewhere cannot be accounted for except by postulating an Irish original of the work in question. The issue of 'national' biblical texts is particularly fraught in this respect, for in order to show that the 'insular symptom' in a biblical codex relates to that in some other text, then one would have to show that it was only through that insular channel that that variant could be encountered. The variant would have to be shown to have originated in the particular locality, such as Ireland, in the

---

50 See P. Sims-Williams, 'Celtomania and Celtoscepticism' in *Cambrian Medieval Celtic Studies* no. 36 (1998), pp 1-35. 51 The 'Irish religious material is distinctive' thesis is ultimately a hang-over from the nineteenth-century fascination with the 'Celtic Church' within 'branch theory' Anglican ecclesiology where every possible distinctiveness was played up for all its worth, as it indicated a 'distinctive' Church by analogy with autocephalous Greek churches. The origins of this explanatory hypothesis, and various more recent mutations, are examined in T. O'Loughlin, *Celtic Theology*, ch. 1.

same way that we suppose the idiosyncracies of the 'national hands' arose in their particular areas. To demonstrate such exclusive paths of contact we would need to assume that we have, if not all, then most of the biblical codices that were ever produced – a clear impossibility.[52]

The fourth element in arguments for an Irish origin for these homily collections is that one can identify many elements between them, and many parallels with other works known to have been used in the insular area.[53] However, not only does this criterion lack exclusivity in its probative force, but it can be turned on its head. Given that these homilies were used on the Continent, the fact that similar materials were in use in texts whose insular origins are certain, implies that there is a general similarity of theological culture in the Latin west in the eighth and ninth centuries. This is not only an assumption masked by the notion that 'Irish' texts were in use on the Continent, but it also excludes the hypothesis that any particular set of overlaps could be indicative of origin in a specific cultural setting.

Finally, arguments from 'characteristic ways of thinking and writing' belong to the *modus inueniendi* of an hypothesis, not to its probation. Every scholar has had hunches that resulted from his or her sheer weight of experience in an area; it is 'the nose' that one acquires through years of familiarity. Without such 'hunches', one would never create an hypothesis which may unlock a text's history. However, evidence for an hypothesis must then be found which does not rely solely on that hunch. The hunch may be a creative starting point, but it is not evidence.

I have laboured these points lest it be said that this chapter avoids a direct assessment of what could be the largest single body of Irish preaching from the early Middle Ages. However, until we have full editions and studies of those collections, to proceed on the assumption that they are Irish is to create a putative history which may have to be pulled down – a common phenomenon in early Irish studies – but which nevertheless continues to contaminate general perceptions long after its dismissal from mainstream scholarship. In

---

52 On the problems of using the biblical text as an indicator of insular connections – an approach which has had many supporters in the late-nineteenth and for most of the twentieth centuries – see O'Loughlin, 'The Biblical text of the Book of Deer (C.U.L. Ii.6.32)'. It should be noted that those scholars such as J. Wordsworth and H.J. White who first grouped manuscripts into regional texts were not guilty of this absurdity – it is a legitimate process in carrying out the *eliminatio codicum* on the way to an edition. The methodological error occurred when later scholars saw the families of manuscripts so assembled by region, and assumed that the variants common in each family could be utilised as a diagnostic tool in determining the origins of otherwise unsourced texts. 53 This has been a major concern of Professor McNamara (see his 'The affiliations and origins of the *Catechesis Celtica*') and it is because of parallel passages in the three collections that he wishes to label the Cracow and Verona collections as *Catechesis Cracoviensis* and *Veronensis* so as to recall links with the so-called *Catechesis Celtica*.

any case, the Cracow collection is not so much an indicator of preaching, as such, but, as Leclercq recognised, part of a larger development in western monastic spirituality. Certainly, when we read them in David's partial edition we are on far surer ground if we regard them as *readings* in spirituality keyed to the liturgical year (an early version of later manuals of 'spiritual reading'), than as homilies committed to writing.

Several caveats expressed with regard to the Cracow and Verona collections do not apply to the collection known as 'In nomine Dei summi' for we have a complete edition,[54] and some studies of the material.[55] It is also clear from the homilies themselves that not only was this collection made for actual preaching at the Eucharist, but it was compiled for preaching to a lay congregation. The collection of seven texts is found in two Vatican manuscripts, Pal. lat. 220 (Anglo-Saxon script, upper Rhineland, early ninth century) and Pal. lat. 212 (from the first half of the ninth century). McNally in his study of these texts concentrated on the first of these manuscripts as it 'generally seems to represent a purer tradition than the latter.'[56] An instance of this for McNally was the presence in Pal. lat. 220 of the opening formula 'In nomine Dei summi' before each sermon, whereas in Pal. lat. 212 it is found only before the first sermon of the collection, forming, McNally supposed, an introduction to the whole collection.[57] He also found that these homilies 'provide convincing evidence of being Irish in character',[58] and this has been widely accepted. Hence the collection is catalogued as the work of an Irish *peregrinus* from the end of the eighth century in Lapidge and Sharpe's *Bibliography of Celtic Latin literature* (item 803); and based upon that entry they now have a number in *Clauis Patrum Latinorum* (item 1163b) with the title *Sermones anonymi vii* which were 'composed in the eighth century by an Irish author.'

To establish their authorial provenance, McNally used a cumulative method. First, they stand 'in the Antiochene rather than the Alexandrian tradition' of scriptural exegesis. That this distinction was real for the seventh and eighth centuries had been a central pillar of much work by medievalists for decades.[59] It had been made a commonplace through the work of M.L.W. Laistner, who saw the continuing presence of an early fourth-century distinction in Greek exegesis having force in Latin writings until almost the time of

---

54 McNally, 'Seven Hiberno-Latin sermons'. Shortly before his death in 1977, Robert McNally was working on the edition of this collection but did not live to finish the work; the collection was later prepared for publication by J.J. O'Donnell (and M.F. Wack). **55** There is a translation of the collection by T. O'Loughlin, 'The Celtic homily: creeds and eschatology' in *Milltown Studies* xli (1998), pp 99-115; and a study of their implicit view of the Christian life in T. O'Loughlin, *Journeys on the edge* (London, 2000), ch. 7. **56** McNally, 'Seven Hiberno-Latin sermons', n.3. **57** McNally, 'Seven Hiberno-Latin sermons', p. 123. **58** 'Seven Hiberno-Latin sermons', his opening sentence, p. 121. **59** See McNally's own *The Bible in the*

the scholastics.⁶⁰ The Antiochene approach was seen as a definite Irish symptom by Bischoff in an article of 1954 to which McNally appeals in support of his argument.⁶¹ This identification of 'Antiochene exegesis' as an 'Irish-symptom' has been one of the consistent criticisms of Bischoff.⁶² But, more radically, we must ask how valuable is it as a distinction. Laistner began with a model of what he considered standard early medieval exegesis (which he considered to be 'allegorical' = 'Alexandrian') and then noted some commentaries that were notably lacking in this kind of exegesis. To him, these formed an 'exception' to the norm. Bischoff, in his turn, noted some of these commentaries as being Irish, and thus had identified a national characteristic, so that in general an interest in the literal text = 'Antiochene' = 'Irish.' However, since before 800 a far wider range of exegesis was being conducted in Latin throughout western Europe than has been recognized,⁶³ these categories cannot be adopted as a firm clue to origins. The terms 'Antiochene' and 'Alexandrian' should be reserved for the fourth century,⁶⁴ and we should foster wider expectations of what the range of exegetical strategies regularly deployed in the seventh and eighth centuries in the Latin west might consist of. McNally supported his case for the Irish origins of these sermons by noting the presence in his principal manuscript of another text linked to Ireland, the presence of Irish abbreviations, and similarities of biblical text with the *Book of Armagh*.⁶⁵ I have already commented on the probative force of these arguments, but for McNally they raised the probability of the Irish origin of these texts beyond real doubt.

McNally was, however, bothered by some features of the collection. It was central to his argument that the collection – which he showed had many points of contact with other texts – was the work of a single author. It thus had a genuine unity of origin and not just a unity conferred by the person who gathered them into the collection (of which two witnesses survive), and this author's theological perspective and homiletic style was to be seen throughout the seven pieces:

early middle ages (Westminster Md, 1959), ch. I, p. 9. **60** See his 'Antiochene exegesis in Western Europe during the middle ages' in *Harvard Theological Review* xl (1947), pp 19-31. **61** McNally, 'Seven Hiberno-Latin sermons' cites Bischoff in n.2, and adds 'The exegetical tradition or spirit of Antioch was sustained by certain Irish exegetes into the ninth century.' **62** Cf. C. Stancliffe, 'Early "Irish" Biblical exegesis' in *Studia Patristica* xii (1975), pp 361-370; and, but with less effect on this particular point, by M.M. Gorman, 'A critique of Bischoff's theory of Irish exegesis: the commentary on Genesis in Munich Clm 6302 (Wendepunkte 2)' in *Journal of Medieval Latin* vii (1997), pp 178-233. **63** See T. O'Loughlin, 'Seeking the medieval view of the Song of Songs' in *Proceeding of the Irish Biblical Association* xviii (1995), pp 94-116; *Teachers and code-breakers: the Latin Genesis tradition, 430-800* (Turnhout, 1999), ch. 5; and 'Christ as the focus of Genesis exegesis in Isidore of Seville' in T. Finan and V. Twomey (eds), *Studies in Patristic Christology* (Dublin, 1998), pp 144-62. **64** Cf. R.M. Grant with D. Tracy, *A short history of the interpretation of the Bible* (2nd edition, London, 1984), chs 6 and 7. **65** McNally, 'Seven Hiberno-Latin sermons', p. 122.

It is likely that the collection originated in the last decade of the eighth century, perhaps even somewhat earlier; and in accord with the evidence of the manuscript the place of provenance can be reasonably located in the upper or middle Rhine valley, a locale which at this time was still frequented by insular *peregrini*. The personal identity of the author is unknown. He was probably Irish by nationality, but certainly the product of that culture; he was a monk in orders with an interest in various apostolic tasks, preaching and catechizing especially. His homiletical work is not original; it tends to be prosaic, at times even ordinary, largely basic, awaiting expansion and development. The collection represents an ancient witness to the character of preaching in the period before the Carolingian reform had set in.[66]

Yet earlier McNally had noted that there was a distinction between the first four items which 'structurally and stylistically merit inclusion in [the] category' of 'sermon' which needed only some 'editing, reshaping and expanding' to turn them 'into homilies in the proper sense.' While the other three texts 'despite their inclusion with' and 'close affiliation with' the first four, 'in no sense ... qualify as sermons', but could only 'provide themes,' 'inspiration' and 'represent the germ out of which the homily or the sermon grows.' McNally then added: 'obviously they have no title to be considered catechetical instructions.'[67]

Here lies a clear problem, recognised in part by McNally himself: should we look on these homilies as having an authorial unity distinct from that of a collector who assembled them in the exemplar from which the two extant manuscripts derive? The first point to note is that in terms of content, length, and tone, texts III, IV, V, VI and VII are all remarkably similar. This similarity is even more pronounced by contrast with the first two homilies that focus on the eschatological Judgement. The five shorter pieces all convey, in a staccato form, basic Christian information: items III and VII are expansions on the Nicene Creed which are, in effect, commentaries by paraphrase; items IV, V and VI are exhortations to a style of Christian living which portrays the way of Christians using simple two-handed comparisons (Christians do x, non-Christians do y; the earthly way is x, the heavenly way is y). Such a style belongs to the class of homily where the distinctions between 'homily' and 'sermon' and 'catechesis' cease to have meaning. In each case the sermon is a direct instruction which is seen as the means of exhorting listeners using a 'know ... and then do' strategy, rather than by any attempt to capture their attention with a narrative or with well developed images.

[66] McNally, 'Seven Hiberno-Latin sermons', p. 132. [67] McNally, 'Seven Hiberno-Latin sermons', pp 122-3.

Equally, both texts IV and VII make the same assumptions about a credal formula which is closely related to the formula known as the Nicaenoconstantinopolitan Creed. While one could make much of textual variants that overlap with texts in use in Ireland (such as the *Antiphonary of Bangor*[68] and the *Book of Dimma*,[69] as McNally does in his notes),[70] there is an even stronger connection between these two texts and the insular region if we assume that both texts are actual catechetical homilies for use at the Eucharist. The creed was introduced into the Eucharistic liturgy in Spain in the late sixth century and located just before the *Pater noster*.[71] The creed spread first to Ireland. There it moved to the now familiar place in the Liturgy of the Word after the gospel, as can be seen from the *Stowe Missal* (the oldest surviving Irish missal and dating to the 790s).[72] Thence it came to Anglo-Saxon England, and from there, through Alcuin, to the Continent where in the early 790s it is found in the palace chapel of Charlemagne at Aachen. It appears that it spread slowly on the continent, despite approval for its use from Leo III in 810,[73] mainly in centres with insular links, for it is mentioned in a few ninth-century Carolingian liturgical sources.[74] This pattern for the use of the creed exactly fits with the assumption of an insular origin for our homilies: they were in use in Anglo-Saxon circles on the Continent in the early ninth century, and came from a liturgical environment in which the creed was firmly familiar. This would argue in favour of Ireland as their original home. Unfortunately, since the *Stowe Missal* is our earliest fixed date, we cannot determine when the use of the creed began in Ireland, but we could presume that it was at least in use by the early eighth century.

That a congregation would be thoroughly familiar with the creed is something that we take very much for granted, for the creed is not only widely used liturgically, but has established itself within Christian consciousness as a summary of 'the core' of Christian belief. Whether or not the agreed symbol of the Fathers of the Council of Constantinople of 381 does contain the core of Christian beliefs is a matter for systematic theologians. However, historically, it was not originally so considered, and the notion that it is 'a statement of core beliefs' is itself a consequence of familiarity with it through its use in

---

68 See Lapidge and Sharpe, *Bibliography*, item 532. 69 See Lapidge and Sharpe, *Bibliography*, item 517. 70 McNally, 'Seven Hiberno-Latin sermons', pp 126-7. 71 Compare B. Capelle, 'Alcuin et l'histoire du symbole de la messe' in *Recherches de Théologie Ancienne et Médiévale* vi (1934), pp 249-60. 72 Royal Irish Academy, Dublin, MS D.II.3, ff 20-1 (Warner (ed.), *The Stowe Missal*, p. 8); and compare F.X. Murphy, 'Creed' in the *New Catholic Encyclopaedia*, iv, pp 432-8 at 436. 73 Cf. J.H. Emminghaus, *The Eucharist: essence, form, celebration* (Collegeville, 1978), p. 150. 74 Cf. J.A. Jungmann, *The Mass of the Roman Rite: its origins and development* (New York, 1951), p. 469. Note, however, that Emminghaus, *The Eucharist*, p. 150, supposes that its use was more widespread: 'In the seventh/eighth century it [the Creed] entered the Gaulish-Frankish Mass'. I take it that Emminghaus was referring to its use in the insular area as witnessed in the *Stowe Missal*.

the Eucharistic liturgy. Before its introduction into the Eucharistic rite, the creed as a single text was a touchstone of theological orthodoxy on particular points relating to Christology, and other creeds (such as the so-called 'Apostles' Creed) were met normally in the course of the baptismal liturgy in the form of questions. These questions were not about Christian beliefs as such, but belief in the revealed nature of God in whose name they, or those they sponsored, were about to be baptised. However, the preacher of these homilies assumes that his congregation not only met the creed frequently and can identify quotations from it, but also view it as a summary of all that they must believe. Is there a better candidate for a country where by the late-eighth or early-ninth century the creed was thoroughly familiar than Ireland?

These five homilies all make their points in a concise manner. In all of them a tight logic holds all those points in sequence, and all have a fondness for listing elements whether it is the qualities of good works in IV or the list of the virtues that God teaches as against the vices that the devil teaches in V, or the list of seven signs (events in Christ's life as professed in the creed paralleling events in our lives through grace) in VII. In each sermon one can easily imagine a preacher listing qualities of Christian behaviour on his fingers as he spoke. Thus the style, and the use of the creed in two of the five texts, argues in favour of a single author for homilies III-VII. These arguments corroborate those of McNally for the unity in authorship. Moreover, they strengthen his argument for the probability of an Irish author from parallels with insular material. This can now be seen as collateral evidence for a probability based on Ireland as having the longest familiarity with the regular use of the creed as part of the Liturgy of the Word. If one accepts McNally's arguments, as I do, when they are restricted to sermons III-VII (while rejecting his distinction between I to IV and V to VII), then in this little collection we have a window, otherwise unavailable to us apart from in homilies surviving in Old Irish, upon the ordinary preaching of the early Irish Church. Two homilies are on belief as encapsulated in the creed: the first with a simple explanatory expansion of the text taken as a narrative of the work of God which ends in human beatitude; the second, a homily that seeks to relate the creed to the basic events of life seen as foreshadowed in Christ, and again ending in the destiny of eternal life with Christ. The other three relate to the moral life of Christians. Sermon IV stresses the passing of this world and the need for good works as a preparation for the kingdom – the homily is based upon part of the Sermon on the Mount (Matthew 5-7) and uses Matthew 6:33, 7:7, and 7:8 in succession so it is possible that it was for use with a pericope running from Matthew 6:33-7:8. Sermon V sets out the good things to be done and the evils to be avoided if we are to remain in the love of Christ and reach salvation; while sermon VI presents a list of changes in the perception of life necessary for the Christian, and again the ability to inherit eternal life is the measure of the success of this conversion. The common features in the underlying theology seem to be that the Christian faith can be laid out as a series of straightforward instructions and demands, and that their end-point is the Christian's reign with Christ in the final kingdom. When these simple didactic sermons are read alongside the 'Tract on the Mass' from the *Stowe Missal* the homiletic character of the 'Tract' becomes far more apparent. The sermons and the 'Tract' share the same ethos: both seek to explain the realities of the Christian life – such as the liturgical actions at the Eucharist or the creed – by listing the perceivable and knowable realities beyond the senses towards which the ones point. It is as if both the sermons and the 'Tract' use the same sacramental semiology that is laid out in Sermon VI: oportet nos excitare animas nortras de presentibus ad absentia ... de terrenis ad celestia, de imis ad alta ... ('it is fitting that we raise our souls from things that are present to things that are absent ... from things earthly to things heavenly, from the depths to the heights').[75]

We must now turn to the first two sermons which not only differ from the rest in style, but have several points of contact with each other. Let us consider each separately. Sermon I is the most interesting since it was not confined to this collection but circulated widely both in manuscripts with insular connections and in manuscripts without any such associations. J.J. O'Donnell added a note about this in the edition when he pointed out that Rudolph Willard had edited the homily from two other manuscripts (Bibliothèque Nationale, Paris, MS Lat. 2628 from the eleventh century, and University College, Oxford, MS Latin 61 from the thirteenth or fourteenth centuries) and that these later texts were fuller than Sermon I, but that 'the text they represent parallels McNally's paragraph for paragraph at all points, sentence by sentence for perhaps 75 per cent of the whole, and word for word for perhaps 30 per cent of the whole.'[76]

The homily first came to notice in 1911 in the doctoral dissertation of Louise Dudley, 'The Egyptian elements in the legend of the body and soul'.[77] Her thesis was that a remnant of a pre-Christian Egyptian motif was detectable in a range of homilies from medieval Europe which involve a

---

[75] The developments in sacramental theory in the centuries between Augustine and the Carolingians is an area that has not received proper attention from historians of theology; for an introduction to the problems involved, see T. O'Loughlin, 'The symbol gives life: Eucherius of Lyons' formula for exegesis' in T. Finan and V. Twomey (eds), *Scriptural interpretation in the Fathers: letter and spirit* (Dublin, 1995), pp 221-52. On how this developed in the sixth and early seventh centuries, O'Loughlin, 'Christ as the focus of Genesis exegesis in Isidore of Seville'; and for its use in Hiberno-Latin, compare T. O'Loughlin, 'Distant islands: the topography of holiness in the *Nauigatio Sancti Brendani*,' in M. Glasscoe (ed.), *The medieval mystical tradition: England, Ireland, Wales* (Exeter Symposium VI, Woodbridge, 1999), pp 1-20. There is a summary of the various approaches in O'Loughlin, *Journeys on the edge*, chs 2 and 5.
[76] McNally, 'Seven Hiberno-Latin sermons', p. 133. [77] Louise Dudley, *The Egyptian*

dialogue between the body and the soul at the moment of death. She considered Homily 36 (on the soul's exit from the body) from the *Leabhar Breac* (a manuscript considered more fully in the following essay) to be one example of such a pagan survival.[78] In an appendix to her dissertation she printed the homily from Bibliothèque Nationale, Paris, MS Lat. 2628 as exemplifying 'the variations which the Egyptian traditions suffered in the Western homilies.'[79] She notes that this homily (our Sermon I) contained 'no speech of the soul to the body, this homily clearly belongs to the same line of tradition as much of the body and soul material ... and in the antithesis between the song of the demons and the song of the angels it should be compared with the Irish homily [from the *Leabhar Breac*].'[80] In the same year that Dudley published her thesis, Carl Marstrander published a 'little tale' from the *Liber Flavus Fergusiorum* I entitled 'The two deaths.'[81] The tale differs from the homily in many respects but contains the homily's dialogue, partly retained in Latin, between the soul and the demons and then with the angels. Marstrander did not comment upon the tale except to note that 'the language gives evidence of considerable age.' This text printed and translated by Marstrander was later commented upon by St John D. Seymour who gave the dialogue involving the angels and demons the title, by which it is now most commonly known, 'the three utterances [of the soul].'[82]

The next stage in the investigation was conducted by Rudolph Willard in the 1930s where he not only found another text of the homily in Latin, already mentioned, but found versions of the homily in Anglo-Saxon in a number of manuscripts.[83] He saw both Irish and Anglo-Saxon versions as derivative from Latin, and this Latin homily he held to be derived from a Greek original.[84] The next person to examine this material after Willard was Réginald Grégoire in *Les Homéliaires du moyen âge*[85] who found the homily in the *Homiliary of Toledo* and noted five other manuscripts containing the homily in Latin.[86]

More recently the homily's theme has again attracted attention from scholars working on Hiberno-Latin. Martin McNamara in his survey *The*

---

elements in the legend of the body and soul (Baltimore, 1911). 78 Dudley, *Egyptian elements*, pp 128-44. 79 Dudley, *Egyptian elements*, p. 164. 80 Dudley, *Egyptian elements*, p. 165. 81 C. Marstrander, 'The two deaths' in *Ériu* v (1911), pp 120-5. 82 'The bringing forth of the soul in Irish literature' in *Journal of Theological Studies* xxii (1921), pp 16-20 at pp 19-20. 83 He first mentioned the theme in 'The address of the soul to the body' in *Publications of the Modern Language Association of America* l (1935), pp 957-83 at pp 960-1. He then produced a study comparing the various Anglo-Saxon and Irish versions, with the Latin text identified by Dudley, in *Two Apocrypha in Old English homilies* (Leipzig, 1935), pp. 31-149 – this is still the most complete study of the theme; and finally he edited the Latin texts upon which the vernacular versions are based in 'The Latin texts of The three utterances of the soul' in *Speculum* xii (1937), pp 147-66. 84 See the stemma in his 1937 article, p. 164. 85 Rome, 1966. 86 Item T80, pp 224-6, and compare p. 177 for the list of manuscripts.

Apocrypha in the Irish Church concentrated on the apocryphal theme, as distinct from the homily that he did not mention as such.[87] He took the version found in *Liber Flavus Fergusiorum* I as the basic text, but recognised the Irish versions as dependent on a Latin original. Charles D. Wright has accepted McNally's position that the homily is originally Irish and that it diffused both in Latin and in the vernaculars from an Irish source.[88] Wright, in association with Mary F. Wack, has now (as of 1993) identified over twenty further manuscripts and intends to produce an edition of the Latin sermon and the Old English versions. We shall have to await that edition to see whether an Irish origin for the sermon will account for all the evidence of diffusion. However, whether or not we have an 'Irish' homily, we can certainly see the homily as providing an insight into sermons preached in early Christian Ireland, and as evidence that the taste in homilies there was very similar to that in many other places in western Europe at the time.

Sermon II resembles Sermon I in that its central concern is with the Judgement, but its imagery is drawn from the Last Judgement passage found only in Matthew's Gospel (25:31-46). The sermon has, to my knowledge, not been found elsewhere, yet it stands apart from sermons III-VII in that it has a developed rhetorical style. It appeals to the congregation directly by name and calls for them to reflect on themselves and their destiny. The staccato listing of 'key-points' is absent, and at no time has it the feel of the school-room: the preacher is a human being addressing other adults. It is, moreover, the only sermon that clearly could not be used within the monastery for it calls on husbands to love their wives, to honour their parents and teach their children. It also has two curious echoes of Christian antiquity aside from the texts now incorporated in the New Testament canon. Its opening command *Ad eclesiam* [sic] *frequenter conuenite* has no parallel in the canon, but does echo a phrase from the final chapter of the *Didache*: 'be gathered [all of you] frequently together seeking those things which will be of profit to your souls' (16:2). Moreover, that chapter of the *Didache* is an ancient sermon on the coming judgement using the same traditions that would find a place in gospel writing in Matthew.[89] Have we here a trace of a much earlier tradition? The answer to that question cannot yet be given, but it does deserve further study.

---

87 (Dublin 1974, and with revisions 1984), Item 102D, pp 127-8.   88 I have not tried to list the many Anglo-Saxon scholars, for example the late J.E. Cross, who have worked on this theme for there is a detailed summary of the state of the question, with particular emphasis on Anglo-Saxon material, in Wright's *The Irish tradition in Old English literature* (Cambridge, 1993), ch. 5, especially pp. 215-8; he had earlier looked at the topic in 'Apocryphal lore and insular tradition in St Gall, Stiftsbibliothek MS 908' in Ní Chatháin and Richter (eds), *Irland und die Christenheit*, pp 134-7.   89 For a convenient summary of the relationship between the materials in the *Didache* which were later recorded as the words of Jesus in the gospels, compare C.N. Jefford, *The sayings of Jesus in the teaching of the twelve Apostles* (Leiden, 1989), especially pp 85-90. On the imperative qualities of passages in the *Didache* as sermons for oral delivery, see I.H.

In contrast to those who have simply accepted McNally's probability that the collection is the work of a single, Irish homilist as a fact, I would point out that the weight of evidence for that position is greatest with regard to the final five sermons, but that the evidence tells against all seven originating in one mind. Was the author of sermons III-VII the one who bound the other two with his work, or was there a collection of five homilies to which two others were added? Such questions cannot be answered. Sermons III-VII are probably of Irish origin, but even if not, they give us our best view of the kind of homily material used in Ireland for ordinary people. As for Sermons I and II, the question of their origin is best left open. However, we can be certain that Sermon I was not only used in Ireland, but was popular there, and therefore it illustrates the sermon tastes of Christians in Ireland just as it does those of Christians in Anglo-Saxon England, the Rhineland, and even further afield. As for Sermon II, its origins are even more obscure. The fact that the compiler of this popular (witness Sermon I) and practical (Sermons III to VII) collection included it, allows us to see it as one more example of the sort of sermon material that circulated in the late eighth century, and so it indicates another sort of homily that was probably used in Ireland.

This chapter's aim has been to survey the evidence for preaching in early Christian Ireland that has survived in the form of homilies and to show some of the problems that need to be addressed with further research. It should be complemented by what is said about preaching in texts such as the laws or in saints' lives, but that is work for another day. A feature of the early Irish Church that struck both Kenney and McNally was just how little homily material has survived: only a few isolated homilies and the *Instructiones* of Columbanus are secure. Other collections show links with Ireland and may contain Irish compositions. In some cases, we can be fairly certain that these are at least representative of actual preaching in Ireland, while more often we can say that they indicate the kind of material used both in Ireland and by Irish clergy on the European mainland. That so little material can be identified as originating in Ireland has troubled many scholars in recent decades. There has been a regrettable tendency to champion as Irish every text proposed as 'possibly Irish' by discovering Irish 'links' and parallels. Such arguments from symptoms ultimately rest on the notion of an Irish taste and theology distinct from the rest of Europe at the time. Yet the very fact that the question has to be raised at all implies that any Irish homily in Latin was just as much to the taste of contemporary Continental congregations as that which they themselves produced! This quest for parallels, overlapping interests, common elements and themes – for example those identified by scholars like

Henderson, 'Didache and orality in synoptic comparison' in *Journal of Biblical Literature* cxi (1992), pp 283-306; and compare A. Milavec, 'Distinguishing true and false prophets: the protective wisdom of the Didache' in *Journal of Early Christian Studies* ii (1994), pp 117-36.

J.E. Cross[90] and Charles Wright[91] – has been too often pursued in the hope of identifying yet another 'Irish text' without recognising what makes these parallels and overlaps truly significant. The preaching of early Irish clergy, in its written expression in Latin, in the period before the ninth century, shows that the religious culture sustaining it was neither consistently trail-blazing nor backwaterish, but that is played an integral part in the contemporary developments in theology, homiletics and liturgy of the Latin Church.

---

90 From among the many writings by Cross which noted the use of Irish materials by Anglo-Saxon writers one could pick out *Cambridge Pembroke College MS. 25: a Carolingian sermonary used by Anglo-Saxon preachers* (London, 1987); and 'On Hiberno-Latin texts and Anglo-Saxon writings' in O'Loughlin (ed.), *The scriptures in early medieval Ireland*, pp 69-79.   91 See the references to his works above.

Preaching in medieval Ireland: the Irish tradition

Brian Murdoch

There are several problems which have to be faced by anyone wishing to examine the early Irish vernacular sermon: first, that there are relatively few extant examples; secondly, that even with those we *do* have, it is sometimes hard to tell whether they really are sermons at all; and thirdly, that scholarship has been most confident in denying to the medieval Irish sermons much in the way of literary value. Whitley Stokes, for instance, described the principal collection of sermons in the *Leabhar Breac* as 'nearly worthless', adding the qualifier presumably only in view of their philological value. More recent critics have rightly drawn attention to the discrepancy between the paucity of surviving written material and the great amount of Irish vernacular preaching there must have been in the middle ages,[1] and there is always a difference between the evaluation of a written text and the attempt to assess actual preaching to a given audience at a given time. Better editions and fuller studies of what we do have are still regularly presented in the secondary literature as desiderata, most recently by Hildegard Tristram, who has herself remedied the situation somewhat by offering two systematic surveys, first as part of her study of the *Sex aetates mundi*, and then independently.[2] As far as other studies are concerned, the writings of the late Frederic Mac Donncha (including his doctoral dissertation), another dissertation by Jean Rittmueller, and a handful of articles, principally on the *Leabhar Breac* homilies, by Gearóid Mac Eoin and others, represent pretty well the full extent.[3]

---

1 Thomas O'Loughlin, 'The Celtic homily: creeds and eschatology' in *Milltown Studies* xli (1998), pp 99-115. I am indebted to Dr O'Loughlin for a copy of his paper, and I owe a considerable debt of gratitude (as often before in the field of Irish studies) to Dr Máire West for copies of hard-to-find material and for much additional information. 2 See Frederic Mac Donncha's summary of his doctoral thesis on the *Leabhar Breac* homilies, 'Medieval Irish homilies' in Martin McNamara (ed.), *Biblical studies: the medieval Irish contribution* (Dublin, 1976), pp 59-71. Hildegard L.C. Tristram, *Sex aetates mundi. Die Weltzeitalter bei den Angelsachsen und den Iren. Untersuchungen und Texte* (Heidelberg, 1985), pp 133-152. Her interim conclusion is, 'ein weites Forschungsfeld erwartet uns hier' ('a rich field of research awaits us here', p. 152). Her later work, published in the *Sitzungsberichte* of the Austrian Academy (Phil.-Hist. Kl. 623) is more specific, *Early Insular preaching: verbal artistry and method of composition* (Vienna, 1995). 3 Frederic Mac Donncha [Finnbar Mac Donnchada],

The medieval Irish sermon is in its basic form a spoken prose instruction in the vernacular (sometimes with a Latin admixture), delivered after the Gospel on any day, but especially on a feast day or a Sunday, and more particularly, perhaps, during Lent. It will more strictly be either a *homily*, expounding biblical verses in detail from one of the lessons of the Mass, or a thematic *sermon*, though this also takes a biblical citation as a starting point. The forms overlap and are confused from an early stage, but there are recurrent shared stylistic features, notably the exordial address – the *karissimi* formula – and the use of the inclusive first person plural, plus a sometimes equally formulaic concluding benediction invoking, say, the intercessionary aid of a saint. Saints' lives themselves are close to the thematic sermon in that they are more or less by definition *exempla* for good behaviour, albeit a saint's *vita* is sometimes more *admiranda* than *imitanda*, and Irish texts (and others) adapt saints' lives with the addition of an exordium and with concluding homiletic prayers, and even with homiletic introductory sections. But these features may be superficial additions to what are principally written readings, *legenda*, with their own different stylistic and generic determinatives.[4] A collection of written sermons in Latin (or later in the vernacular, or both), a *homiliarium*, might contain examples of the different types. A somewhat truncated relative is the preaching-aid or handbook, and we are again clearly in the area of written texts. Later on, of course, the techniques of preaching were categorized in writing in the *ars predicandi*.

Preaching in the vernacular was encouraged at an early stage and various Church Councils decreed the use of native-language sermons, probably largely translations of Latin originals. Charlemagne's *Admonitio generalis* in 789 called for preaching to all the people in Continental Europe, and

'Na hoimilí sa Leabhar Breac, i Lebor na hUidhre, i Leabhar Mhic Cárthaigh Riabaigh, agus i Vita Tripartita Sancti Patricii, a mBunús, a nÚdar, agus nDáta', PhD thesis, University College, Galway, 1972 and his 'Seanmóireacht in Éirinn ó 1000 go 1200' in Máirtín Mac Conmara (ed.), *An léann Eaglasta in Éirinn 1000-1200* (Dublin, 1982), pp 77-95; see on the Irish texts Hildegard Tristram in *Medieval Sermon Studies Newsletter* no. 14 (Spring 1984), p. 13 and Mac Donncha, 'Medieval Irish homilies', pp 59-71; Gearóid Mac Eoin, 'Observations on some Middle-Irish homilies' in P. Ní Cháthain and M. Richter (eds), *Irland und Europa im frühem Mittelalter: Ireland and Europe in the early middle ages* (Stuttgart, 1996), pp 195-211 Jean Rittmueller, 'The *Leabhar Breac* Latin and Middle-Irish homily *"In cena Domini"*: an edition and source analysis', PhD thesis, Harvard University, 1984. Parts of this thesis (available via University Microfilms) appeared in the *Proceedings of the Harvard Celtic Colloquium* i (1982), pp 1-8 and ii (1983), pp 1-10. The former was expanded as 'The Gospel commentary of Máel Brigte Ua Máeluanaig and its Hiberno-Latin background' in *Peritia* ii (1983), pp 185-214. The dissertation still provides very useful summary of the *Leabhar Breac* and its homilies in general. 4 See the divisions made by Honorius Augustodunensis for his own *Speculum Ecclesiae*, a collection of Latin sermons much-used by vernacular preachers in *Patrologia Latina* [hereafter *PL*] 172, 1085. It is cited among others by Rudolf Cruel, *Geschichte der deutschen Predigt im Mittelalter* ([Detmold, 1879], Darmstadt, 1966), p. 2. The intent of all, however, was *instruere populum*.

sermons, probably Latin ones, by Irish preachers were clearly translated during the mission to southern Germany. Ermenrich of St Gall, Walahfrid Strabo and others laud Irish preaching, and we are told of Hibernian preachers, including St Gall himself, giving sermons which were translated immediately into German.[5]

There is, finally, an early link between sermons and poetry. The German term *Reimpredigt* was used in 1882. A century later a study of Welsh texts used the terms 'sermon poetry' and 'sermon songs' and the relationship between the two genres has been examined in detail for Middle English.[6] There is a German poem from about 1150 which gives the story of St Martin and also expounds the Gospel pericope of Zachaeus the tax-collector. It is almost certainly the work of a canon regular of the Minster of St Martin in Colmar, and it was clearly read out to an aristocratic, secular, married, and most importantly *moneyed* audience, telling them that in spite of Matthew 19:24, the rich could indeed enter the kingdom of heaven, provided they gave alms. Its style is almost completely homiletic, with the inclusive voice, biblical exposition and a link either to the *dedicatio* (for which the Zachaeus-pericope is a lesson) of the Martinsmünster, or to Martinmas itself, the day on which taxes were traditionally collected and the patronal feast of that church. But whether we can really call it a sermon, and when it was delivered, remain unclear.[7]

Stokes referred to twenty-two Irish sermons (with a footnote adding the Cambrai Homily), mainly in the *Leabhar Breac* and the *Lebor na hUidre*, which he grouped into classes according to subject.[8] This has not been expanded upon greatly, even though not everything has been printed – Tristram has drawn attention to some unedited sermons in the *Liber Flavus Fergusiorum* and in a Paris manuscript. It is useful to take Tristram's survey in her *Aetates*-book as a starting point, because it is comprehensive, succint, and honest about the nature of the texts.[9] Of the material that she includes, the sermons of St Columbanus – the *Instructiones* – are derivative (their editor points out that plagiarism was hardly a stigma) and they are in Latin. The rhetoric and emotional grand style of Columbanus's sermons noted by

5 Cruel, *Geschichte*, p. 7f; J. M. Clark, *The abbey of St Gall* (Cambridge, 1926), pp 18-54. 6 Eduard Schröder, 'Reimpredigt' in *Zeitschrift für deutsches Altertum* xxvi (1882), pp 199-200; E. I. Rowlands, 'Religious poetry in late medieval Wales' in *Bulletin of the Board of Celtic Studies* xxx (1982), pp 1-19; Siegfried Wenzel, *Preachers, poets and the early English lyric* (Princeton, 1986) and the comments in Alan Fletcher's essay below. 7 I have discussed the work in detail in my study 'Treasures stored in heaven: the early Alemannic "Scopf von dem lône" from Colmar' in *Amsterdamer Beiträge zur älteren Germanistik* xxxiii (1991), pp 89-115. The small work is culturally of considerable significance in view of its context. The search for comparable Irish works in this mode would take us beyond the scope of this brief survey. 8 Whitley Stokes, 'A Middle-Irish homily on S. Martin of Tours' in *Revue Celtique* ii (1873-5), pp 381-402. 9 Tristram, *Sex aetates*, pp 133-52. I omit the Rennes sermons referred to by Jean Rittmueller in her dissertation.

Tristram are especially clear in sermon VII, for example, an exemplary set-piece on the human will,[10] but its connection with vernacular preaching requires special argument. The *Catechesis Celtica*, too, is a series of Latin excerpts from the Fathers with a few Celtic (Brythonic) glosses, and might have been used in the compilation of sermons, but speculation on this particular text has led to an interesting double jeopardy as far as Irish studies are concerned: the (very few) glosses in it are Welsh or possibly Cornish, but Paul Grosjean considered that the work was Irish in origin. However, he did *not* think that it was used as an aid to preaching; André Wilmart, who part-edited the text, on the other hand, while considering it to be a preaching-aid, did not think that it was Irish. The evidence is more fully reviewed in Thomas O'Loughlin's essay above. At best the case remains not proven, though the role of the exegetical handbook in preaching is important. Other Irish(-influenced) exegetical works – Tristram lists a number – do provide evidence for the particular use of emotional rhetoric, eclecticism, and above all, a preference for eschatology.[11]

Stokes and Tristram both include with the early Irish sermons two further categories of vernacular texts which are at least on the edge of preaching. First comes a group of works placed by Tristram under the heading of 'sermons in the *Lebor na hUidre*', whilst she makes it clear almost immediately that they are (with one possible exception) not sermons at all, but theological tractates with virtually none of the characteristic stylistic features,[12] in spite of a quasi-homiletic final formula.[13] Irish apocryphal texts such as these have been shown to have provided the *source* for homilies in other languages altogether, such as the Old Norse *Homiliu-Bok*,[14] but they are not really sermons themselves. Secondly, and with similar problems, come the saints' lives, principally the *Vita tripartita* of St Patrick and a number of others in the *Leabhar Breac*, in the *Book of Lismore* (*Leabhar Mhic Cárthaigh Riabaigh*) and elsewhere.

10 G.S.M. Walker (ed.), *Sancti Columbani opera* (Scriptores Latini Hiberniae 2, Dublin, 1957, rept 1970), pp xxxix-xliv for a general introduction and pp 90-3 for *Instructio* VII. 11 Tristram, *Early Insular preaching*, pp 34-8 gives details of editions and a bibliography for the various relevant works. On the *Catechesis Celtica* and its particular problems, see Peter O'Dwyer, *Célí Dé: spiritual reform in Ireland, 750-900* (Dublin, 1977, rev. ed. 1981), pp 166-7 and the comments of Thomas O'Loughlin in his essay above. The links to the Culdee movement are a separate issue. 12 Tristram, *Sex aetates*, pp 137-43. 13 See Gearóid Mac Eoin, 'Na críocha déanacha i seanmóirí na Sean- agus na Méan-Ghaeilge' in *Diagacht/Theology: Bulletin of the Western Theology Research Association* ii (1997), pp 20-6. Other papers in that issue, introduced by Martin McNamara and devoted to eschatology, are also relevant. 14 Mattias Tveitane, 'Irish Apocrypha in Norse tradition? On the source of some medieval homilies' in *Arv* xxii (1966), pp 111-35 is of interest, but does not refer to any of these tracts. See also Charles Wright, 'The Irish enumerative style in Old English homiletic literature, especially Vercelli Homily XVI' in *Cambridge Medieval Celtic Studies* no. 18 (1989), pp 27-74 (based on a Cornell PhD dissertation from 1984).

The relevant texts in the *Lebor na hUidre* include the two apocalyptic works *Dá Brón Flatha Nime*, the 'Two Sorrows of Heaven' (which was not considered by Stokes to be a sermon), and the *Fís Adomnán*, the 'Vision of Adomnán', plus the *Scéla Lái Brátha*, the 'Tidings of Doomsday', and *Scéla na hEsérgi*, the 'Tidings of the Resurrection'. Tristram (cautiously) takes the *Scéla Lái Brátha* as exhibiting homiletic elements (or at least containing an exordium apparently addressed to a public), but this is by no means clear, and none of these works is unequivocally a sermon. However, they do have something to say *about* preaching, and they say it in Irish. One might add to them a further well-known Irish apocryphal text (though neither Stokes nor Tristram do so), namely *An Teanga Bithnua*, 'The Ever-New Tongue', known in several recensions, and allowing us to hear, as it were, expositions of parts of the Bible in a theological question-and-answer session in which the Tongue speaks, so to speak, in tongues. The connecting element of all these works is once again a stress on a dominant eschatology.

Dá Brón Flatha Nime and *Fís Adamnán* are both apocalyptic visions told in the third person as straightforward narratives.[15] In the case of the first, the substance of Elijah's sermon to the birds in Paradise in this Irish-language offshoot of the eastern Enoch-and-Elijah/Antichrist tradition would certainly have been familiar as he spoke about the benefits of heaven and the fate of the wicked in hell, the need to do good works and the coming of Christ. His preaching was presumably in the form of a thematic *sermo;* Elijah takes a Gospel-book with him, opens it to begin with a Gospel passage, and preaches to the birds about the day of judgement. His avian audience reacts in terror after quite literally a hell-fire sermon, an unlikely response, perhaps, for birds who have been feeding on the berries of the tree of life, but clear enough for a human audience. *Dá Brón Flatha Nime* served as one of the sources for the rather longer 'Vision of Adomnán', in which we are allowed first to see with Adomnán the torments of the souls in hell, and then to hear preaching at second-hand again. Adomnán preached, we are told, to the crowds as long as he lived, teaching (in Irish to a secular audience) about the rewards of heaven and the eye-wateringly specific tortures to be meted out to the souls in hell that have just been revealed to the reader or listener in the more clearly apocalyptic portion of the work. The last part tells how Adomnán preached to the great assembly and to the nobles of Ireland. The continuity of this hell-fire preaching is underlined when we are told that this is what Patrick had done, as had Peter, Paul and Silvester to Constantine (an

15 On the two texts, see Martin McNamara, *The Apocrypha in the Irish Church* (Dublin, 1975), pp 24-7 and 126. Both works are in R.I. Best and Osborn Bergin (eds), *Lebor na hUidre* (Dublin, 1929), pp 47-4 and 67-76. The former, however, is imperfect in *Lebor na hUidre*, but there are other recensions; see G. Dotin, 'Les deux chagrins du royaume du ciel' in *Revue Celtique* xxi (1909), pp 349-83. Both works are translated in Máire Herbert and Martin McNamara (eds), *Irish Biblical Apocrypha* (Edinburgh, 1989), pp 19-21 and 137-48.

allusion to the familiar narrative in the *Donation of Constantine* and many later works), as well as Elijah again, whose attentive birds this time emit cries of lamentation and draw blood from their own bodies.[16]

The 'Tidings of Doomsday', a text dubbed 'an early-middle-Irish homily' by Stokes, and its companion-piece in *Lebor na hUidre*, 'The Tidings of the Resurrection', may be taken together,[17] though their precise relationship to the sermon is again tenuous. They open with general injunctions, and they describe the end of the world, heaven and hell, but specific sermon features are otherwise limited, though both bear further witness to preoccupation with the eschaton. In the presentations of heaven and hell, the first draws perhaps upon *Saltair na Rann*, the vision of hell which also has a close verbal connection to that presented in a genuine sermon in the *Yellow Book of Lecan*. That same sermon has, indeed, a concluding prayer also found in one version of the 'Ever-New Tongue', while the 'Vision of Adomnán' is also cited in sermons proper.[18]

Saints' lives also represent, as indicated, a generic problem-area between the sermon and the devotional reading-text (*legenda*).[19] Stylistic determinatives of the sermon need to be present beside those of the *vita* (specific elements of *imitatio Christi*, such as childhood wisdom, healing and other miracles). The saint's life is a fluid genre, however, overlapping into a whole variety of other genres, including the literary narrative proper, and even straightforward adaptation into the vernacular can be problematic.[20] The best-known (and most important for sermon studies) of the Irish examples of saints' lives is the *Vita tripartita* of St Patrick, known in the main from Bodleian Library, Oxford, Rawlinson MS B 512, a fourteenth or fifteenth century manuscript which contains other *vitae* and indeed further sermons,[21] and also

---

16 The description of judgement day is strongly reminiscent of related works like the Old High German poem *Muspilli*, 'The destruction of the world by fire', a tenth-century work probably aimed at a secular aristocratic audience and designed for moral amelioration. Heinz Finger, *Untersuchungen zum Muspilli* (Göppingen, 1977) does note some Irish parallels, though not to sermons.   17 In the Best/Bergin edition of *Lebor na hUidre*, pp 77-81 and 82-8 (in the MS they follow the *Fís Adomnán*). Both are edited and translated by Whitley Stokes, 'The tidings of Doomsday' in *Revue Celtique* iv (1879-80), pp 245-57 and 'Tidings of the Resurrection' in *Revue Celtique* xxv (1904), pp 232-59.   18 Mac Eoin, 'Na criocha', p. 25, has shown links with *Leabhar Breac* Sermon XXXVI on the soul's exit from the body. See his 'Observations' on the *Scéla Laí Brátha* and the *Saltair na Rann*.   19 On the genre as such, see Dieter von der Nahmer, *Die lateinische Heiligenvita* (Darmstadt, 1994), esp. pp 131-45 and 175-7. The standard study as far as the Irish Latin material is concerned remains Richard Sharpe's *Medieval Irish saints' lives: an introduction to the Vitae Sanctorum Hiberniae* (Oxford, 1991). 20 See Hugh Magennis, 'Listen now all and understand: adaptation of hagiographical material for vernacular audiences' in *Speculum* lxxi (1996), pp 27-42; Clare Stancliffe, 'Early "Irish" Biblical exegesis' in *Studia Patristica* xii (1975), pp 361-70 has some interesting brief comments on the point, esp. p.369, but there she separates (at least implicitly) the sermon from the *vita*. 21 See the monumental edition by Whitley Stokes for the Rolls Series, *The tripartite life of St Patrick, with other documents relating to that saint* (2 vols, London, 1887). The text is in vol. i and

from the British Library, London, Egerton MS 93 as well as in the *Leabhar Breac* and *Book of Lismore* homilies. The *Vita tripartita* seems to have been composed in the tenth century, but was given sermon elements in the eleventh.[22] This Irish vernacular *sermo de sanctis* is essentially a hybrid, formed by grafting sermon elements onto a narrative life without much in the way of integration. Only the first part of each section reads like a brief homily which is, however, used only as a lead-in to details of the life, which is not itself treated in the same way, and is usually long. All three introductory sections adopt the standard homiletic procedure of interpreting biblical verses associated with a Mass pericope. The work begins with a familiar verse, Isaiah 9:2, central to the Mass of the Nativity (but in a non-Vulgate form, with *sedebat* instead of *ambulabat*), in Latin and then Irish, which is interpreted with reference to Jerome. The interpretation is detailed, and Christ is seen as the light of the world, and one of the rays of this light is St Patrick. The rest of the first section presents the miracles of Patrick without particular commentary, until we are told (in the Egerton text): *Biat na ferta conicci so indiu* – 'Let the miracles be as far as this today', a recurrent marker for oral presentation, but not an appropriate conclusion for a sermon, though there is a brief summary. In the second part, the verse is the words of the Christ after the Resurrection in Matthew 28:19, the Gospel for Trinity Sunday. The text is given in Latin and after a very brief interpretation in Irish and Latin comes another passage in Latin on the importance of teaching before baptism and of the unity of the Trinity. We are shown Patrick preaching, but then come further miracles until we again come to a suitable break: *Biit dano na ferta coso indiu*, 'so far today are the miracles.' The injunction to venerate Patrick's relics is not necessarily homiletic. The third section begins with a single sentence from Psalm 67:36, associated with saints' feasts, and leading therefore easily and briefly into the final part of the miracles. None of the sections *ends* with an homiletic feature except perhaps the last, which concludes with the briefest of prayers 'Alme trocairi, et reliqua', 'we beseech mercy, etc.'. The text seems indeed to have been read in three sections. The *Leabhar Breac* homily on St Patrick elaborates the life, but does end with a very brief formulaic prayer: 'I implore God's mercy through Patrick's intercession! May we all attain to that unity. May we deserve it. May we dwell therein for ever and ever! Amen'. This prayer, with slight variations, becomes a stock feature in Irish sermons on the saints. The *Book of Lismore* Patrick-homily has a briefer, final benediction.[23]

additional material including the *Leabhar Breac* homily based upon it is in vol.ii. See i, pp xxvi ff. on the homilies on the Passion and on the Nativity found elsewhere in the principal MSS. The more recent edition of the *Tripartite life* is that by Kathleen Mulchrone, *Bethu Phátraic* (Dublin, 1939). **22** Máire Herbert, *Iona, Kells and Derry* (Oxford, 1988; reprinted Dublin, 1995), p. 195. See Gearóid Mac Eoin, 'The dating of Middle Irish texts' in *Proceedings of the British Academy* lxviii (1982), pp 127-34 and Frederic Mac Donncha, 'Dáta Vita Tripartita Sancti Patricii' in *Éigse* xviii (1980), pp 125-52 and xix (1983), pp 354-72. **23** Stokes, *Tripartite life*, ii, 488f. 'Alim trócaire nDé tria impide Pátraic. Roissam uli inoentaid sin:

Other vernacular saints' lives in homiletic adaptation are found in *Leabhar Breac*, *Book of Lismore*, and various other manuscripts; that of Colum Cille, for example, is found in seven different places. It is worth considering the homiletic aspects of those collected in *Book of Lismore*, since these illustrate again the generic problem.[24] The most frequent state of affairs is the addition to a straightforward *vita* of an homiletic introduction linked with the feast day, and then a concluding prayer. As far as the latter is concerned, however, we must remember that such a brief comment (in the inclusive we-form) is also a standard feature of narrative literature of all kinds, religious: ('ȝif ous grace for to winne/þe ioie þat Adam now is inne,), quasi-religious ('do besâzen si gelîche/daz ewige rîche./alsô müezez uns allen/ze jungest gevallen!/ den lôn, den si dâ nâmen/des helfe uns got! âmen.') and secular ('Ihesu bryng vs to hys blys/That neuyr schall haue ende!'). My examples are deliberately from different languages, although the first two relate the final prayer to the (religious) story that has just been told.[25]

The *Book of Lismore* life of Colum Cille resembles the *Vita tripartita* in that it begins with an exposition of Genesis 12:1 according to the *sensus litteralis*, expounding in fairly simple terms the motivation of Abraham as *pater omnium fidelium*. This shifts to the notion of *peregrinatio*, and thence to the life and miracles of Colum Cille. Again the bulk of the text is plain narrative without intrusive comment, and not until the concluding prayer invoking the saint's aid is there another homiletic element. These elements frame the narrative, rather than inform it. There is a similar but briefer introduction (based on Matthew 7:12 and 10) exhorting charity, in the life of St Ciarán of Clonmacnoise; in this case the ending is more extended, though the final prayer is the same. The homily on St Mochua of Balla, finally, opens with an allegorical exposition of the parable of the talents in Matthew 25: 14, and then moves to the life; the ending in the *Book of Lismore* is abrupt and there is no prayer.

rosairillem: rosaitreuam in saecula saeculorum! Amen.' (=LB. The whole homily is on pp 428-89). For the *Book of Lismore* text, see Whitley Stokes (ed.), *Lives of saints from the Book of Lismore* (Oxford, 1890), pp 1-19 and 149-67. Here the prayer does not even invoke the saint. **24** Stokes (ed.), *Lives of saints from the Book of Lismore*. See also his *Three Middle-Irish homilies on the lives of Saints Patrick, Brigit and Columba* (Calcutta, 1877). For studies of Irish saints' lives Frederic Mac Donncha, 'Bunús Beathaí Bhrighde, Cholm Cille, Chiaráin, Ghrigóir agus Mhartain', MA thesis, University College, Galway, 1965, and Herbert, *Iona, Kells and Derry* on Colum Cille in particular; see p. 291 for bibliographical references to other Irish hagiography in Latin and Irish. Herbert includes (pp 218-69) an edition and translation of the *Leabhar Breac* life of Colum Cille, with a list of the MSS on pp 210-13. **25** The quotations are from: the Auchinleck *Life of Adam and Eve*, ed. C. Horstmann, *Sammlung altenglischer Legenden* (Heilbronn, 1878), pp. 139-47, v. 779f., p. 147; Hartmann von Aue, *Der arme Heinrich*, ed. Hermann Paul, 16. ed. by Kurt Gärtner (Tübingen, 1996), vv. 1515-20, p. 63 ('they both entered the eternal kingdom. May this happen to us all at the end of time. May God grant us the reward that they received. Amen.'); and a romance, the British Library, Cotton MS version of *Sir Eglamour of Artois*, ed. Frances E. Richardson (Early English Text Society OS 256, London, 1965), v. 1376f., p. 97.

There is some variation in the extent to which homiletic elements have been grafted onto these *vitae*; the expository introduction may well be from a known Latin work – Bede on Luke in that on St Martin, and in that for St Ciarán the homiletic portion is in fact the Irish Sermon XIV in the *Leabhar Breac* on charity. The actual life is usually also from a known source – Sulpicius Severus on St Martin, for example, in the *Leabhar Breac* homily and the concluding formula is usually along the lines seen already for St Patrick: 'I beseech the lord's mercy through St Martin's intercession. May we all reach that bliss and may we dwell therein *in secula seculorum*. Amen, Amen'.[26]

As sermons, these were presumably designed for reading aloud, but the superimposed rather than integrated homiletic elements in these usually long Irish pieces keep the texts closer to saints' *vitae* proper than to sermons in other languages which actually use the saint as an *exemplum* (see St Bernard's sermon on St Martin (*Patrologia Latina* 183, 484)), or which are briefer and maintain more consistently the invocatory style (see the sermons on St Martin by Honorius Augustodunensis in the *Speculum Ecclesiae* (*Patrologia Latina* 172, 1021-4) or by Godfrey of Admont (*Patrologia Latina* 174, 1047-52)). Honorius, for example, complains about the fact that if even such a holy man as St Martin was attacked by the devil, what of the poor sinner in general? So, too, a later and well-integrated hagiographic sermon by St Bonaventure on St Francis begins with a biblical interpretation, but presents the details of the saint's life with frequent *karissimi* interpolations and addresses to the audience. Bonaventure's relatively short sermon ends with the standard Latin prayer ('Rogabimus Dominum ...'. 'Let us beseech the Lord ...') in the name of St Francis. The early Irish examples are rarely as thoroughgoing in their adaptation.[27]

It is with the so-called Cambrai Homily,[28] probably of the late seventh or early eighth century, that we find the first concrete example of an Irish vernacular homily in a contemporary manuscript (rather than in a far later one, that perennial bugbear in dating conservative Irish texts). Although we

---

26 Stokes, 'Middle-Irish homily on S. Martin', p. 402, 'Ailim trócaire inchoimded triaimpide naem martain. corisam uli infáilte sin. 7 corosaittrebam. in saecula saeculorum. amen. amen.'.
27 Honorius (PL 172, 1024): 'heu, karissimi, quid fiet de miseris omnibus flagitiis involutis, si turba daemonum Martino occurrit, qui omnibus virtutibus floruit?' Bonaventure is edited by Robert E. Lerner, 'A collection of sermons given in Paris *c.* 1267' in *Speculum* xlix (1974), pp 466-98 (text pp 491-8). Again these sermons have been chosen to demonstrate the regularity of specific features over a temporal and geographical range.   28 Text and translation in Whitley Stokes and John Strachan (eds), *Thesaurus Palaeohibernicus* (2 vols, Cambridge, 1901-3; rept Dublin, 1975), ii, pp 244-7; this text includes material surrounding the sermon in the MS but not part of it. There is a separate text, without translation, in Rudolf Thurneysen, *Old Irish reader*, trans. D.A. Binchy and Osborn Bergin (Dublin, 1949), pp 35f. The fullest study is that by Pádraig Ó Néill, 'The background to the Cambrai Homily' in *Ériu* xxxii (1981), pp 137-48. Ó Néill points out that the Latin Biblical citations are not always Vulgate readings, and considers that they are from memory, p. 139.

do not have much of this earliest vernacular example (strictly a combination of Irish and Latin) of prose in sermon form, what we have (placed in the manuscript amongst material to do with bribes) interprets in detail a selection of biblical verses, but then focuses upon the theme of martyrdom. There is a brief liturgical introduction, an invocation, and then a Gospel verse (Matthew 16:24), one associated with Masses in commemoration of martyrs (which gives a putative context), followed by a development of that theme and a close interpretation of other verses. There is use of the inclusive first person plural throughout, and one identifiable extra-biblical Latin source, Gregory's *Homilia in Evangelia*, one of the most widely used texts of the Middle Ages and from which two homilies are cited. The theme moves from the necessity to abjure sins to the participation of all men in the sins of others, and thus to the notion of fellow-suffering (*tollat crucem*). Homiletic in its interpretation of a series of verses, if not of a complete pericope, overall it has the feel of a thematic *sermo*, turning as it does from self-denial to the three types of martyrdom, white, green and red.

This last section, considered by Ó Néill to be of native Irish origin, has occasioned considerable and inconclusive discussion. White martyrdom is the retreat from the world and red (the liturgical colour for the commemoration of martyrs in any case) the actual martyr's death; both are fairly predictable. However, *glasmartre*, 'green martyrdom', seems to imply simply penance, fasting and suffering, perhaps on a large scale. Sources have not been established for this concept. There are of course various classifications of types of martyrdom and penance: Ó Néill cites the Hiberno-Latin *Prebiarium de Multorium Exemplaribus*, but the relationship is not close. Various forms of penance (inluding martyrdom) are also enumerated and categorized in works such as the (Irish) *Poenitentiale Bigotianum*, but without the colour reference. This may be a native motif; certainly the combination itself is unusual.[29] On the other hand, various sources suggest themselves; colour symbolism is extensive in medieval exegesis and often linked with the symbolism of the lapidary. Red for martyrdom is familiar: 'Sardius' says Bede on the description of heaven in the penultimate chapter of the Apocalypse, 'is the colour of blood, and signifies the glory of martyrdom', and parallel

---

29 Ó Néill, 'Background', p. 143. On the penitential, see John T. McNeill and Helena M. Gamer, *Medieval handbooks of penance* (New York, 1938, rept 1990), p. 152. On the question of the colours of martyrdom, see (inconclusively) Robert E. McNally, 'The imagination and Early Irish Biblical exegesis' in *Annuale Medievale* x (1969), pp 5-27, esp. pp 24 f. and the brief comments in Pádraig Ó Fiannachta, 'Briathar Dé agus briathra daoine sa tSean-Ré' in *Irisleabhar Mha Nuad* 1980, pp 71-84, see pp 81 f. and Mac Eoin, 'Na criocha', p. 20. On the other hand, the footnote reference in Stokes and Strachan's *Thesaurus*, ii, p. 247 to the colours of death in the *Arabian Nights* must rank as one of the least informative parallels ever. However, the exhaustive study of exegetical triads in Heinz Meyer, *Die Zahlenallegorese im Mittelalter* (Munich, 1975), pp 117-23, demonstrates nothing that could serve as a basis.

examples are numerous. White indicates purity, and an earlier commentary on the Apocalypse talks of white as the colour of the innocent life. Green is also usually a positive colour, and it is possible that the source of this triad might lie either in an interpretation of the Apocalypse, in a lapidary, or in an encyclopaedic treatment of colour symbolism. A (late) French lapidary translated into English talks of the *grenehede in þe feith* of patriarchs and prophets. Saints, too, are seen as clothed in different colours in encyclopaedic writings.[30]

Fuller and somewhat clearer, although not without problems, is the ninth-century sermon (rather than homily) edited first by Kuno Meyer from a Royal Irish Academy manuscript and then from the *Yellow Book of Lecan* by John Strachan.[31] It has an opening statement of the theme of thanking God for forgiveness, in the sense of Psalm 144:10, and supports this, as is customary, by citing a related verse, Psalm 102:22 as part of the *concordantia* process, although this is not an homiletic exordium proper, nor a known pericope. The development section introduces and interprets a passage ascribed to 'Peter', but not identifiable from the Gospels, Acts or general epistles. The caution with which St John Seymour suggested that the passage might refer to the apocryphal *Apocalypse of Peter* is echoed by McNamara's firm refusal to make any definite comment, although Tristram seems to think that it actually is the source. In fact this is very unlikely; nothing in what we have of the Peter-Apocalypse (what there is survives partly in Ethiopic) makes this plausible. As David Dumville points out, we need to stay within the limits of historical probability. Nor, indeed, is there anything relevant in the apocryphal *Acts of Peter (and Paul)*. What is more likely is that the source is an exegetical text of some kind, since the passage voices what is a (later) medieval commonplace of the need for man to acknowledge with gratitude the gifts of God, and then damns the souls of those who fail to do so (*ingraciam animam malus possidet demon*); an interpretation of Job, for example, might be a possibility.[32] One of

---

30 *Sardius, qui ex integro sanguinei coloris est, martyrum gloriam significat*' (Bede, *PL* 93, 199); '*simplices ... et innocentes qui propter vitae puritatem per lapidem candidum [= sardonyx] designantur*' (Berengaudus, *PL* 17, 954); the healing power of the emerald and the linking of green with human striving for perfection is also common: all examples are taken from Christel Meier, *Gemma Spiritalis* (Munich, 1977), pp 148, 156 and 165. For the English lapidary, see Joan Evans and Mary Serjeantson, *English medieval lapidaries* (Early English Text Society OS 190, London, 1933), p. 21. Eadmer refers to the colours of different virtues for 'the saints (*PL* 159, 592f.) and this is used in Honorius' *Elucidarium*. 31 Kuno Meyer, 'Eine altirische Homilie' in *Zeitschrift für celtische Philologie* iv (1903), pp 241-3 (in Irish only); J. Strachan,'An Old Irish homily' in *Ériu* iii (1907), pp 1-7. 32 McNamara, *Apocrypha*, p. 102 f.; see St John D. Seymour, 'Notes on Apocrypha in Ireland' in *Proceedings of the Royal Irish Academy* xxxvii sect. C (1924-7), pp 107-17, esp. pp 112f which suggests a patristic work. M.R. James, *The Apocryphal New Testament* (Oxford, 1924, repr. 1975), pp 505-21 gives the fragments of the Peter-Apocalypse. Tristram, *Sex aetates*, p. 137 uses the word *vermutlich*, 'presumably', and refers otherwise simply to heterodox views. The reference to the soul as an ingrate might on the other hand point to an interpretation of, say, the first part of Psalm 102. See finally D.N.

the manifestations of pride – in a scheme based ultimately on Gregory's *Moralia in Job* which became an exegetical commonplace in various of the pre-scholastic and scholastic writers – is the refusal to acknowledge that the gifts enjoyed by man come from God.[33] Rather unusually, however, the Irish text refers to a *temple* and habitation of the devil ('*is tempul 7 is atrab do Diabul*'). This division is rounded off with a second blessing, based on Matthew 10:40. The substance of the work, however, is a sequence of rhetorically presented antitheses, the joys of heaven contrasted with the pains of hell. The eschatological point is made with some force. Such contrasts are found, of course, in works in Irish like those in *Lebor na hUidre* described already, and are not uncommon in much medieval literature depending upon the Apocalypse. There are English examples, and there is also a striking and eminently comparable early German text in rhythmic prose from a twelfth-century manuscript in Munich known as *Himmel und Hölle*, 'Heaven and Hell'.[34] More striking, however, is the comment in the Irish text, with hell presented first, that 'there are ... likenesses of the kingdom of heaven and of hell in this world'. The cold of winter, age, decay and death are contrasted then with summer and youth, and although the view of winter as adversity and summer as prosperity is hardly original,[35] this is still effective eschatology in a developed antithetical and amplificatory style, taking Matthew 13:50 as its starting point, and bewailing those judged worthy of hell at doomsday. The imagery of hell is rooted in the Apocalypse, that of heaven in the *locus amoenus / patria paradisi* tradition. What is of particular interest concerning this set of images is the use of the same passage in the *Lebor na hUidre* 'Tidings of Doomsday', a work far more like a tract, in which it is, however, considerably extended; but even here the anaphoric *accumulatio* remains forceful:

> [Hell] is a prison to keep, it is a flame to scourge, it is a net to hold fast, it is a scourge to lash, it is an edge to wound, it is night to blind, it is smoke to stifle, it is a cross to torture, it is a sword to punish.[36]

Dumville, 'Biblical Apocrypha and the early Irish' in *Proceedings of the Royal Irish Academy* lxxiii sect. C (1973), pp 321f.   33 See Gregory's *Moralia*, i, xxiv, 32, for example, and writers such as Peter Lombard in the *Sentences* (*PL* 176, 114).   34 On Old English see Hildegard C. Tristram, 'Stock descriptions of heaven and hell in Old English prose and poetry' in *Neuphilologische Mitteilungen* lxxix (1978), pp 102-13. There is a text and modern German translation of *Himmel und Hölle*, which is in rhythmic prose, in balanced units (cola) and occasional endrhyme, in Karl Wolfskehl and Friedrich von der Leyen, *Älteste deutsche Dichtungen* (Frankfurt, 1964), pp 18-29. The standard text is in Elias von Steinmeyer's *Die kleineren althochdeutschen Sprachdenkmäler* (Berlin and Zurich, 1916, 2nd ed., 1963), text no. 29. Here heaven is presented first, then hell.   35 Strachan, 'An Old Irish homily', p. 5: 'Ataat dano cosmuiliusa flatha nime 7 iffirnn isin bithso'. The winter/summer allegory is found, for example (with a reference back to Aristotle) in the fourteenth-century treatise and preaching aid *Fasciculus Morum*, ed. Siegfried Wenzel (University Park, Penn., 1989), p. 141.   36 Strachan, 'An Old Irish homily', p. 5, 'is carcar do chomét, is breó do loscud, is lín do astud, is

This is countered with another anaphoric accumulation, this time of the virtuous deeds that will permit God to call the righteous on the day of judgement, and the ultimate reward is in the *Venite* of Matthew 25:34. The concluding portion of the text is a warning against the world, and here the anaphoric imagery is not dissimilar to that used already for hell, followed by the ideal of heaven, again expressed in a sequence of specific poetic images rather than literal details. This is not unknown in early medieval literature; again we may find the rhetoric of eschatology in Old English examples, while Otfrid of Weissenburg's Old High German metrical *Gospel-Book* of about 860 demonstrates in his picture of heaven the mixture of antitheses and straightforward description found also in the 'Tidings of Doomsday': 'there is life without death, light without darkness, the company of angels and eternal delight'.[37] The way in which the picture is presented in the Irish sermon is rather different, the extended images matching those for hell: 'a flame for its beauty ... a harp for its melodiousness ... a banquet for its abundance of wine ...'.[38] It is heaven that appears in the final position, however, and this is followed logically by the final blessing, a typical homiletic indicator with the inclusive first person plural which is, as indicated, close to one found at the end of one version of the 'Ever-New Tongue'. The whole is a neat and beautifully balanced sermon, although one wonders if the proposed date of the mid-ninth century is not too early.

The main repository of medieval Irish vernacular sermons is the collection of clearly homiletic texts, which mix (as does the Cambrai Homily) Latin and Irish, in the *Leabhar Breac*. The eleventh-century texts are *sermones de tempore* based on a pericope (such as the homily for the first Sunday in Lent, on the temptation in the desert), or are on liturgical themes, and there is an additional and unusual *sermo ad reges*. With these sermons are associated saints' lives which have been, as indicated, slightly adapted to provide a series of *sermones de sanctis*. These sermons and saints' lives, plus perhaps the eschatological works of the *Lebor na hUidre*, may have constituted an early Irish *homiliarium*, but this is a moot point. The collection presents certain problems, one of which is the absence of a reliable and indeed user-friendly edition. Another is the question of unity. Although it has been thought to contain the basis of a *homiliarium* comprising the

---

srogell do essorcain, is fáibur do atchumbu, is adaig do erdallad, is dé do múchud, is croch do phíanad, is claideb do dígail'. See Stokes, 'Tidings', p. 254, 'isbréo doloscud. Is(s)raigell do escorgain. Isfaebur do athchumma. isadaig doerdalldud. Is dethach domuchad. Iscroch dophianad. Isclaideb do digail'. 37 *Otfrids Evangelienbuch*, ed. Oskar Erdmann, 4. ed. by Ludwig Wolff (Tübingen, 1962), p. 39 (= I, xviii, 9f.): 'Thar ist líb ana tód, líoht ana finstri,/ éngilichaz kúnni joh éwigino wúnni'. It is a measure of the antiquity of the ideas that the first of these lines is one of only two in Otfrid's extensive work that does not rhyme. Otfrid's poem is datable by its dedications to before 873 and he must have known the line as a set phrase. See Stokes, 'Tidings', pp 256 f.   38 Strachan, 'An Old Irish homily', p. 7, 'is log ara sochraidi, is crot ara ceolbindi, is fledol ara finamiri ...'.

passions and homilies (with other saints' lives and the eschatological texts from the *Lebor na hUidre*), it is not clear which texts the *homiliarium* might have contained, even taking works from the *Leabhar Breac* alone. Some of the *Leabhar Breac* texts have been shown on linguistic grounds to be far later than the supposed eleventh-century date of the whole, and Mac Eoin has made clear that 'the collection in *Leabhar Breac* is not a uniform set of texts but that they derive from widely differing periods'. The passions have even fewer homiletic features than the saints' lives, and there are also catechetical texts in the *Leabhar Breac* which may or may not be treated as sermons (the exposition of the Creed is a case in point).[39] In Whitley Stokes's enumeration of what he saw as homilies in 1873, he omitted several of the passions and catechetical texts from a list which he did not take as a *homiliarium* anyway. The form and purpose of such a collection, if indeed there was ever such a homogeneous unit, can only be a matter of speculation.

For all that, we can still affirm that *Leabhar Breac* contains a number of sermons in Latin (with some Irish), plus Irish versions, and some without Latin. Jean Rittmueller examined in detail the sermon *Ad Cenam Domini*, however, providing some support for the date (for some texts) between 1050 and 1150 and for the suggestion of Máel Ísu Ó Brolcháin of Armagh (who died in 1086 at Lismore) as compiler and translator. Rittmueller established the sources for the sermon (Mac Donncha had done so for others), asserting however (against Tristram) that the eclectic Irish exegesis was not necessarily to be linked with any contemporary European *homiliaria*. Indeed, Rittmueller saw the separation of the senses of Scripture as a specifically Hiberno-Latin phenomenon, which need not, however, be seen as exclusive to Irish writing, the more so as the sources are nearly all from Patristic or Carolingian exegesis. Otfrid's German *Gospel-Book*, for example, referred to already and perhaps the work of a teacher for pupils, takes biblical pericopes and offers literal expositions, separating off those according to the other senses as distinct sections (headed *mystice, spiritualiter* or *moraliter*, the last very much like rhymed sermons). The same pattern is clear in the Latin/Irish sermon (*Leabhar Breac* Sermon X) for the first Sunday of Lent, for example, where detailed literal presentation is combined with typological prefigurations of the temptation (Moses in the desert, the three temptations of Adam) and cul-

---

39 *Leabhar Breac* texts are in Robert Atkinson (ed.), *The passions and homilies of the Leabhar Breac* (Dublin, 1887); Edmund Hogan (ed.), *The Irish Nennius from L. Na Huidre and homilies and legends from L. Brecc* (Dublin, 1895); Frederic Mac Donncha, 'Don Tarmchrutta: an 11th century homily on the Transfiguration' in *Collectanea Hibernica* no. 25 (1983), pp 7-11. Atkinson's edition, which virtually every critic condemned as inadequate, is far from user-friendly in that his editorial method, whilst claiming to provide translations, sometimes uses the Latin texts as such, without making it clear what is going on. See the review by Whitley Stokes in *Transactions of the Philological Society* (1888-9), pp 203-34. The citation from Mac Eoin is from 'Observations', p. 211.

minates in an exhortation to maintain the Lenten fast. The pattern is standard.[40]

Probably the most interesting of the *Leabhar Breac* Irish sermons is the so-called *Sermo ad reges* (*Leabhar Breac* Sermon VII, with a full text in Irish and a briefer Latin version). It takes as a starting-point Proverbs 17:7 and its theme is the correlation of just rule on earth with divine rule in heaven. It is based on a mid seventh-century Hiberno-Latin text, *De duodecim abusivis seculi*, much used in later writing in Continental Europe, where it is ascribed to Cyprian or Augustine.[41] Once again, the concluding contrast in eschatological terms between the punishments of the wicked kings and the rewards of the 'righteous, pious, merciful' kings is striking; hell is the reward of the former, with 'an eternity of various penalties', infernal darkness and permanent longing for a second death, whilst the just kings will enjoy the everlasting delights of the heavenly paradise. But the eschatological contrast is really the conclusion of the sermon, apart from a formulaic hope at the end that we might all enjoy paradise. The most interesting elements of the sermon are the requirements for a king on earth to rule justly so that the kingdom is not disturbed. The source material, then, is an Irish tractate used in other, Carolingian, homilies, such as that in Pembroke College, Cambridge, MS 25.[42] Our text begins with a general righteous/unrighteous contrast, and moves to the notion of kingship by way of the necessity for mankind to follow God-given leaders in the spirit of Romans 13, which is cited, and then moves on to the direct address to kings to rule wisely. The implications for the kind of audience remain interesting, although the concluding benediction is generalized.

One of the most noticeable features of the existing vernacular Irish sermons surviving is the concentration upon the eschaton, something which has regularly been noticed, of course, and which is matched in Latin.[43] Sermons of widely diverging content – even those to kings – climax upon the contrast between hell and heaven, and this is reinforced by the evidence of the apocalyptic tracts. A further recurrent element is the largely non-integrated adaptation of saints' lives in Irish *sermones de sanctis*. Finally,

---

[40] Mac Donncha was perhaps too concerned about the supposed far-fetchedness of the typological prefigurations in the homilies as such, 'Medieval Irish homilies', p. 60, though this one is not referred to directly. On Quadragesima homilies, see my book *The recapitulated Fall* (Amsterdam, 1974). The text is Sermon X in Atkinson (ed.), *Passions and homilies*, pp 172-81 and 425-30 (= Latin text). [41] Mac Donncha, 'Homilies', p. 67. The text is in *PL* 4, 947-60 as Pseudo-Cyprian and *PL* 40, 1079-88 as Pseudo-Augustine. See M.L.W. Laistner, *Thought and letters in Western Europe AD 500 to 900* (new ed. London, 1957), pp 144 f. on the importance and influence of this text. [42] The sermon *De principibus et populis* in James E. Cross (ed.), *Cambridge, Pembroke College MS 25: a Carolingian sermonary used by Anglo-Saxon preachers* (London, 1987), pp 156-60. [43] Thus Tristram, *Sex aetetes*, p. 137, plus the 1997 issue of *Diagacht* mentioned above. See also O'Loughlin, 'The Celtic homily'.

specific small elements in the existing texts may or may not be exclusively Irish, such as the motif of green martyrdom in the Cambrai Homily. Other elements, however, match Continental patterns, such as the use of different senses of Scripture and the employment of standard texts, even when they are themselves Irish in origin.[44]

If the apocalyptic tracts may afford a glimpse of actual vernacular preaching, the direct material we have is, of course, written. As D.H. Green, in a recent work on medieval listening and reading, points out, the written sermon-collection itself had a variety of possible audiences: its separate elements could have been delivered as sermons to clerics or laity, it could be used as a quarry for sermons and it could be read devotionally.[45] So too, the precise nature of discourse in the sermon as an oral product demands attention. Gloria Cigman, in a short but illuminating paper on Lollard sermons, distinguishes between the extrinsic approach (sources, contextualisation) and the examination of the way sermons work, whether they are addressing an audience directly or whether the preacher is indulging in what she calls 'speaking-aloud meditation'.[46] Early sermons in Irish need to be looked at more closely both as written and oral monuments in terms of function and discourse. Such examination may ultimately prove more useful than the speculative pursuit of *homiliaria* which may or may not have existed.

---

44 See Stancliffe, 'Early "Irish" exegesis' on the European-ness of some of the material. Thomas O'Loughlin also makes some sensible comments on the Irishness of some Latin texts in 'The Latin sources of medieval Irish culture' in Kim McCone and Katharine Simms (eds), *Progress in medieval Irish studies* (Maynooth, 1996), pp 91-105. **45** D.H. Green, *Medieval listening and reading: the primary reception of German literature 800-1300* (Cambridge, 1994), pp 152-4 and the comments below pp 58-60. **46** Gloria Cigman, '*The keyes of kunnynge*: unlocking the texts' in 'Volker Mertens and Hans-Jochen Schiewer (eds), *Die deutsche Predigt im Mittelalter* (Tübingen, 1992), pp 256-67. In spite of the title of the collection Cigman's paper is concerned with English sermons.

Preaching in late-medieval Ireland: the English and the Latin tradition

Alan J. Fletcher

In one important sense, the title of this chapter introduces a doubtful distinction. To cordon off an 'English' and a 'Latin' tradition of preaching in Ireland is to ignore the fact that at least some preachers, especially ones whose mobility brought them to areas of the island where Irish was the dominant, in many places the exclusive, vernacular, would not have recognized such a distinction as either particularly significant or appropriate. Such men would have needed to be linguistically amphibious in order to fulfil their charge. The Orders of friars come principally to mind in this respect, for while the secular clergy, and those of the religious who preached, operated mainly at a local level, it was the essence of the mendicant movement to undertake preaching tours that ranged over wide territory. Egregious in their response to the evangelical precept to preach the gospel to all nations (Matthew 28:19), the friars became associated with itinerancy, so much so that their detractors would seize upon it as a sign of their lapse into vagrancy and interloping. The career of a mid-thirteenth century Irish Franciscan, Tomás Ó Cuinn, illustrates well this holy wanderlust. At one stage he had been guardian of the Franciscan house in Drogheda, that most English of towns in late-medieval Ireland, and yet he was evidently an indigenous, Gaelic-speaking Irishman. The English compiler of the late-thirteenth century *Liber exemplorum*, a work to which we shall return, wrote approvingly of a sermon that Friar Tomás had preached against local superstition – it seems to have been against popular belief in the fairy folk – in the diocese of Clonfert, Connacht province. Ó Cuinn had evidently gone on tour. The (lay) congregation at his Clonfert sermon must have comprised Irish speakers, and thus it must have been in Irish that he preached.[1] But it is likely that he reported what he said to the English friar compiler of the *Liber exemplorum* in English, since the latter, a native either of Warwickshire or of Worcestershire, would no doubt have been less familiar with Irish than Friar Tomás was.[2]

---

[1] See J. Watt, *The Church in medieval Ireland* (2nd ed., Dublin, 1998), pp 77-8. Ó Cuinn became bishop of Clonmacnoise in 1252; his Connacht preaching had occurred before that date. [2] A.G. Little (ed.), *Liber exemplorum ad usum praedicantium* (Aberdeen, 1908), p. vii, believed

Although the distinction proposed at the outset may therefore be far from watertight, it nevertheless remains for the purposes of the present discussion convenient. The medieval preaching tradition in the Irish language has been more extensively considered by Brian Murdoch above, and the diaspora of the friars, notably the Franciscans, throughout the Irish-speaking territories is discussed by Colmán Ó Clabaigh below. Yet, more may be said for the distinction than mere taxonomic convenience, for in another sense, it is historically justified. As is well known, the Church in medieval Ireland was plagued by the factionalism of the two nations.[3] Demarcation lines drawn up between the Church *inter Anglicos* and *inter Hibernicos* would necessarily complicate, if not compromise, the Church's mission as a single, coordinated enterprise. Even certain of the friars, famous boundary-crossers between different ethnicities, as Friar Tomás's career eloquently testifies, eventually succumbed to a partitionist thinking that a combination of historical circumstances conspired to bring about.[4] If we take as illustration a manuscript well known in literary circles, the Franciscan miscellany of verse and prose now preserved as British Library, London, Harley MS 913, we could arguably regard it as epitomizing this polarizing drift. Its palæography suggests that it was assembled, probably by one scribe, in the 1330s, by which time the sorting even of the friars in Ireland into the 'two nations' was well under way. And what we discover on opening it is its presentation in the three chief languages of late-medieval England (that is, English, French and Latin). Its English is undoubtedly Hiberno-English, a dialect variety whose distinctiveness depends in part on its occasional lexical borrowings from Irish, but in Harley MS 913 there is no Irish per se to be found. On the face of it, therefore, the manuscript seems to be very much the product of such polarized cultural circumstances, and indeed, the balance of the evidence suggests that its provenance, entirely consistent with such circumstances, was the anglicized walled town of Waterford.[5] We will return to this manuscript too in the course of the chapter since, like the *Liber exemplorum*, Harley MS 913 also serviced the culture of preaching.

So our isolation of an English and Latin from an Irish preaching tradition may have some historical justification provided, that is, that the distinction be not insisted upon too rigorously nor allowed to harden into a fixed orthodoxy. For even in the era of the Church *inter Anglicos* and *inter*

that the English compiler originated in Warwickshire, but the place names of Arley and Astley occur also in close proximity in Worcestershire. **3** See J.A. Watt, *The Church and the two nations in medieval Ireland* (Cambridge, 1970). **4** The support of some Franciscans for the Bruce invasion of 1315, for example, was divisive within the Order (Watt, *Church in medieval Ireland*, p. 80). **5** M. Benskin, 'The style and authorship of the Kildare poems – (I) Pers of Bermingham' in J. Lachlan Mackenzie and R. Todd (eds), *In other words: transcultural studies in philology, translation and lexicography, presented to Hans Heinrich Meier on the occasion of his sixty-fifth birthday* (Dordrecht, 1989), pp 57-83; see p. 59.

Hibernicos, the situation on the ground was not entirely diametrically opposed, nor were the different ethnicities hermetically sealed off from one another quite as tightly as the administrative categories *inter Anglicos* and *inter Hibernicos* might suggest. Whatever the early fourteenth-century Harley MS 913 might seem to imply about a segregation is countered by another Franciscan product of the century to follow, probably copied *c.*1455 in a conventual house in County Clare,[6] which witnesses to a rapprochement of the English, Latin and Irish traditions in a remarkably telling way. Apart from the fact that the manuscript, Trinity College, Dublin, MS 667, contains English, Irish and Latin texts presented in comfortable proximity to each other, the very hybridity of the *mise en page* of the texts in the Irish language testifies, in the face of any notions of segregation, to ethnic cross-fertilization and exchange (see fig. 1). The style of the *litterae notabiliores*, rubricated and complemented by trailing pen flourishes (see for example the four letter A's in the left-hand column), is wholly consistent with contemporary English, as opposed to insular Irish, manuscript layout. Conversely, the script of the text is otherwise unmistakeably Irish in character. Trinity College, MS 667 is another to which we shall return.

Having justified and qualified our focus, then, we next need to establish a corpus of manuscripts for study. Medieval preaching, no less in Ireland than everywhere else, is notoriously ephemeral. Like any oral performance pre-dating the era of recording technology, it comprised evanescent words carried away on the air in the moment of their utterance. Such traces as survive do so, necessarily, only in written form, and for a host of reasons written form may not fully reflect what was actually preached. Sermons in manuscript may, for example, have been originally conceived as model sermons, designed not for preaching as they stood but as quarries for subsequent preachers to excavate in their search for their own *materia predicabilis*. Again, manuscript sermons may be literary, more sophisticated workings of what was actually said after the event itself, as may be the case with the sermons preached between 1348 and 1356 and recorded in the sermon diary of Richard FitzRalph, archbishop of Armagh;[7] and so forth. Thus for a variety of cultural considerations, sermons on the page may stand at a remove from their counterparts in oral delivery. Perhaps the best evidence for what early preachers actually said is to be found in the *reportatio* (that is, an account taken down of the sermon as preached), but from medieval Ireland there survive, as far as I am aware, no such *reportationes*; indeed,

---

[6] R. Flower, 'Ireland and medieval Europe' in *Proceedings of the British Academy* xiii (1927), pp 271-303; see p. 282. But see also below p. 90, where the possibility is also aired of its origin in either Nenagh or Limerick. [7] Aubrey Gwynn, 'The sermon-diary of Richard FitzRalph, archbishop of Armagh' in *Proceedings of the Royal Irish Academy* xliv sect. C (1937), pp 1-57.

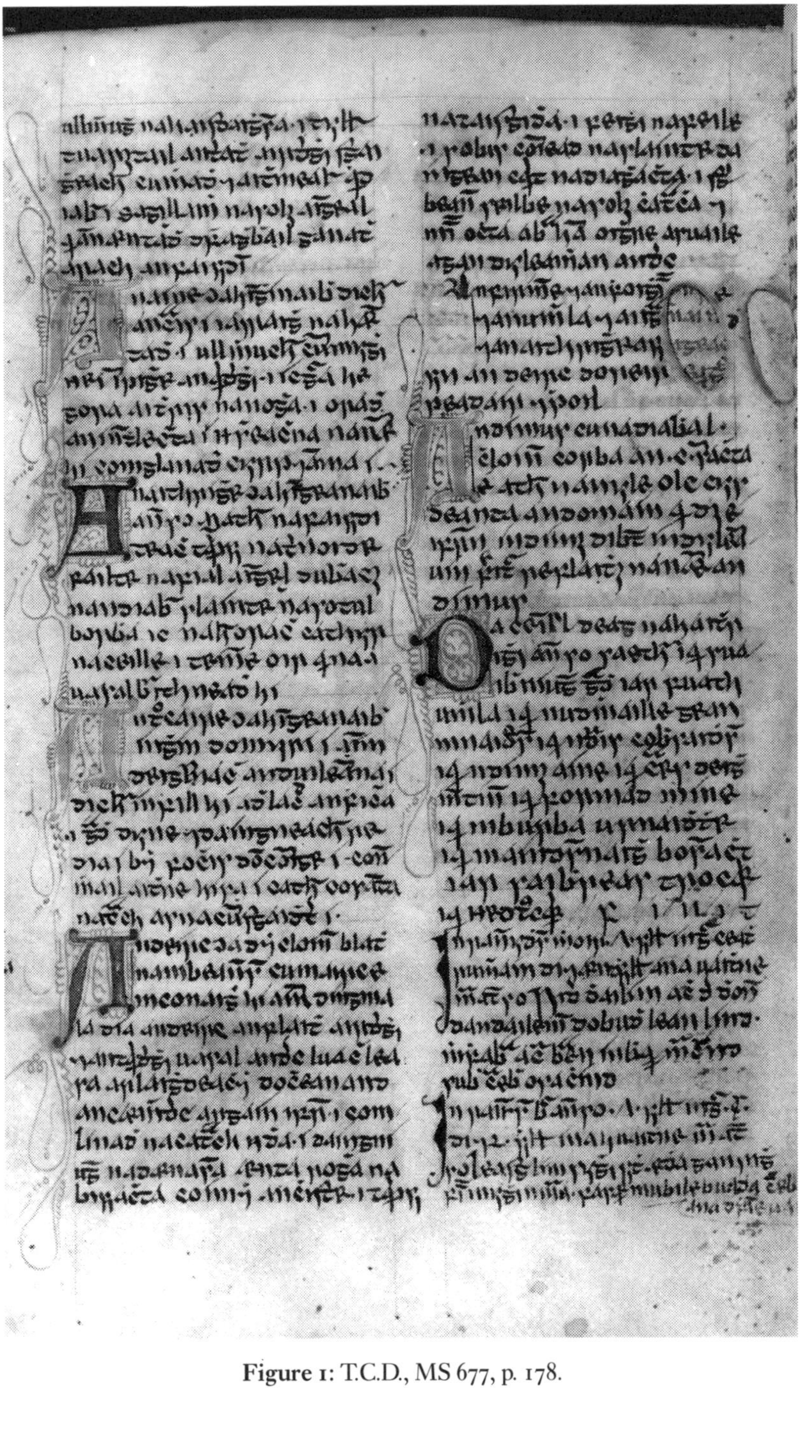

Figure 1: T.C.D., MS 677, p. 178.

they are rare enough in the medieval British Isles in general. We only approach, and that obliquely, something having *reportatio* status in the account that Friar Tomás Ó Cuinn gave of his own preaching as related to the English compiler of the *Liber exemplorum*. But the account is fleeting. If we take a little liberty with this category, it could be widened to include a discourse that features in the earliest morality play known from these islands, *The pride of life*, a play possibly written in medieval Dublin at the beginning of the fifteenth century.[8] In this play, whose former manuscript context suggests that it may have been produced under the aegis of the canons regular of the Rule of St Augustine – men in the forefront of late-medieval preaching – there occurs a scene in which a bishop preaches to an arrogant anti-hero, the king of life, about life's transitoriness and the futility of earthly pride. What the play's audiences and the king of life were evidently being treated to was a facsimile, albeit in the context of a play, of an actual sermon. That the bishop, like the other characters in the play, spoke in verse does not necessarily detract from the possible resemblance between the play sermon and a real one. There existed such things as verse sermons, and indeed, British Library, Harley MS 913 contains one that, both in terms of its metre and content, resembles the sermon of the bishop in the play very closely.[9] But again, the play sermon is a lone witness, and thus its inclusion would extend the '*reportatio*' category only marginally.

Ireland is therefore no exception to the rule, and we are heavily reliant for our understanding of the English and Latin traditions of late-medieval preaching on texts of the sort liable to represent whatever may have been preached in reality filtered according to taste and preoccupation. The evidence consists in manuscripts containing sermons (principally or exclusively), in clerical miscellanies and anthologies in which sermons are included, or in materials intended for the use of preachers when they came to compose sermons of their own (from such materials it may be possible to conjecture the sort of preaching to which they may have given rise). The evidence also consists in library catalogues (which, at the very least, illustrate what sermons or sermon-related materials were in circulation, even if the catalogued originals may have subsequently vanished),[10] or in references to the activities of preachers and to preaching that occasionally appear in historical documents of other sorts. For the purposes of this essay, I propose to concentrate on the first, second and third classes of evidence (since the second and third sometimes overlap, however, they should not be regarded as absolutely exclusive): that is, manuscripts principally or exclusively containing sermons;

---

8 For the play, see N. Davis (ed.), *Non-cycle plays and fragments* (Early English Text Society, SS 1, Oxford, 1970), pp 90-105. Its auspices are discussed in A.J. Fletcher, *Drama, performance, and polity in Pre-Cromwellian Ireland* (Toronto, 2000), pp 82-3 and 121-3.   9 As Davis, *Non-cycle plays*, p. xcviii, pointed out.   10 The library catalogue of the Franciscans of Youghal discussed by Colmán Ó Clabaigh below is a famous example.

sermons in clerical miscellanies and anthologies; and finally, sermon-related materials. The first and second classes are easier to identify than the third because, irrespective of what their exact nature may have been if they were indeed preached, the sermon status of a written text, more often than not, is relatively self-evident,[11] while the homiletic applicability of a text of the third class may be much less so. St Paul's sanguine maxim that everything that is written is written for our learning promises a cornucopia from which preachers in future ages might choose, but at the same time holds out a depressing prospect for academic pigeonholing. Nevertheless, at the risk of appearing arbitrary, I will confine discussion of works of the third class to ones that have overt and ostensible relation to preaching, compilations like the *Liber exemplorum* cited earlier.

John Watt was in essence right to regret a 'virtual disappearance of sermon literature' from medieval Ireland (and the examples of it that he cites suggest that he was thinking chiefly of sermons from the English and the Latin tradition before ones from the Irish tradition surveyed above by Brian Murdoch). However, a little more survives for investigation than his bleak statement might suggest, especially if we include material that may have been imported from England for use in Ireland.[12] It is striking that both of the earliest manuscripts to have survived from the late-medieval period are associated with the mendicant Orders, although one, New College, Oxford, MS 88, arrived in Ireland, it is to be presumed, only from some date in or after 1397. In that year its owner, Thomas Cranley (1337-1417), became archbishop of Dublin.[13] Although nothing of his own work is known to survive, Cranley was a noted preacher. Thus New College, MS 88 was precisely the kind of manuscript that he would have found useful, containing as it mostly does sermons *de tempore* and *de sanctis*. A note on f. 1v declares that he purchased it in Oxford.[14] It is a stocky little compilation (493 leaves, these measuring 152 mm x 107mm),[15] and its portable format is wholly typical of many manuscript books produced by mendicant preachers for use in their travels. Indeed, the other manuscript of this earliest group, Trinity College, Dublin, MS 347, is of comparable dimensions, measuring 159mm x 110mm. Internal indications also put the original mendicant auspices of New College, MS 88 beyond any doubt, although whether it was a product of mendicants in Oxford, where Cranley acquired it, is less clear.[16] In addition to items of

---

11 On what constitutes a sermon, see H.L. Spencer, *English preaching in the late middle ages* (Oxford, 1993), pp 3-4 and 112-13.   12 Watt, *Church in medieval Ireland*, p. 210. New College, Oxford, MS 88 was imported and National Library of Ireland, Dublin, MS 9596 may have been, though this is not clear.   13 A.B. Emden, *A biographical register of the university of Oxford to A.D. 1500*, (3 vols, Oxford, 1957-9), i, pp 510-11.   14 F. 1v: 'Liber Magistri Thome Cranle quem emit Oxon'. ('The book of Master Thomas Cranley which he purchased in Oxford.')   15 British Library, London, Harley MS 913, discussed below, is roughly comparable. Its leaves measure approximately 140mm x 95mm.   16 Dr Margaret Laing, to whom I am grateful for

mendicant (and particularly Franciscan?) interest,[17] on f. 491v the following inscription can be seen under ultraviolet light: 'Iste Liber ... conceditur fratre Roberto ... ad terminum vite sue. qui hunc titulum deleuerit anathema sit. fiat/fiat amen.' ('This book ... is granted by Friar Robert ... to the end of his life. May whoever shall have deleted this inscription be anathema. Fiat, fiat. Amen.') It seems that Friar Robert's book never returned to his Order from the unknown grantee, but eventually passed by some route into Cranley's hands. In it he would have found not only the wide selection of ready-made Latin sermons mentioned earlier, but also extensive sermon materials, some of which included occasional verses in Middle English.[18] Selected examples of these verses are worth citing, since they crystalize favourite sermon motifs and give some impression of what the thematic centres of preaching were around which many medieval sermons *ad populum* tended to converge.

The first piece of verse in New College, MS 88 was written *c.*1300 in the hand of a contemporary annotator who supplied marginalia throughout the entire manuscript:

> Wanne Ich þenche þinges þre,
> Ne mai [Ich] neure bliþe be.
> Þat on is, Ich sal awe.
> Þat oþer is, Ich ne wot wilk day.
> Þat þridde is mi meste kare:
> I ne woth nevre wuder I sal fare.[19]

(When I think on three things I may never be happy. The one is, that I must pass away. The other is, I don't know which day. The third is my greatest care: I have no idea where I shall fare to.)

This lyric introduces the mind-focusing prospect of death, and induces fear of an uncertain hereafter (purgatory and hell were traditionally presented as being more populous than heaven, moreover), in order to make those who heard it pliably receptive to the Church's prophylaxis for the two post-mortem states that were to be feared. The lyric's strategy is common enough in the British Isles, but considered in a specifically Irish context, it begs comparison with the *memento mori* emphasis of the sermon of the bishop in

---

advice, would tentatively locate the dialect of the Middle English appearing in New College, Oxford, MS 88 in the region of south-east Herefordshire or south-west Worcestershire. **17** A tract *de modo confitendi*, ff 211-14, begins: 'Frater qui confessiones auditurus est ...' ('The friar about to hear confessions ...'). And a note running across the foot of ff 89v-90 reads: 'Contra illos qui dicunt quod mundus melior ante aduentum fratrum ...' ('Against those who say that the world was better before the coming of the friars ...'). **18** There is also a little French, as for example in the sermon on St Thomas Becket (ff 31-2), and a prayer to Jesus (f. 477). **19** New College, Oxford, MS 88, f. 32. The lyric seems to have been popular; for discussion, see R. Woolf, *The English religious lyric in the middle ages* (Oxford, 1968), p. 86.

The pride of life play,[20] or with sentiments expressed in the song of Michael of Kildare (a British Library, Harley MS 913 lyric whose author names himself as a Franciscan friar), or with sentiments in another Harley MS 913 text, this time an actual verse sermon,[21] or again with the moralized digits in Trinity College, Dublin, MS 667 (see fig. 2) discussed at the end of this chapter. The lyric seems to be a reflex of this particular contemporary preoccupation, one whose appearance as late as Trinity College, Dublin, MS 667 shows how resilient it would prove to be within the preaching of the mendicant Orders.

Another New College, MS 88 lyric that commandeers and Englishes a favourite sermon theme, this time copied by one of the manuscript's three principal scribes and embedded into a set of notes on the Passion, runs as follows:

> Man and wyman, loket to me
> U muchel pine Ich þolede for þe.
> Loke up one mi rig, u sore Ich was i-biten.
> Loke to mi side, wat blode Ich haue i-leten.
> Mine uet an mine honden nailed beth to þe rode.
> Of þe þornes prikung min hiued urnth a blode.
> Fram side to side, fro hiued to þe fot,
> Turn mi bodi abuten, oueral þu findest blod.
> Man, þin hurte, þin hurte þu turne to me,
> For þe vif wndes þe Ich þolede for þe.[22]

(Man and woman, look upon me, how much torment I endured for you. Look at my back, how grievously I was beaten. Look at my side, how much blood I have shed. My feet and my hands are nailed to the cross. My head streams with blood from the pricking of the thorns. From side to side, from head to foot, turn my body about, you find blood everywhere. Man, turn your heart, your heart, to me, for the five wounds that I suffered for you.')

Here, the verses offer a version (whose opening lines have evidently also been influenced by one of the *improperia* from the Good Friday liturgy, *O vos omnes qui transitis per viam*) of a preceding Latin text beginning *Respice in faciem Christi tui* (Psalm 83:10; this Psalm verse was itself frequently chosen

---

20 Davis, *Non-cycle plays*, pp 100-2, lines 327-406, and pp 103-4, lines 435-48. **21** Respectively, A.M. Lucas (ed.), *Anglo-Irish poems of the middle ages* (Dublin, 1995), p. 74, lines 17-18, and pp 82-4, lines 153-68. This latter text also, incidentally, identifies the typical stuff of mendicant preaching as being heaven, hell, joy and torment (Lucas (ed.), *Anglo-Irish poems*, p. 80, lines 109-10): '... freris prech of heuen and helle, / Of ioi and pine to mani man.' **22** New College, Oxford, MS 88, f. 181.

as a theme for sermons).[23] The lyric, patently in touch with the widespread, late-medieval tradition of affective piety, evokes a speaking Christ intent on requisitioning, ultimately for their spiritual benefit, the audience's attention and pity. To that extent, the lyric's manipulation of salvific emotion compares with that of 'Wanne Ich þenche þinges þre'. And once again, though here in an unequivocally Irish context, British Library, Harley MS 913's poem Fall and Passion, which versifies a selection of key Bible narratives from the fall of Lucifer until the Resurrection, nevertheless elects to dwell on the Passion preponderantly.[24]

A third lyric in New College, MS 88 appears alongside other snippets of Middle English within a set of memoranda concerning those who dangerously defer penance. In order to illustrate how most of the theological notes in this manuscript await the finishing touches of their actual users for their final arrangement and presentation – the notes of New College, MS 88 are sermon materials in the most fundamental sense – their immediate Latin context has also been provided here:

> *Exemplum:* difficile est auem senem docere ad loquendum, scilicet, 'Richard'. Similiter, equum senem ad ambulandum. Exemplum: de malo garcione qui necgligenter surgit, uocante eum domino suo, 'Robin, Robin, up aris!' Iacet autem et dormit donec tercio uel quarto uocetur. Augustinus, *Libro confessionum:* 'Non erat quid responderem tibi ueritate conuictus dicenti mihi, "Surge qui dormis, et exurge a mortuis, et illuminabit tibi Christus" (Ephesios 5) nisi uerba lenta et sompnolenta, "Modo, ecce modo, sine paululum." Sed "modo" et "modo" non habebat modum, et "sine paululum in" longum ibat. Similiter est de differentibus penitencie:
>
> Louerd, þu clepedest me
> An Ich nagt ne ansuarede þe
> Bute wordes scloe and sclepie.
> Þole yet, þole a litel.

---

[23] Woolf, *English religious lyric*, p. 43, n. 1, notes that the lyric's opening is not an exact verbal parallel to *O vos omnes*. True, but the opening is possibly responsive to sermon protocols, where the expression 'good men and women', certainly by the fourteenth century, was a favoured form of opening audience address. For a repertoire of sermons on the theme *Respice in faciem Christi tui* by named preachers active in the later-thirteenth century, see J.-B. Schneyer, *Repertorium der Lateinischen sermones des mittelalters*, (11 vols, Münster, 1969-90), i, p. 312; ii, pp 662, 673; iii, pp 287, 289, 291; iv, p. 45. Interestingly, the authors of these were all friars.   [24] Lucas (ed.), *Anglo-Irish poems*, pp 102-14 (especially pp 108-12, lines 113-79). Friars' sermons were typically wont to capitalize on Passiontide emotions too, even if Passiontide was not explicitly named as a mendicant preaching favourite in the poem of British Library, London, Harley MS 913 entitled 'Sarmun'.

Bute yiet and yiet was endelis,
And pole a litel a long wexis.²⁵

(*Exemplum*: it is hard to teach an old bird to speak, that is, [to say] 'Richard'. Likewise, [it is hard to teach] an old horse to amble. *Exemplum*: concerning the bad boy-servant who gets up negligently as his master calls him, 'Robin, Robin, get up!' But he lies and sleeps until the third or fourth time he is called. Augustine, in [his] *Book of Confessions*: 'There was nothing that I, convinced by [your] truth, might reply to you as you said to me, "Get up, sleeper, and arise from the dead, and Christ will give you light" (Ephesians 5:14), other than slow and sleepy words. "Soon, see now, soon, endure a short while." But "soon" and "soon" had no measure, and "endure a short while" was long lasting.' It is similar with those who defer penance: 'Lord, you called me and I answered you nothing except slow and sleepy words. "Endure yet, endure a little." But "yet" and "yet" was endless, and "endure a little" grows into "a long".')

If Cranley ever preached material such as this before his Irish audiences, he would first have had to trim it into sermon shape. By the late middle ages, preaching and the practice of confession and penance were often twinned enterprises and thus understandably, the centrality of the sacrament of confession was frequently preached about, or affective sermons might be contrived to induce in their hearers the preliminary disposition, namely, contrition, from which effective confession could grow.²⁶ If art had power to move, it could be enlisted to the preacher's purpose, and this is the purpose that probably called the New College, MS 88 lyric into being. Compare, again, the song of Michael of Kildare in British Library, Harley MS 913, which urges confession and due penance upon its hearers.²⁷

Equally pragmatic, if less emotionally evocative, is this final illustration which, in versifying one of the essentials of catechesis that from the Lambeth Council of 1281 preachers were widely enjoined to communicate, the Decalogue, dresses it in mnemonic rhyme.²⁸ Thus set forth, it would have been more liable to lodge in the heads of the audience:

---

25 New College, Oxford, MS 88, f. 181v; the reference to St Augustine is to Book viii, section 5, subsection 12 of his *Confessions* (L. Verheijen, ed. *Sancti Augustini Confessionum Libri XIII* (Corpus Christianorum Series Latina 27, Turnhout, 1981), p. 120, lines 42-7). 26 For further discussion of the late medieval consortium of preaching and confession, see A.J. Fletcher, 'The essential (ephemeral) William Langland: textual revision as ethical process' in *Yearbook of Langland Studies* xv (2001), forthcoming. 27 Lucas (ed.), *Anglo-Irish poems*, p. 72, lines 117-24. 28 For the relevant section of the Lambeth Constitutions of 1281 (the decree beginning *Ignorancia sacerdotum*), see F.M. Powicke and C.R. Cheney (eds), *Councils and synods, with*

> On God þu sal aue in wrchepe,
> Ne takyn natte is name in idelchepe.
> Hold wel þe haliday.
> Fader a[nd] moder þu wrchep ai.
> Ne sclo þe nevre no man.
> Lecherie ne do þu non.
> Loke þat nast þu ne stele,
> Ne no fals withnesse þu ne bere.
> Affeter oþer mannes wif nast te ne longe,
> Ne nast of his haue wid wronge.[29]

(You shall worship one God. Do not take his name in vain. Keep the holy day well. Always honour father and mother. Never slay any man. Do no lechery. See that you do not steal, nor bear any false witness. Do not hanker wrongfully after another man's wife, nor after anything that he has.)

And again, finally, we may compare a poem devoted to the Decalogue in British Library, Harley MS 913 and which, with four other poems in this manuscript, has the formal stylistic features of sermon register. These would have suited it for preaching.[30]

We turn now to another manuscript of approximately similar date and also produced in a mendicant context, though this time actually in Ireland. Trinity College, Dublin, MS 347, in being so remarkably similar to New College, MS 88 in format and in the general complexion of its content, witnesses to a degree of consistency in the late-thirteenth century mendicant approach to pastoral care throughout the British Isles. A note of ownership in an early-fifteenth century hand on f. 1 declares: 'notandum quod iste liber est fratris Iohannis knoces accomodatus domino Iohanni hothum rectori de clogheran sine pecunia et quicumque istum titulum deleuerit anathema sit.' ('It is to be noted that this is the book of Friar John Knock, loaned to Master John Hothum, rector of Cloghran, without money. And may whoever deletes

---

other documents relating to the English Church (2vols, Oxford, 1964), ii, pp 900-5. Archbishop John Pecham, who issued the Consitutions, was himself a Franciscan. Only one reference to the Irish adoption of '*Ignorancia sacerdotum*' is currently known, and appears in the registers of the late-medieval diocese of Armagh.   **29** In the manuscript, the line 'Lecherie ne do þu non is written finally, and marked to replace the line originally written, 'Bute bi þi wif ne li þu bi no wiman', which has accordingly been omitted here. The annotating hand adds this rhymed Decalogue at the foot of f. 49ov. I am indebted to Dr Margaret Laing for checking and correcting my transcriptions from New College, Oxford, MS 88.   **30** Lucas (ed.), *Anglo-Irish poems*, pp 116-21. There are five 'sermon poems' in this manuscript (using Lucas' titles, they are: Sarmun, Fifteen Signs before Judgement, Fall and Passion, Ten Commandments, and Seven Sins).

this inscription be anathema.') It seems that Trinity College, MS 347 had stayed in mendicant hands from the time of its copying (the various scribes at work in it were all roughly contemporary, c.1300) until it passed to John Hothum, rector of Cloghran (possibly the place situated a few miles north of Dublin). In this respect again like New College, MS 88, therefore, Trinity College, MS 347 was permitted to migrate from mendicant to secular clerical use. This suggests some mendicant collaboration with and support for the seculars in their exercise of the *cura animarum*, irrespective of the hostility that sometimes marred relations between them. In Ireland that was especially characteristic of the campaign of Richard FitzRalph, of which more later; if any intra-clerical hostility registers in Trinity College, MS 347, it is not against the seculars but against the monastic regulars that it is directed.[31] The manuscript was possibly assembled at the Franciscan house at Multyfarnham, County Westmeath.[32]

It principally contains Latin sermons, *de tempore* and *de sanctis*, and sermon materials, and its occasional vernacular verses, like those of New College, MS 88, are used to vivify and enliven fundamental Christian catechesis. The prime example of their use occurs within a passage against dancers, in which six aspects of dancing are each envisaged as profaning one of the Church's sacraments. The verses, in English and French, are interpolations into a passage which derives ultimately from the influential *Summa de vitiis* of the thirteenth-century French Dominican, William Peraldus.[33] (The passage is itself an interpolation into a larger work, the *Distinctiones* of Gilbert the Minorite.)[34] The passage is worth quoting, since it shows how an Irish preacher, obliged, in accordance with Church injunction, to discant annually on the sacraments, was being offered the resources to do so imaginatively. The passage's simultaneous attack on dancing has the additional advantage of serving as a device whereby the individual sacraments might be remembered:

> Qve choreas ducunt faciunt quodammodo contra omnia sacramenta ecclesie. Prima contra baptismam, quia frangunt pactum quod inierunt cum Deo in baptismo cum patrini earum dixerunt pro eis, 'Abrenuncio diabolo et pompis eius.' Pompam siue processionem diaboli intrant cum choreas intrant. Vnde patrini earum possunt timere, ne de promissione illa rei apud Deum inueniantur, si non admonuerint eas diligenter ne choreas intrent. Contra sacramentum ordinis. Sunt enim qui simie clericorum et tale seruicium diabolo offerunt, quale clerico

---

[31] Note its verses on bad monks (f. 9), for example; compare also the anti-monastic satires of British Library, London, MS Harley 913. [32] Its contents are fully catalogued in M.L. Colker, *Trinity College Library Dublin: descriptive catalogue of the mediaeval and Renaissance Latin manuscripts* (2 vols, Aldershot, 1991), i, pp 710-40. [33] As S. Wenzel, *Preachers, poets, and the Early English lyric* (Princeton, 1986), p. 216, has observed. [34] Its incipit is: *Accidiosus*

Deo, et per cantus earum impediuntur [*lege* impeditur] cantus ecclesiasticus et contempnitur, quia qui deberent interesse uesperis, intersunt choreis. Contra matrimonium, quia maritis multum detrahitur, quibus dicitur:

'Pur mun barun, fi!
Vn plus bel me at choisi'.

Et Anglice dicitur:

'Of my husband giu I noht.
Another hauet my luue y-bohit
For tuo gloues wyht ynoht.
If Hic him luue,
Y naue no woht.'

Multi et incitantur ad faciendum contra matrimonii fidem. Aperte uero contra legem matrimonii predicatur cum cantatur quia pro prauo viro uxor dimittere non debeat quin amicum faciat. Vnde:

Lete þe cukewald syte at hom
And chese þe another lefmon.
Lete þe chorl site at hom and pile,
And þu salt don wat þu wile.
God hit wot, hit nys no skile.'

Cum secundum legem Dei et leprosum dimittere non debeat, quin loco et tempus [*lege* tempore] debitum ei reddat si ipse uoluerit. Contra confirmacionem, in quo [*lege* qua] in fronte signum crucis susceperunt, tanquam empte Passione Christi. In choreis uero signo Christi abiecto, signum diaboli pro eo in capite posuerunt; signum, scilicet, uenalitatis, quasi Christus non emerit eas. Christus posuerat uexillum suum in eminenti parte, scilicet, in fronte, tanquam in eminen |fol. 200| ciori parte castri, et ipse uexillum diaboli pro eo posuerunt, non absque magna contumelia Christi. Sicut faciunt qui furantur equos signatos, delent enim signum et ponunt signum suum. Contra sacramentum penitencie, per quam Deo reconsiliate erant in quadragesima, dum pacem illam frangunt, et in excercitum diaboli uadunt. Contra sacramentum altaris, quia ad mensam Dei panem celestem susceperunt et postea nichilominus Dei terram igne infernali incendunt. Similes inde qui cum comedisset ad mensam Domini, accepit choortem a pontificibus et phariseis, uenit contra Ihesum.[35]

(Those women who lead dances in a certain way act contrary to the Church's sacraments. First, against baptism, because they break the agreement with God that they entered in baptism when their godparents said on their behalf, 'I renounce the devil and his pomps.'

---

siue piger est fertilis ad multiplicandum uicia.   **35** I have ignored the scribe's mechanical copying errors and self-corrections.

They enter into the pomp or procession of the devil when they enter into dances. Wherefore their godparents may fear lest they be found guilty before God because of that promise, if they have not admonished them diligently not to enter into dances. Against the sacrament of Orders. For there are those who ape clerics and offer such service to the devil as a cleric does to God, and through their songs the song of the Church is impeded and despised, because those who ought to attend vespers attend dances. Against marriage, because husbands are much disparaged, of whom it is said, 'Fie upon my husband! I have been chosen by one more handsome.' And in English it is said, 'I care nothing for my husband. Another has bought my love for two very white gloves. If I love him, I have no sorrow.' Many are also driven to behave contrary to the faith of marriage. Indeed, it is openly preached against the law of matrimony when it is sung, because a wife ought not dismiss [her husband] on account of a faithless man but rather make him her friend. Whence [the verses], 'Let the cuckold sit at home and choose yourself another lover. Let the churl sit at home and pluck [his hair] and you shall do what you will. God knows, it's entirely appropriate.' Since according to God's law she might not abandon even a leper, but that at the right place and time let her repay [her husband] his debt if he wishes it. Against confirmation, in which they received the sign of the cross on their forehead, as if purchased by Christ's Passion. But in dances, having thrown aside Christ's sign, they have set the devil's sign in its place on their head, a sign, that is, of venality, as if Christ may not have bought them. Christ had set his banner in a prominent place, that is, the forehead, as if in the higher part of a camp, and they have set up in its stead the devil's banner, not without great insult to Christ. Those who steal horses behave similarly, for they remove the sign and impose a sign of their own. Against the sacrament of penance, by which they were reconciled with God in Lent, until they shatter that peace and enter the devil's army. Against the sacrament of the altar, because they have received heavenly bread at God's table and nevertheless afterwards they set God's land ablaze with infernal fire. Thereupon they are like the man who, when he had eaten at the table of the Lord, received a troop of soldiers from the priests and Pharisees and came against Jesus.)

The last of the late-thirteenth century preaching compilations needing notice has already been mentioned, so it can be dealt with summarily. It is the collection of sermon *exempla* known, appropriately enough, as the *Liber exemplorum*, preserved in University Library, Durham, MS Cosin B.IV.19. Though the manuscript itself was copied about the middle of the fourteenth century, the work was composed, as Little has shown, between 1270 and 1279, and probably in the latter part of this period, between 1275 and 1279. The peppering of sermons with short, lively narratives or *exempla* was a condiment that many friars applied liberally, doubtless because the laity, whose taste for tales and vivid illustrations had long been acknowledged by preaching theorists and practitioners alike, were especially targeted by friars. They also sought the laity out in those regions which the seculars often did not reach, fastened as they generally were to their local livings.[36] The appearance of mendicant *exempla* collections as preaching resources is therefore no surprise, and the *Liber exemplorum*, among the more substantial specimens of this genre to have survived, is of Irish origin. Its anonymous compiler, an English friar, distributed the *exempla* he gathered – some from common pan-European sources, others by word of mouth from friars active like himself in Ireland – between two broad categories, the 'higher' and the 'lower matters'. He classified as 'higher' *exempla* on topics like the life of Christ, the sacrament of the altar, and the Virgin Mary.[37] As 'lower' he classified, for example, *exempla* about the Seven Deadly Sins (perennial preaching matter since, like the sacraments itemized in the passage on the evils of dancing quoted above, these too were part of the established preaching programme).[38] Also classified here are *exempla* on assorted, more mundane topics, including specific social ones like the vices of lawyers, merchants, evil clerics and executors.[39] Since it can be safely assumed that the substance of some of the material in this *exempla* collection was indeed preached, portions of the *Liber exemplorum* open a window onto things actually heard by medieval Irish audiences.[40]

Just as certain topics of the *Liber exemplorum* were similarly favoured in the other early mendicant sermon manuscripts that have been considered, so too they would echo later in the first of the fourteenth-century compilations to which we may now turn, another Franciscan product, British Library,

---

[36] Even if the clergy did not reside in their livings, provision was normally made for resident vicars and deputies to serve in their stead.   [37] A very large number concern the Blessed Virgin Mary (twenty-six); compare too the way in which the *exempla* on her cluster in Trinity College, Dublin, MS 667. Other *exempla* topics classified under the 'higher' section concern, for example, the cross (the well known story of the nun and the lettuce features here), the angels, and St James.   [38] Sloth x 4; Avarice x 5; Gluttony x 6; Envy x 2; Wrath x 2; Lechery x 17; Pride is not present, because the collection, arranged alphabetically, is atelous, with the result that Superbia is missing. (The Seven Deadly Sins were staples of Pecham's programme; see note 28 above.)   [39] Also included are *exempla* about carnal thoughts, baptism, marriage, confession, alms, excommunication, those who injure the Church, those who work on feast days, those who tithe badly, inordinate games, backbiting, humility, indulgences, vainglory, the joy of heaven, oaths, Judgement (including the 'Fifteen Signs'), the memory of death, etc. The original topical emphasis of this section on 'lower things' is distorted because the manuscript is atelous, but judging by what survives, the prominent themes are social complaint, Christian living and catechesis.   [40] Friar Tomás Ó Cuinn's sermon, for example.

London, Harley MS 913.[41] Such thematic consistency suggests that between *c.*1270 and *c.*1330, mendicant preaching in Ireland wove variations on a repertoire of characteristic themes. On the basis of the evidence considered in this chapter, this repertoire could fairly be summarised as having comprised affective preaching about cardinal New Testament (and apocryphal) narratives and persons (for example, about Passiontide and about the Blessed Virgin Mary), and elementary catechetical preaching and moral exhortation. (Indeed, this consistent picture would not be disturbed by any apparent departures in the content of fifteenth-century sermons either, as will be seen.) If we take, for example, two topics from the *Liber exemplorum*'s 'lower matters', the Seven Deadly Sins and the Fifteen Signs before Doomsday, we find them again centrally positioned in two of the 'sermon poems' of Harley MS 913.[42] Harley MS 913 has five 'sermon poems' in all. A third 'sermon poem', on the Decalogue, refurbishes another catechetical chestnut (recall the vernacular verse Decalogue prominent in New College, MS 88), while a fourth and a fifth, respectively the Fall and Passion 'sermon poem' and the 'sermon poem' simply entitled Sarmun by its recent editor, rehearse, respectively, summaries of key biblical narratives from the fall of Lucifer to Christ's Resurrection and Ascension, accenting the Passion, and contempt for the vanity of this fleeting world. Harley MS 913 additionally keeps company with the earlier Franciscan manuscripts New College, MS 88 and Trinity College, Dublin, MS 347 in terms of its small, portable format (University Library, Durham, MS Cosin B.IV.19, the *Liber exemplorum* manuscript, is substantially bigger, but this work was made to be consulted, not to provide a friar with a vademecum).

It seems impossible to determine whether significance, or mere coincidence, should be attached to the fact that this early clutch of manuscripts are mendicant (indeed, Franciscan) products. Unquestionably, the mendicants comprised an important preaching corps in medieval Ireland; were manuscript quantity alone a reliable indicator, the mendicants would emerge as the most important, the prime movers on the preaching scene. Whatever the historical truth of this, it is interesting to note that it was partly in reaction to mendicant activity that the first major name to emerge among secular preachers in fourteenth-century Ireland defined his mission. The career of Richard FitzRalph (1299/1300-1360) has been amply charted elsewhere, but here some notice of his Irish preaching is warranted.[43] He came to Ireland twice, as archbishop of Armagh, first between April 1348 and the early summer of 1349, and next from about the summer of 1351

---

41 An edition of the entire manuscript is projected by Michael Benskin and A.J. Fletcher. 42 Lucas (ed.), *Anglo-Irish poems*, pp 90-101 and 140-9. 43 In addition to Gwynn's study (cited in note 7 above), see Katherine Walsh, *A fourteenth-century scholar and primate: Richard FitzRalph in Oxford, Avignon and Armagh* (Oxford, 1981).

until the early summer of 1356.[44] In this time his sermon diary records him having preached some twenty-eight sermons, all but two of which were in English. All were committed to parchment, however, in Latin.[45] The two sermons preached in Latin were, unsurprisingly, to clerical congregations, and delivered at synods held in Drogheda, on 7 February 1352 and 5 February 1355 respectively.

FitzRalph's first recorded sermon in Ireland, delivered the previous year also in London, was preached on 24 April 1348 in Dundalk on the six petitions of the *Pater noster*. The *Pater noster*, like the Decalogue and sacraments, was one of the staples of catechesis, and eminently suitable fare for a sermon *ad populum*. He managed to work into his preaching other catechetical favourites, too. The Seven Deadly Sins, for example, feature in a sermon of his delivered at Louth on 27 April 1348.[46] As occasion required, he was also prepared when preaching to make topical references, though these seem to have touched on the moral conduct of particular social groups rather than on broad political issues. Thus his memorandum of a sermon delivered in Drogheda on 2 December 1352, for example, notes that 'ibi fiebat dilatacio sermonis ad mercatorum fraudes et falsitates' ('at that point the sermon was expanded to touch on the frauds and deceits of merchants'),[47] and in another sermon delivered at Skreen on 21 June 1355 he noted that there existed in the deanery there 'vsurarij, falsidici et receptores furtorum et furum tanquam collectores' ('usurers, liars and harborers and collectors, as it were, of thieves and robbers').[48] Since all of the sermons delivered in Ireland were recorded in Latin, and most were preserved as précis or digests, we cannot know precisely what FitzRalph said, with the exception, perhaps, of the two synodal sermons, and of the obiter dicta, like those at Drogheda and Skreen, that he notes having made. FitzRalph's sermons were cast in the 'modern' form of preaching (discussed further below), and he favoured *exempla*, especially in sermons preached *ad populum*, as might be expected.

During his first visit FitzRalph is known to have preached in Dundalk, Louth, Ardee, Drogheda and Mansfieldstown, all in county Louth. His second visit saw him again in these places, excepting Louth and Mansfieldstown, but now also including to the south of Dundalk his manor at Dromiskin and to the north-east of Drogheda his manor at Termonfekin. On this second visit he ventured a little further afield, preaching also in co. Meath at Trim, Athboy, Kells, Skreen and Greenock, and in one notable

---

44 He was probably absent with the king for most of summer and autumn of 1353. **45** None of the sermon diary manuscripts is holograph. (For a catalogue of these, see Gwynn, 'Sermon-diary'). **46** Bodleian Library, Oxford, MS Bodley 144, ff 42v-3. **47** Bodleian Library, Oxford, MS Bodley 144, f. 63. Criticism of merchants was a sermon commonplace but in Drogheda, which had an established mercantile community, FitzRalph's comments, even if they were not actually intended as imminently topical, would doubtless have seemed so. **48** Bodleian Library, Oxford, MS Bodley 144, f. 72.

case, even travelling to the northernmost part of his diocese to preach on 8 September 1351 in Coleraine. But most of his time was spent in the relatively more domesticated reaches of the Pale.

FitzRalph's activity, however, seems to be something of an exception to prove the rule, for precious little preaching ascribable to seculars is in evidence before the fifteenth century, and even then, some preachers, like Archbishop Thomas Cranley of Dublin, were content to use mendicant materials. Of the four fifteenth-century manuscripts to which we must finally turn (Trinity College, Dublin, MSS 201, 204 and 667, and National Library of Ireland, Dublin, MS 9596), three were certainly produced in Ireland (Trinity College, MSS 201, 204 and 667), while the fourth (National Library, MS 9596) possibly was. Of these four, one may have served secular clergy (Trinity College, MS 201), another probably did (National Library, MS 9596), another may have been produced by mendicants (Trinity College, MS 204) and the last certainly was (Trinity College, MS 667).[49] The earliest of them, Trinity College, MS 201, is the only late-medieval sermon manuscript surviving from Ireland whose contents are almost entirely in English. It contains an (incomplete) copy of the massively popular *Festial* of John Mirk, Augustinian canon of Lilleshall Abbey, Shropshire. Mirk authored it probably in the period *c.*1382-90.[50] The name of one 'Dominus Thomas Norreys' copied at the top of f. 22 seems to be in the hand of the principal scribe of the manuscript. Norreys's hand dates to the first half of the fifteenth century (possibly the second quarter) and, given that the dialect of Middle English that he reproduced is Hiberno-English, it is likely that he was trained to write in Ireland.[51] In fact, a Thomas Norreys, chaplain, who is conceivably the same man, appears first on record in Dublin on 3 May 1447, when along with two other chaplains he was granted a messuage in High Street.[52] He also appears in one of the deeds of Christ Church Cathedral, Dublin, for 10 December 1455. Here, along with two other chaplains, he was granted two messuages and three gardens in Dublin by one William Hogge.[53] His last recorded appearance is in June 1470. He is referred to as chaplain again but now also as a warden, with one Henry Yonge, of the Guild of St Anne.[54] It is not known whether Norreys, like the author of the sermon

---

49 In certain cases their content is older, antedating the fifteenth century. **50** A.J. Fletcher, 'John Mirk and the Lollards' in *Medium Ævum* lv (1987), pp 59-66. **51** A. McIntosh and M.L. Samuels, 'Prolegomena to a study of medieval Anglo-Irish' in *Medium Ævum* xxxvii (1968), pp 1-11; unless, of course, Norreys was copying *literatim*. **52** H.F. Berry, 'History of the religious gild of S. Anne, in S. Audoen's Church, Dublin, 1430-1740, taken from its records in the Haliday Collection, R.I.A.' in *Proceedings of the Royal Irish Academy* xxv sect. C (1904-5), pp 21-106; see p. 68, item 75. He also appears in property deeds connected with St Anne's Guild dated 20 February 1451, 12 May 1468 and finally June 1470 (see respectively Berry, 'Gild of S. Anne', p. 69, item 77, p. 70, item 84 and pp 87-8, item 135). **53** M.G. McEnery and R. Refaussé (eds.), *Christ Church deeds* (Dublin, 2001), no. 961. **54** Berry, 'Gild of S. Anne', pp 87-8, item 135.

collection he copied, John Mirk, may have been an Augustinian canon too, though with three houses in medieval Dublin, the canons were well represented, and would have contributed significantly to the city's clerical complement. Furthermore, it was in connection with one of those houses, Christ Church, that the Norreys of the deed of 1455 appeared. In any event, Norreys's possession of the *Festial* is evidence of the importation into Ireland, and presumably use there, of one of England's most influential vernacular sermon collections.

The writing of the *Festial*, a work stoutly orthodox and stocked full of *exempla*, some of which are tastelessly sensational, may partly have been prompted in reaction to other contemporary preaching propagated by those opponents of orthodoxy, the Lollards. Such people had set their faces against the sort of fables and tales in preaching that Mirk, like the friars, relished. Yet the avoidance of racy narrative was not simply a means whereby Lollard radicals implicitly declared their opposition to the conservatives within the Church; even amongst the conservatives, including the friars, can be found sermons of chaster pitch. The second fifteenth-century manuscript from Ireland containing the sermons of a single author, this time ones in Latin, is Trinity College, Dublin, MS 204, and it conceivably had mendicant auspices.[55] The two major sermon cycles in it, the *Sermones dominicales* and the *Sermones de sanctis et festis* of Nicholas de Aquevilla, were the work of a Franciscan who flourished early in the fourteenth century, and Trinity College, MS 204 represents an Irish appropriation of this other, highly popular but far less flamboyant, sermon collection. The style of Nicholas de Aquevilla's sermons, in utter contrast to John Mirk's, is restrained, and they tirelessly employ a tight, schematic form of sermon composition known as the 'modern' mode of preaching. 'Modern' sermons opened with the announcement of a theme of Scripture which was then systematically subdivided for discussion, the subdivisions providing the bulk of the sermon.[56] The manuscript's exact provenance within Ireland is unknown, nor is anything known of the identity of one Nicholas Katwell, who declares his ownership in a fifteenth-century hand on f. 278v.[57]

Whether or not Trinity College, MS 204 originated within the Pale, the third fifteenth-century sermon manuscript of present concern, if indeed it originated in Ireland, may have done. At least by the sixteenth century, it was

---

55 Fully described by Colker, *Descriptive catalogue*, i, pp 391-2. Aquevilla was a Franciscan. Though his sermons were also copied widely beyond the mendicant Orders, T.C.D. MS 204 additionally contains the *Super Deuteronomium* of Thomas Docking OFM. (Two snatches of Middle English, the words 'dysclosyd' and 'deseysyd', appear on f. 145v.)   56 For a valuable study of late medieval sermon form, see Spencer, *English preaching*, pp 228-68.   57 Not Kantwell, *pace* Colker, *Descriptive catalogue*, i, p. 392, although, to be sure, an -n- may have been omitted; the name Cantwell had strong associations with the Kilkenny region. Some names of Gaelic Irish owners, listed in Colker, ibid., are also to be found.

circulating in Drogheda. National Library of Ireland, Dublin, MS 9596 has no perceptible affiliation with any particular Order within the Church, though that said, mendicant auspices seem perhaps the least likely. The late-medieval core of this manuscript was copied by two scribes in the second half of the fifteenth century. By the sixteenth, it had come into the lay possession of a Drogheda burgess family, the Burnells, and parchment leaves originally left blank between many of its items were subsequently used by Burnell family members (notably by Robert Burnell, mayor of Drogheda in 1570) for preserving pious or practical memoranda. Perhaps the most important of these post-medieval insertions, from the historian's point of view, is a unique, but hitherto unnoticed, account of the land-gavel of Drogheda, copied between ff 41v-52v in the first half of the sixteenth century.[58] However, our concern here is with the manuscript's late-medieval core. Its first substantial item is a set of notes on the Decalogue,[59] each commandment being accompanied by commentary and illustrated with *exempla* of the type that many preachers, as has been seen, would have approved. For example, the second commandment, not to take God's name in vain, includes telegraphic notes such as the following which seem to assume in their readers a previous acquaintance with the narratives alluded to:

> Quidem lusor ad taxillos, cum semel perdidisset, multum iratus cepit iurare et blasphemare Deum. Et in signum perdicionis, iecit sagittam contra celum, quasi volens Deum sagittare. Mox que sagitta ad pedes eius ad detestacionem peccati redijt cruentata. Nota et de illo qui perdiderat primogenitum, vxorem et oculum dextrum, et tandem diuina vlcione percussus interijt. Nota et de periurio et iuramento super reliquias in libro de Alphabeto narracionum.[60]

> (A certain dice player, when he had lost on one occasion, was greatly enraged and started swearing and blaspheming God, and shot an arrow against heaven as a sign of his perdition, as if wishing to pierce God. To his detestation, this arrow soon returned bloodstained to his feet. Also, note about the man who had lost his first-born son, his wife and his right eye, and at length he died, struck by divine vengeance. Also, note in the book of the *Alphabet of Tales* about the perjurer and his oath upon the relics.)

58 This invaluable source for Drogheda history, which merits publication, was not noticed in S. O'Connor, 'Tudor Drogheda' in *Journal of the Old Drogheda Society* x (1996), pp 86-110 or in John Bradley, *The topography and layout of medieval Drogheda* (Drogheda, 1997). 59 National Library of Ireland, Dublin, MS 9596, ff 2-19. 60 National Library of Ireland, Dublin, MS 9596, f. 5v. The *Alphabetum narracionum* (the 'Alphabet of Tales') was an alphabetically arranged collection of *exempla*.

Next, a discussion of lechery is followed by a series of alphabetically arranged topics with accompanying notes.[61] The sermons proper start on f. 124v with an opening for a Palm Sunday sermon, followed by full sermons for, respectively, the fourth Sunday in Lent (ff 125 col. a – 127v col. b), the first Sunday in Lent (ff 127v col. b – 131 col. a),[62] the fourth Sunday in Advent (ff 131 col. a – 134 col. a), and Passion Sunday (ff 134 col. a – 136v col. b). Since Advent, Lent and Passiontide were prime preaching seasons, the content of the manuscript at this point may reflect preaching's traditional seasonal investment. Then follow two openings of sermons, respectively for the first and second Sundays in Advent (f. 136v col. b), and lists of sermon themata (Temporale themata on ff 137r-v and on ff 137v-8v Sanctorale themata, plus themata for visitation and synodal sermons, and sermons to congregations of religious and solitaries).[63] Next comes an opening for a sermon on the feast of relics (f. 141),[64] and finally an atelous sermon of unknown occasion (f. 144v).[65]

These sermons, cast like FitzRalph's and de Aquevilla's in the 'modern' form, are probably all fifteenth-century compositions, and at least seven are likely to be by the same anonymous author.[66] He may have been addressing a clerical congregation, comprised as this was of 'Reverendi domini et amici carissimi'.[67] Conceivably, therefore, the sermons were delivered, as recorded, in Latin, even though four also mark their thematic divisions with verses in Middle English.[68] Were they preached in Drogheda? Certainly, as remarked, the manuscript was kept there by the sixteenth century, and we have seen how in the fourteenth, FitzRalph had set a precedent for 'modern' Latin preaching in Drogheda when he twice addressed clerical congregations. But the importation of National Library of Ireland, MS 9596 from somewhere in England cannot be absolutely ruled out.

---

61 Respectively, ff 20-5 and ff 26-110. Various interpolations were later made on the folios originally left blank, the land-gavel of Drogheda being one such.   62 This sermon concludes (f. 134 col. a): 'quod Rychmund'. It is hard to know whether the name Rychmund was scribal or authorial.   63 Note that the themes of the earlier sermons appear in these lists.   64 References to the Normandy campaigns of Henry V here must date the sermon to some time in his reign, or later, post-1422). The date of those other sermons in this manuscript that may be by the same author (see further below) is likely to be similar.   65 However its theme (Hebrews 7:26) derives from the epistle reading for the feast of several confessors in Sarum Use, so it may be for then. (The manuscript concludes with an alphabetical list of topics on f. 145.)   66 The incomplete sermon on f. 141 that refers to the Normandy campaigns of Henry V is one of those addressed to 'Reverendi domini'.   67 Compare the opening terms of address of one of FitzRalph's synodal sermons in Drogheda on 7 February 1352: 'Reuerendi domini, patres et fratres, et amici carissimi' (Bodleian Library, Oxford, MS Bodley 144, f. 49).   68 Those for the fourth Sunday in Lent, for the first Sunday in Lent, for the fourth Sunday in Advent, and for Passion Sunday. All are also addressed to 'Reverendi'. On the use of verses in sermons, see S. Wenzel, *Verses in sermons: Fasciculus Morum and its Middle English poems* (Cambridge, Mass., 1978), pp 61-100.

Our final fifteenth-century manuscript takes us beyond the Pale and back once more to the friars with whom we began, and this time, Irish origin is beyond dispute. Trinity College, Dublin, MS 667, cited earlier as witnessing to a close association, indeed symbiosis, of the material forms of two ethnic religious cultures on the island, includes amongst its varied contents two Latin sermons for the feast of Corpus Christi.[69] A modest investment, to be sure, but other sermons are in Gaelic, and the remaining contents would have commended the manuscript to friars whether *inter Anglicos* or *inter Hibernicos* as a preaching resource. Its pertinence to preachers is clear from such items as a passage comparing the attributes and habits of a cockerel to those of a preacher, for example, or the notes on preaching's sister enterprise, confession.[70] Also of pulpit use were its several Latin *exempla*, many on familiar and favourite sermon topics (on death and the last things, for example, and on the Blessed Virgin Mary).[71] Trinity College, MS 667 also contains what may be considered the ultimate template for a sermon, supremely portable in the best mendicant tradition: a moralized diagram of the human hand appears on p. 252 (see fig. 2). With the moral significance of its digits committed to memory, a preacher would never have lacked a sermon of perennial (if gloomy) relevance: 'You don't know how greatly, nor how often, you have offended God', says the thumb; 'Your ending is bitter, your life brief, and you have entered the world in sin', says the index finger; 'You will take nothing hence other than your deeds, nor can you prolong your life nor evade death', says the middle finger; 'You don't know whence you come, nor how nor when you will die', says the fourth finger; and the little finger says, 'You will soon be forgotten by those dear to you, your heir will seldom make provision for you [presumably, by commissioning post-mortem spiritual suffrages for your soul], nor will those do any differently to whom you leave your wealth.'[72] Thus without needing either book or sermon notes, the preacher's very hand might serve as an aide-mémoire.

The fact that the two actual sermons chosen for preservation in Trinity College, MS 667 are both for Corpus Christi is itself of interest. The second, being the more substantial, may conveniently serve for illustration. It is organized according to the 'modern' form, and like some of the 'modern'

---

69 Trinity College, Dublin, MS 667, pp 130-1 and 184-8 respectively. At least the second of these Corpus Christi sermons may be a fifteenth-century composition; its sensitivity to lay debate about the nature of the Eucharist leads one to suspect a composition after the 1380s when Eucharistic controversy was becoming topical among laity. (For further discussion of MS 667 within a Franciscan context, see Colmán Ó Clabaigh's essay below.)   **70** Trinity College, Dublin, MS 667, p. 82 col. a and pp 105 col. a – 106 col. a respectively; in addition, a list of what sins are reserved to bishops to absolve appears on p. 81 cols a-b, and an Irish text on confession on p. 165 col. a.   **71** Respectively Trinity College, Dublin, MS 667, pp 32 col. b – 36 col. a; pp 199 col. b – 214 col. b and 222 col. a – 231 col. b.   **72** Though termed a *manus meditacionis*, the diagram stocks the mind with preachable matter.

sermons noted previously in National Library of Ireland, MS 9596, it too introduces a threefold rhymed division of its matter in Middle English into its Latin.[73] But unlike the National Library, MS 9596 sermons, the likelihood seems stronger that this Corpus Christi sermon may originally have been preached in the vernacular. It is aware that some among the laity were asking many questions about the sacrament of the altar, and that more properly they ought simply to believe what the Church told them.[74] Advice of this sort is familiar in orthodox sermons to the laity in England at about this date. Moreover, the sermon's admonitions would remain unheeded if left ring-fenced in priestly Latin, a language normally beyond the laity's reach. Recommendations that the laity be acquiescent also strongly suggest that the sermon was composed some time in the wake of the Eucharistic controversies of the 1380s. Evidently, some of the friars in fifteenth-century Ireland felt moved to champion orthodox teaching on the Eucharist, as friars had been doing in England, and choosing as its forum a singularly appropriate feast day.

It is difficult to be confident that any summary of what this small collection of manuscripts suggests about the history of the English and Latin preaching tradition in late-medieval Ireland may not suffer from partiality: Watt was essentially right, after all, when he regretted Ireland's scarcity of medieval sermon literature. This being so, the picture is necessarily incomplete. Yet, a few points have emerged that are worth drawing together, especially since they are consistent with what other classes of evidence described at the beginning of this chapter suggest, but whose discussion here was prevented by limitations of space. The aggregated manuscript evidence suggests that in late-medieval Ireland, the Church's preaching mission was being staunchly undertaken by the friars, a point that Colmán Ó Clabaigh's essay will further elaborate. Indeed, mendicant efforts seem to eclipse those of the seculars, though it must be admitted that since the activity of seculars was in the nature of things more locally circumscribed, it would have been somewhat less conspicuous. And as if by way of corollary, we find cases where the preaching of the seculars was directly facilitated by resources originally mendicant. The mendicant preaching machine was also being serviced in Ireland as early as the second half of the thirteenth century with preaching aids like the *Liber exemplorum*. It may, therefore, be more than a mere cliché of antimendicant propaganda that Richard FitzRalph uttered when he lamented the ubiquitousness of the friars: in Ireland, it seems, he would indeed have been surrounded by them. Nor did any division of the late-medieval Irish Church *inter Anglicos* and *inter Hibernicos* hamper their collaborative activity on the preaching front, at least not in the fifteenth

---

73 The division is summarized at the foot of p. 184: 'Condiciones corporis Christi: hyt ys dredefull in takyng; hyt ys nedefull in reseuyng; hyt ys medefull to belyuyng.' 74 Interestingly, this sermon seems to have been copied by the Irish scribe Donald O Maelechlan.

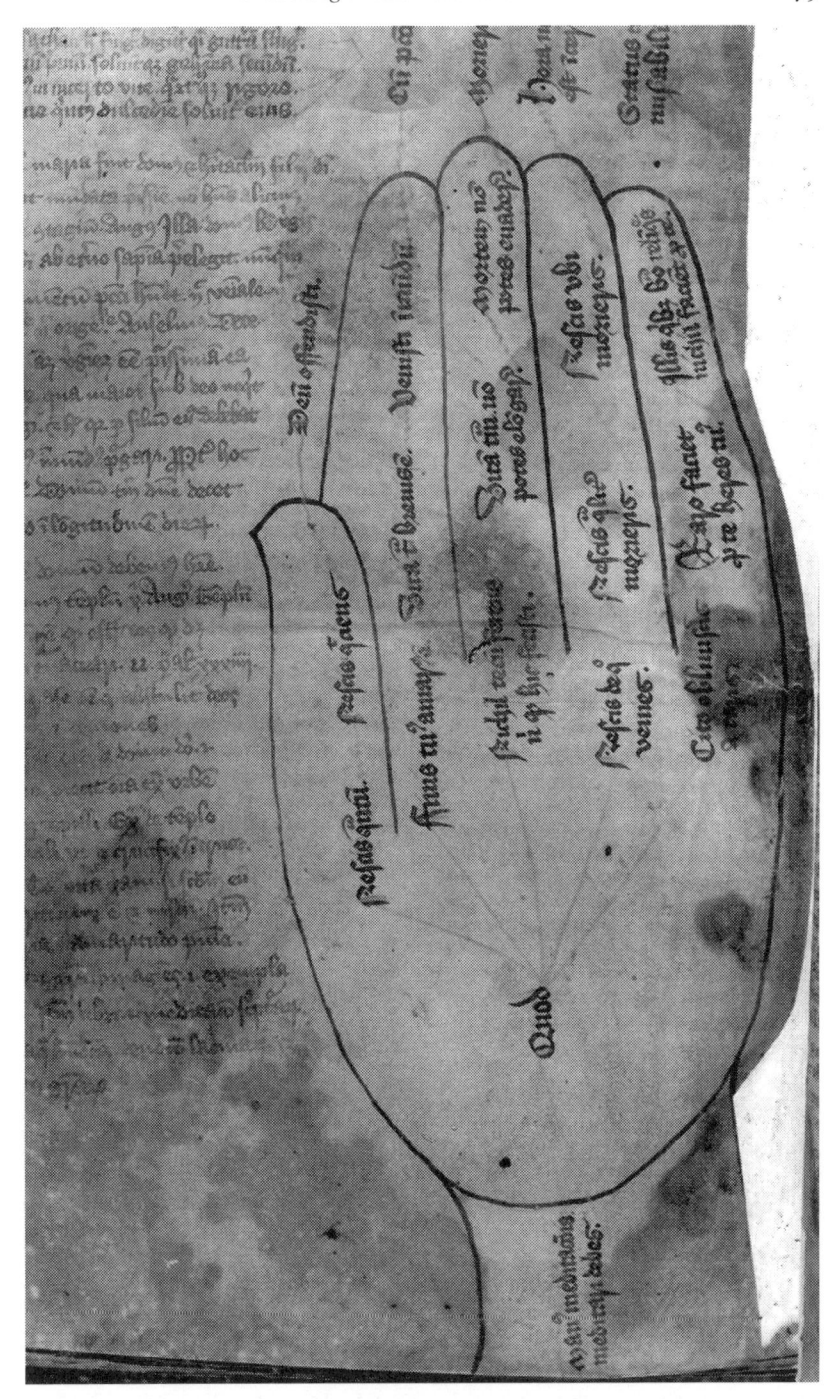

Figure 2: The moralised hand (T.C.D., MS 677, p. 252).

century. And as for the matter that they most typically preached, it combined key biblical (sometimes Apocryphal) narratives with practical moral exhortation. This matter might be artistically and imaginatively vivified – here *exempla* played an important part – to render it at once palatable and memorable. Little that was preached, judging by what the manuscripts disclose, was historically unique and specific. When the inhabitants of Drogheda and Skreen were admonished by FitzRalph, for example, it seems to have been more for such venalities as the flesh is ever heir to, as well as for besetting class sins, than for circumstances peculiar to Drogheda and Skreen. This does not, of course, necessarily imply that preaching, indifferent to contemporary politics, confined itself exclusively to timeless matters of morality.[75] However, the prevailing impression is of a relative consistency in the matter preached that is remarkable. Its longevity over nearly three centuries, moreover, is impressive. Such was its tenacity in Ireland that its characteristic concerns echoed into the sixteenth century and beyond. But this early modern afterglow is another essay's story.[76]

[75] The friars in Ireland were commissioned to preach the crusades on various occasions: for example, in 1250, Henry III requested that they do so (H.S. Sweetman, (ed.), *Calendar of documents, relating to Ireland, preserved in Her Majesty's Record Office, London* (5 vols, London, 1875-86), i, p. 457). Amongst the seculars, FitzRalph preached topically when he targeted the claims of the friars. And indeed, topical preaching was not shunned by preachers in a later age, as Bernadette Cunningham's essay below makes clear. [76] See especially Bernadette Cunningham's essay below.

Preaching in late-medieval Ireland: the Franciscan contribution

Colmán N. Ó Clabaigh, OSB

In 1515 the anonymous compiler of the well-known report on the 'State of Ireland and a plan for its reformation' listed clerical negligence and the lack of preaching as one of the chief reasons for the disordered state of the country:

> Some sayeth, that the prelates of the churche, and clergye, is much cause of all the mysse order of the land; for ther is no archebysshop, ne bysshop, abbot, ne pryor, parson, ne vycar, ne any other person of the Churche, highe or lowe, greate or smalle, Englyshe or Iryshe, that useyth to preach the worde of Godde, saveing the poore fryers beggers; and ther wodde of Godde do cesse, ther canne be no grace and wythoute the specyall [grace] of Godde, this lande maye never be reformyd...[1]

Recent work has shown that the extent of clerical negligence may be exaggerated but confirms the reputation of the friars as the pre-eminent preachers of the period.[2] The preaching activities of the Franciscans, or Friars Minor, the largest and most influential of the mendicant orders in late medieval Ireland, form the subject of this essay.

The fifteenth and early sixteenth centuries witnessed a remarkable second flowering of the Franciscan movement in Ireland.[3] Unlike the thirteenth- and fourteenth-century friars who gravitated to the towns and boroughs of the Anglo-Irish colony, the fifteenth-century expansion was largely concentrated in the territories of Gaelic chieftains in Connacht, Munster and Ulster. Another important difference was their cultivation of links with reformed Franciscan circles on the Continent rather than with the more conservative friars of the English province.[4] From at least 1417 the Gaelic friars were in contact with the various reform movements emerging among the friars in

---

1 'State of Ireland and plan for its reformation' in *State papers for the reign of Henry VIII* (11 vols, London, 1830-52), ii, p. 15. 2 Henry A. Jefferies, *Priests and prelates of Armagh in the age of Reformations* (Dublin, 1997), pp 15-82. 3 See Colmán N. Ó Clabaigh, OSB, *From reform to Reformation: the Franciscans in Ireland, 1400-1534* (Dublin, forthcoming). 4 For the early history of the friars see Francis Cotter, OFM, *The Friars Minor in Ireland: from their*

Germany, France and the Netherlands. The most influential of these was the Observant movement which, after a long period of gestation, emerged as a distinct juridical entity in Ireland by 1460.[5] The Observants adopted a strict ascetic lifestyle based on the 1223 rule of St Francis as interpreted by three thirteenth- and fourteenth-century papal declarations. For the reformers north of the Alps (the Ultramontane group) to which the Irish friars belonged, further legislation was provided by statutes known as the *Abbreviatio Statutorum* adopted by the Barcelona general chapter in 1451.[6] Part of the Observants' success lay in their effective use of the system of visitation whereby each house and province of the reform was regularly visited by a superior or his delegate. This ensured maintenance of a uniformly high standard of religious life and fostered a strong sense of *esprit de corps* not only among the houses of individual provinces but between the provinces themselves. Each friary was subject to regular visitation by the provincial superior or his commissary and a report on the house and the conduct of its superior was given to the provincial chapter which met triennially. Similar visitations and reports on the state of entire provinces were made to the general chapter which also met triennially. This was the supreme governing body of the Observants that was held at various locations on the Continent. The surviving evidence shows that the Irish friars were diligent attenders. As well as maintaining standards, these links brought the Irish friars into contact with Continental ideas, texts and practises that demonstrably influenced their preaching ministry.

The high regard in which the Irish Observants were held is demonstrated by the widespread patronage that they enjoyed. Between 1458 and 1508 ten new friaries were established for Observants while by 1540 the reform had been accepted by twenty-eight of the province's forty-eight houses.[7] One result of the Observants' activities was the emergence of the Third Order Regular, groups of religious which emerged out of the lay fraternities or Third Order groups attached to the Observant friaries. These were bound by vows and lived in community but were a distinct entity from the Observant friars. Between 1426 and 1539 they established forty-eight friaries, mostly in Connacht and Ulster, from which they operated as schoolmasters and assistants to the secular clergy.[8] The same period also witnessed a modest expansion of the Conventual, or unreformed, friars in Gaelic territories.

---

arrival to 1400 (New York, 1994). **5** For the development of the Observant reform in general see Duncan Nimmo, *Reform and division in the Franciscan Order (1225-1528)* (Rome, 1987). **6** Michael Bihl (ed.), 'Abbreviatio Statutorum tam Papalium quam Generalium edita apud Barchinonam in Conventu Beatae Mariae de Iesu Familiae Cismontanae de Observantia [1451]' in *Archivium Franciscanum Historicum* xxxviii (1942), pp 106-97. **7** Aubrey Gwynn and R.N. Hadcock, *Medieval religious houses: Ireland* (London, 1970), pp 235-66. **8** Gwynn and Hadcock, *Medieval religious houses*, pp 263-75.

The thirteenth-century friars were swiftly co-opted to implement the pastoral programme adopted by the fourth Lateran council in 1215. To ensure a supply of qualified and competent preachers the Franciscans adopted the tiered education system pioneered by the Dominicans. This provided a basic education for each friar and established a structure by which the brightest students could advance to other centres for further studies. Ideally each friary had a *studium* in which a lector gave the young friars a basic training in the liberal arts, philosophy, theology and the *ars predicandi*. Such local centres were probably where the majority of friars received their training. Some students were sent to the province's or custody's advanced *studium* for further training while the best could be appointed to study at one of the *studia generalia* of the Order by the provincial chapter or the minister general. There is evidence for the presence of Irish friar-students at the *studia* in Oxford, Cambridge, Paris, Cologne, Strasbourg and Bologna from the thirteenth to sixteenth centuries and a number of these also availed of the opportunity to take a university degree.[9] This network, with Paris at its apex, brought young friars into contact with confrères from all parts of Europe and provided an important channel for the transmission of texts and ideas to all levels of the Order.[10] One of the earliest Irish Franciscan texts to survive, the *Liber exemplorum*, discussed in Alan Fletcher's essay above, provides proof of this, compiled as it was from a network of sources extending throughout the British Isles and into the Continent.[11]

The friars' activities as preachers were governed by the Order's own legislation as well as by canon law. The Franciscan Rule was the first to contain instructions on preaching and this was developed in subsequent legislation enacted by the Order. Among the Observants permission could only be granted by the provincial superior with the consent of the provincial chapter and only if the candidate was recommended by trustworthy friars.[12] From their earliest days in Ireland the friars followed the practice of their English and Continental confrères and travelled in pairs on preaching tours. The *Liber exemplorum* contains a number of incidental references to this practice, including Friar Tomás Ó Cuinn's preaching tour in Connacht discussed in Alan Fletcher's essay above.[13] Other references indicate that, even when the majority of their houses were concentrated in the Anglo-Irish colony, they frequently undertook missions to Gaelic areas.[14]

The expansion of the friars into these Gaelic areas in the fifteenth century increased the number of bases from which they could launch such missions,

9 Cotter, *The Friars Minor in Ireland*, pp 114-22.   10 David L. d'Avray, *The preaching of the friars: sermons diffused from Paris before 1300* (Oxford, 1985)   11 A.G. Little (ed.), *Liber Exemplorum ad usum praedicantium saeculo XIII compositus a quondam Fratre Minore Anglico de Provinciae Hiberniae* (Aberdeen, 1918).   12 *Abbreviatio Statutorum*, ch. V, no. 9.   13 Little (ed.), *Liber Exemplorum*, pp 85-6.   14 Little (ed.), *Liber Exemplorum*, p. 51, has an account of a preaching tour conducted by Friar Adam Habe in Ulster.

and though references are few, it is clear that they continued to conduct extensive preaching tours. The 1486 description of Friar Donal O'Fallon as the most effective preacher in Ireland since the time of St Patrick may indicate a widespread ministry,[15] while the obituary of Friar Patrick O'Feidhil in 1505 leaves no room for doubt as he is described as a noted preacher throughout Ireland and Scotland. The fact that his death is recorded in the *Annals of Ulster* but that he was buried in Timoleague in County Cork also provides indications both of his reputation and his travels.[16] The long account given by Friar Donatus Mooney of the activities of Friar Brian MacGrath (or Gray) of Donegal includes references to how he once travelled one hundred and fifty miles to preach before the earl of Kildare and also alludes to a prophecy made by him during a sermon preached in Clogher.[17] The complaints of the people of Kilkenny in 1537 against the tolls levied by the constables of Athy, Leighlin and Carlow on those travelling to hear the friars preach provide evidence both for extensive preaching tours throughout Leinster and for their popularity.[18] Certain representations of St Francis are also of interest in this respect: those in Ennis and Creevelea, County Leitrim, show him carrying a preacher's staff, the long staff surmounted by a cross borne by the friar while on a mission.[19]

Apart from the preaching tours, the regular cycle of sermons in friary churches constituted the other main occasion for the friar's work as preachers. Thirteenth- and fourteenth-century Irish friary churches, such as the one surviving at Nenagh, were long halls designed so that the maximum number of people could both see and hear the preacher. In the fifteenth century large transepts were added to many of the earlier houses, as at Ennis, or built as a matter of course in new foundations, as at Adare. This greatly increased the space available for congregations as well as providing room for additional altars and chapels. Fifteenth-century Irish friaries were also characterized by the construction of a slender square church tower. As well as providing a division between the choir and the nave and transept, the crossing of these towers provided a space for a wooden preacher's platform, and a number of friaries preserve the stone corbels used to support them. In Rosserrilly this *pulpitum* is a stone feature incorporated into the fabric of the tower.

The season of Lent was generally the friars' most active time for preaching as the emphasis on repentance and the requirement that all confess and

---

[15] W.M. Hennessey and B. MacCarthy (eds), *Annála Uladh: Annals of Ulster* (4 vols, Dublin, 1887-1901), iii, p. 305. [16] *Annals of Ulster*, iii, p. 477. [17] Brendan Jennings, OFM (ed.), 'Donatus Moneyus: De Provincia Hiberniae S. Francisci' in *Analecta Hibernica* no. 6 (1934), pp 12-138, reference on pp 46-7. [18] *S.P. Henry VIII*, ii, I. Quoted in Brendan Bradshaw, *The dissolution of the religious orders in Ireland under Henry VIII*, (Cambridge, 1974), p. 12. [19] In Creevelea he is depicted preaching to birds from a pulpit formed from the calyx of a flower, the preacher's staff behind his right shoulder.

receive communion at Easter provided ideal subjects for the preacher. On the Continent such Lenten missions were highly developed affairs with towns and cities vying to secure the services of noted preachers for a course of daily sermons.[20] While there is no reference to such Lenten missions in Ireland in the medieval period it seems unlikely that the friars would have let such an important pastoral opportunity pass.[21] The Youghal friars were certainly aware of the practice as their library contained several collections of Lenten homilies. The earliest reference occurs in 1611 when Friar Donatus Mooney reconciled an apostate Conventual friar during a Lenten mission he conducted at Monahincha near Roscrea.[22] It is possible that this represents the survival of the medieval tradition.

The mendicant friars revolutionized medieval pastoral practice by their actions and, more importantly, through the writings they produced.[23] For preachers these works included treatises on the *ars predicandi*, editions of model sermons and collections of *exempla* or moral tales which could be incorporated into sermons to illustrate points and maintain interest. Other resources included biblical concordances and commentaries, excerpts from classical writers, and encyclopaedias that provided interesting and entertaining references and gave an air of erudition to the preacher.[24] The most representative of all these medieval preaching aids were the small format books, easily carried and designed for use by itinerant preachers, examples of which are discussed in Alan Fletcher's essay above. A number of Irish examples dating from the thirteenth to fifteenth centuries survive.[25]

The only codex known to survive from the library of the Franciscan friary in Youghal is Theologischen Lateinischen folio 703 of the Staatsbibliotek Preussicher Kulturbesitz in Berlin. It contains a number of Franciscan liturgical texts, but folios 150v-152 contain the catalogue of the friary library compiled at three different stages between 1491 and 1523. This catalogue provides an unique insight into the intellectual interests and pastoral resources of the friars.[26] By 1523 the community had amassed a collection of

---

20 Larissa Taylor, *Soldiers of Christ* (Oxford, 1992) gives an account of Lenten preaching in early Reformation France and the Netherlands.   21 Cotter, *The Friars Minor in Ireland*, p. 78.   22 Jennings (ed.), 'Donatus Moneyus: De Provincia Hiberniae S. Francisci', p. 76.   23 d'Avray, *The preaching of the friars* is the most comprehensive survey. See also J. Longère, *La prédication médiévale* (Paris, 1983).   24 d'Avray, *The preaching of the friars*, pp 64-89.   25 See generally on these, David L. d'Avray, 'Portable vade-mecum books containing Franciscan and Dominican texts' in A.C. de la Mare and B.C. Barker-Benfield (eds), *Manuscripts at Oxford* (Oxford, 1980), pp 60-4.   26 The catalogue was first published by William Maziere Brady in his *Clerical and parochial records relating to Cork, Cloyne and Ross* (Dublin, 1864), pp 319-23. Despite its many inaccuracies and omissions this was re-published by James Coleman, 'A medieval Irish monastic library catalogue', in *Bibliographical Society of Ireland Publications* ii (1925), pp 111-20 and has become the standard edition. A new edition, with identifications, is given in Ó Clabaigh, *From reform to Reformation*, appendix I.

150 volumes of which twenty-three were collections of sermons. A number of other works could also have been used by preachers in the preparation of their homilies.

The sermon collections, though extensive, contain few surprises and consist of works by the best-known medieval preachers. The sermons of St Bernard of Clairvaux (1090-1153) head the list in the preaching category of the 1491 section of the catalogue. It is not specified which of St Bernard's sermons are referred to, but the collection probably contained some of his most popular works: the *Sermones super cantica canticorum* or his liturgical work, the *Sermones per annum*. Surprisingly, there are no references to any sermons by St Augustine, St Ambrose or the early Church Fathers in the collection. The only patristic works are the *Letters* and *Dialogues* of Gregory the Great (c.540-604). Of these the *Dialogues*, with their emphasis on the lives and miracles of Italian saints, would have provided useful preaching material. Sermons by mendicant preachers, particularly Dominicans, from the thirteenth to the fifteenth centuries are the most numerous. Thirteenth-century works include the sermons of the Italian Dominican, James of Voragine (c.1230-1298), as well as a copy of the *Legenda aurea*, his highly influential work on the lives of the saints. The presence of the *Sermones dominicales* of the Franciscan Luke of Bitonto (fl. 1233) is unusual, as this work did not circulate widely outside Italy. Fourteenth-century works include the widely read *Sermones dominicales* of the Dominican, James of Lausanne (d. 1322),[27] which generally circulated with his series of Lenten sermons.[28] The last work listed in the catalogue, and almost certainly a printed book, is the sermons of Graeculus, a fourteenth-century Austrian Franciscan.[29] The library had two copies of the *Quatuor novissima*, a collection of thirty-eight sermons on the four last things. Though generally attributed to Bonaventure, it was the work of Gerard of Vliederhoven, a late fourteenth-century Dutch Teutonic knight.[30]

The advances of printing account for the preponderance of late fifteenth- and sixteenth-century Continental works in the collection. These include works by authors who were still alive when the first version of the catalogue was compiled in 1491. The two references to works by the chancellor of the University of Paris, Jean Gerson (1363-1429), may refer to some of his sermons. The *sermones quondam Ricardi Flemeng de pergameno* could be a rare reference to the sermons preached by Richard Fleming (1360-1431), bishop

---

27 He is erroneously described as a Franciscan by the cataloguer. **28** J.B. Schneyer, *Reportorium der Lateinischen sermones des mittelalters für die Zeit von 1150-1350* (11 vols, Münster, 1969-1990), iii, p. 54. **29** Schneyer, *Reportorium*, ii, pp 206-40. **30** R.F.M. Bryn, 'The Cordiale Auszug: a study of Gerard van Vliederhoven's Cordiale de IV novissimis', PhD thesis, University of Leeds, 1976, ii and pp 23-38. I am grateful to Dr Bryn for this reference.

of Lincoln, at the Council of Constance, or alternatively a reference to a collection of sermons by an otherwise unknown Anglo-Irish friar.

The presence of four works by Robert Carraciolo of Lecce (1425-95) is particularly interesting. Robert of Lecce was the most famous and influential Italian preacher of his day. He initially joined the Observant Franciscans but left them in 1452 and joined the Conventuals, becoming one of the harshest critics of his former confrères. In 1455 he was appointed preacher of the crusade and became successively papal nuncio to Lombardy, bishop of Aquino and bishop of Lecce. The Observants regarded him as an apostate, which makes the presence of four of his works in an Irish Observant house all the more intriguing. His sermons circulated widely and a number of editions were printed in his lifetime. The Youghal friars had two copies of his *Sermones de laudibus sanctorum* which was first published in Venice in 1489 and ran to ten editions before 1495. The reference to the *Sermones Roberti de licio in uno volumine* in the 1491 section of the catalogue may be to a copy of one of the earlier editions of his *opera varia*, a collection of his sermons for Lent and Advent. This was first published in Venice in 1479 and ran to three editions before 1490. The library also had a copy of his collected dominical sermons.

The library also contained a copy of the *Thesaurus novus*, an anonymous fifteenth-century work formerly attributed to the thirteenth-century Dominican, Peter of Palude. It consisted of three sermon series, for the Sundays of the year, the feasts of the saints and for the days of Lent, and gave a number of model sermons for each occasion.[31] By 1491 the Youghal friars had acquired two volumes of the sermons of the Dominican preacher, Leonard of Udine (d.1469), though which of his works these were is not clear. It seems likely that these were two printed volumes because his work survives in very few manuscripts. In view of their date of acquisition the volumes could possibly be an edition of his *Sermones aurei de sanctis*, printed in Cologne in 1473 or his Lenten sermons, printed in Venice in 1471.[32] By 1523 the friars possessed an edition of the sermons of the prolific German Dominican, John Herolt or *Discipulus* (d.1468). Herolt produced four series of sermons but it is impossible from the reference to ascertain which one the Youghal friars possessed. He also produced a number of other preaching aids including a collection of *exempla* and a work on the miracles of the Virgin Mary.[33]

Other series of sermons include the Temporale and Sanctorale sermons of Master Paul Van, twenty-three sermons for feast days by Michael Lochmayr and four unidentifiable collections. The 'Antiquus liber predicationis' listed as reserved for the use of Patrick Hel was probably a vade-mecum compilation such as one of those described in Alan Fletcher's essay above. Its description as 'antiquus' confirms that these remained in circulation for long periods and continued to be used by other friars.

31 Schneyer, *Reportorium*, v, pp 525-56.   32 T. Kaepelli, *Scriptores ordinis praedicatorum medii aevi* (4 vols, Rome, 1980), , iii, pp 80-5.   33 Kaepelli, *Scriptores*, ii, pp 450-60.

Apart from these sermon collections, the Youghal library held other material which would have been useful for preparing sermons. *Exempla* or entertaining moral anecdotes were available in the *Gesta Romanorum* which the friars had acquired by 1523. This was not, as its name suggests, a classical text but a compilation of anecdotes and stories assembled by an anonymous English Franciscan in the late 1330s. It rivalled the *Legenda aurea* of James of Voragine in popularity and circulated widely throughout Europe. Latin versions were printed in Utrecht and Cologne between 1472 and 1475 and the Youghal copy may have been one of these editions.[34] Another work frequently quarried for *exempla* by preachers was the *Vitae Patrum* with its accounts of the lives and miracles of the first monks of the Egyptian desert.

In his study of the preaching of the thirteenth-century friars, David d'Avray stresses the importance of biblical concordances, lives of the saints and encyclopedias as resources in the preparation of sermons.[35] The Youghal catalogue, though compiled two centuries later, provides strong confirmation of this. By 1523 the friars possessed three biblical concordances and two encyclopedias: the *De proprietatibus rerum* of the thirteenth-century Franciscan, Bartholomaeus Anglicus, and the *Catholicon* of John Balbus of Genoa. (Mention has already been made of the Youghal friars' copy of the *Legenda aurea* of James of Voragine). Increased contact with the Continental Observants, particularly in Germany, explains the presence of works by John Herolt (*Discipulus*) and John Nider, as well as the *Summa vocabulorum cum expositione in lingau tuetonica* in the library.[36] Surprisingly, there are no references to any works by the Breton Olivier Maillard or the Italian John Capistran. These were two of the most noted Observant Franciscan preachers of the period and their sermons circulated widely. The presence of so much preaching material and the extensive collection of penitential manuals in the library indicates that the collection was primarily geared to the friars' activities as preachers and confessors.

An examination of the preaching material in the Irish Franciscan manuscript now in the public library at Rennes gives some idea of how material like that in the Youghal library was used by Franciscan preachers. The manuscript, which a colophon indicates was written in the Observant friary at Kilcrea in 1475, contains the texts of seventeen sermons or sermon notes, as well as a number of other works.[37] A number of these sermons have been published but have attracted very little attention.[38] They are written in Irish

---

34 R. Aubert, 'Gesta Romanorum' in *Dictionnaire d'Histoire et Géographie Ecclésiastique*, xx, cols. 1111-13.   **35** d'Avray, *The preaching of the friars*, pp 64-89, but see particularly p. 279.   **36** This was possibly a German scriptural concordance or dictionary.   **37** G. Dottin, 'Notice du manuscrit Irlandais de la bibliothèque de Rennes' in *Revue Celtique* xv (1894), pp 79-91.   **38** G. Hoey (ed.), 'An Irish homily on the passion: text and translation' in *Catholic University Bulletin* xvii, pp 459-71, 558-67; J. Geary (ed.), 'Homilies on the resurrection, poverty, confession and the eucharist' in *Catholic University Bulletin* xviii, pp 175-86, 266-79, 344-66, 460-75.

and on grounds of style, language and sources cited, they appear to have been written by the same person. The presence of a series of sermon notes on poverty probably indicates that their author was a Franciscan. There is a great overlap between the material found in the Rennes manuscript and that found in other fifteenth-century Irish codices. A Franciscan provenance cannot be demonstrated for these others, with the exception of Trinity College, Dublin MS 667 discussed in Alan Fletcher's essay above and further below. The relationship between the various manuscripts is highly complex and further work on it may be expected to shed much light on how such texts circulated in fifteenth-century Ireland.[39]

The Rennes sermon on the Resurrection draws almost entirely on the writings of St Bonaventure and in particular on his commentary on the *Sentences* of Peter Lombard.[40] The sermon on the Eucharist draws on Ambrose, Augustine, James of Voragine and Peter Lombard.[41] In the homily on the Passion the chief authorities are Ambrose, Augustine, Bede, Bernard, Cassiodorus, Gregory the Great and the Lombard[42] while the sermon on the Blessed Virgin ends with a quotation from James of Voragine.[43] The two texts on confession are very different in content. The first, and more theologically developed of the two, consists of a list of sixteen conditions for proper confession attributed to Thomas Aquinas, while the second gives a list of sins and is designed as an aid to penitents preparing for confession.[44]

The sermon notes on poverty consist entirely of quotations from scripture and patristic and later writers, including Ambrose, Aristotle, Augustine, Bede, Boethius, Cassiodorus, Gregory and Jerome. The absence of any Franciscan authorities on a topic of interest chiefly to the friars themselves is curious.[45] Similar collections of notes on the virtues of patience and charity cite Augustine, Bernard, Origen, as well as passages from scripture, while another treatise on patience begins with a quotation from the *Soliloquium* of St Bonaventure. The sermon notes dealing with the pains of hell draw from the work of Augustine, Bernard, Jerome, John Chrysostom and Hugh of St Victor as well as from various scriptural texts.[46]

---

39 The closest relationship is between the Rennes MS and Bibliothèque Nationale, Paris, MS Celt. 1 described by H. Omont, 'Catalogue des MSS. celtiques et basques de la Bibliothèque Nationale' in *Revue Celtique*, xi (1890), pp 389-433. For the general literary background to these works and the involvement of the Mac an Legha scribal family in transcribing them see J.E. Caerwyn Williams and Patrick Ford, *The Irish literary tradition* (Cardiff, 1992), pp 119-26. For their theological content see M. Mac Conmara, *An léann Eaglasta in Éirinn, 1200-1900* (Dublin, 1982), pp 102-38.   40 Geary (ed.), 'Homilies', pp 175-86 but particularly pp 175-7.   41 Geary (ed.), 'Homilies', pp 460-75, especially pp 460-1.   42 Hoey (ed.), 'An Irish hom- ily on the Passion'.   43 Dottin, 'Notice du manuscrit Irlandais', p. 82.   44 Geary (ed.), 'Homilies', pp 344-66, especially pp 344-9.   45 Geary (ed.), 'Homilies', pp 266-79.   46 Dottin, 'Notice du manuscrit Irlandais', pp 85-7.

Though some of the authors quoted (for example, Aquinas, Bede, Bonaventure, Gregory the Great and Peter Lombard) are found in the Youghal library, the author of the Rennes sermons had access to a wider range of patristic sources than his Youghal confrères. He seems to have been less aware of more modern texts. This may indicate a date in the early fifteenth century for the composition of these sermons, before the Continental authors represented in the Youghal collection became widely available in printed editions.

Trinity College, Dublin MS 667, already introduced in Alan Fletcher's essay above, is one of the most important Franciscan codices to survive from late medieval Ireland. It contains a number of Irish translations of Continental works which have as their exemplars Latin editions in the same volume. Copies of these Irish translations can be found in other fifteenth-century manuscripts and the manuscript seems to have had a central role in the dissemination of this material in late medieval Ireland. Robin Flower suggests that it was compiled in a Franciscan house in Clare in 1455.[47] This view is based on the predominance of O'Brien entries in a short chronology contained in the manuscript.[48] It should be noted, however, that the O'Briens were also patrons of the friars at Nenagh and Limerick. Both these houses, with their long established *studia*, would have had the resources to produce a text such as this.

The manuscript is too large to be classed as a vade-mecum and much of its content would have been as useful in the classroom as in the pulpit. It does, however, contain a large amount of preachable material. This, for the most part, is loosely arranged into categories and consists of lists of quotations on particular topics drawn from patristic sources, collections of *exempla* and miscellaneous canon law and theological notes. Though *exempla* are found scattered throughout the work, one section is devoted entirely to them. Its fifty-four examples chiefly deal with the Virgin Mary.[49]

The preaching material shows the friars' concern with preaching key Christian doctrines in a straightforward and accessible fashion. There is a large section on purgatory, the afterlife and the importance of prayers and Masses for the dead. Augustine, Jerome, Gregory the Great, Peter of Cluny and Peter Damian are among the authorities cited, and the section also includes supporting *exempla*.[50] The importance of worthy reception of

---

47 R. Flower, 'Ireland and Medieval Europe' in *Proceedings of the British Academy*, xiii (1927), pp 271-303 but particularly pp 282-97. 48 Trinity College, Dublin MS 667, p. 66; M.L. Colker, *Trinity College Library Dublin: descriptive catalogue of the medieval and Renaissance Latin manuscripts*, Dublin (2 vols, Aldershot, 1991), ii, pp 1132-3. This text was printed by M. Esposito in *Romania*, lxii (1936), p. 539. 49 Trinity College, Dublin MS 667, pp 199-214; Colker, *Descriptive catalogue*, ii, pp 1155-61. Colker identifies sixty-nine *exempla* in the codex. 50 Trinity College, Dublin, MS 667, pp 32-6; Colker, *Descriptive catalogue*, ii, pp 1123-4.

communion is the subject of numerous *exempla* and other texts,[51] and logically linked to them are the texts that stress the importance of frequent confession.[52] Great emphasis is laid on the efficacy of the intercession of the Virgin Mary.[53]

The preaching concerns of the Irish friars were those which were central to late medieval spirituality. The Eucharist, the life, death and Resurrection of Christ, repentance, right living, hope of salvation, dread of damnation, intercession for the dead, the cult of the saints (particularly that of the Virgin Mary) all find their place. The Irish Observants, like their Continental confrères, were charged with preaching and promoting the crusades. This continued the tradition of preaching the cross by the Irish friars which is first recorded in 1234.[54] The over-enthusiastic promotion of the crusade indulgence by the Irish Observants, including the vicar provincial Donal O'Fallon, brought them into conflict with Archbishop Octavian of Armagh in 1482.[55]

The surviving sermon material is sufficient to indicate that the Irish friars in this period practised the same style of popular preaching for which their predecessors and Continental confrères were noted. Though a preacher might quote numerous theologians in support of his argument, the sermons were not sophisticated theological expositions but exhortations to shun vice, seek virtue and to reconciliation with God and neighbour. That they could be extremely effective is shown by the obituary notice for Tuathal Balbh O'Gallagher (d.1541) in the *Annals of the Four Masters*. As a young man he had been profoundly influenced by a sermon on the sanctity of human life preached by a friar in Donegal. In his subsequent military career he took prisoners in preference to taking lives.[56]

Nor were sermons the only methods of evangelization used by the friars. There was a long tradition in the Order of composing songs and carols on religious or moral themes for the instruction of the laity.[57] Important examples of this practice are found in several of the poems collected in British Library, Harley MS 913, also mentioned in Alan Fletcher's essay above. Most of the poems in Hiberno-English and Latin in this manuscript are on various devotional and moral themes.[58] Not all of the works are devotional, however, and other texts such as the 'Abbot of Gloucester's feast' and the

---

[51] Trinity College, Dublin, MS 667, pp 184-8; Colker, *Descriptive catalogue*, ii, p. 1153. [52] Trinity College, Dublin, MS 667, pp 38-9; Colker, *Descriptive catalogue*, ii, p. 1125. [53] Trinity College, Dublin, MS 667, pp 199-214; Colker, *Descriptive catalogue*, ii, pp 1155-62. [54] Cotter, *The Friars Minor in Ireland*, pp 78-9. [55] A. Lynch (ed.), 'Documents of Franciscan interest from the episcopal archives of Armagh, 1265-1508' in *Collectanea Hibernica* nos 31 and 32 (1989-90), pp 9-102, reference pp 47-50. [56] John O'Donovan (ed.), *Annála ríoghachta Éireann: annals of the kingdom of Ireland by the Four Masters* (7 vols, Dublin, 1851), v, p. 1463. [57] D.L. Jeffrey, *The early English lyric and Franciscan spirituality* (Lincoln, 1975). [58] A.M. Lucas (ed.), *Anglo-Irish poems of the middle ages* (Dublin, 1995).

'Land of Cokaygne'⁵⁹ are scurrilously entertaining satires on Cistercian and Benedictine monks.

The Franciscans were also noted composers of popular hymnody and wrote religious songs to be sung to popular secular tunes. In Ireland this tactic was adopted by the English friar-bishop of Ossory, Richard Ledrede (1317-61), to counteract the lewd songs being sung by the clergy and people of Kilkenny. His hymns, set to popular tunes and preserved in the *Red book of Ossory*, include works on the Virgin Mary and the name of Jesus.⁶⁰ The recruitment of Gaelic friars in the thirteenth and fourteenth centuries attracted members of the hereditary bardic families to the Order. These men, trained in the complex and stylised art of bardic composition, included the late fourteenth-century Tadhg Camchosach O'Daly and the fifteenth-century Observant friar Philip Bocht O'Higgins. The latter was described as 'the best versifier of devotion in the latter time' by his obituary writer in the *Annals of Ulster*.⁶¹

The high reputation of the Franciscans as preachers is confirmed by a number of contemporary references. Of the twenty-six Observant superiors listed by Friar Francis O'Mahoney before 1534, five were described as noted preachers.⁶² Surprisingly, the list makes no mention of Friar Donal O'Fallon who was vicar provincial from 1472 to 1475 and bishop of Derry from 1485 to 1500 for in recording his presence at a synod in Drogheda in 1486, the *Annals of Ulster* describe him as 'the preacher who did most service to Irishmen since Patrick was in Ireland',⁶³ while his obituary refers to his 'laborious and successful preaching' throughout the country during the previous thirty years.⁶⁴ The same annals also record the deaths of two other Observant preachers: Angus MacNulty in 1492 and Patrick O'Feidhil who died in Timoleague in 1505.⁶⁵

Despite their reputation as excellent preachers, no full description survives of what a late medieval friar preaching may have been like. Friar Donatus Mooney's brief account of denunciations of vices by the Donegal friar, Bernard MacGrath (d. 1547 or 1549), during a sermon in Clogher, conveys something of the impact that a powerful preacher could have on his congregation.⁶⁶ Mooney's account of the preaching of Friar Eoghan O'Duffy (minister provincial 1580-3), perhaps conveys a good impression of what the late medieval Franciscan sermon was like:

59 Lucas (ed.), *Anglo-Irish poems*, pp 46-55. 60 T. Stemmler (ed.), *The Latin hymns of Richard Ledrede* (Mannheim, 1975). Not all of the hymns are Ledrede's work, however; see A.G. Rigg, 'The Red Book of Ossory', *Medium Ævum* xlvi (1977), pp 269-78. 61 *Annals of Ulster*, iii, p. 317. 62 Brendan Jennings, OFM (ed.), 'Brevis Synopsis Provinciae Hiberniae Fratrum Minorum' in *Analecta Hibernica* no. 6 (1934), pp 139-91, reference on pp 166-9. 63 *Annals of Ulster*, iii, p. 305. 64 *Annals of Ulster*, iii, p. 451. 65 *Annals of Ulster*, iii, pp 305 and 477. 66 Jennings (ed.), 'Donatus Moneyus: De Provincia Hiberniae S. Francisci', pp 46-7. During the sermon he had been contradicted by an abbot whose imminent death he then predicted.

> [Eoghan O'Duffy] was a most renowned preacher, and not less distinguished for his austere and saintly life. His fame extended to the most remote parts of the kingdom, and is yet on the tongues of all ... He always travelled barefooted, rejecting even the slight protection which sandals would have afforded him. He preached with such wonderful force and unction that he never seemed tedious to his hearers, although he spoke at great length, sometimes for three hours together. While delivering his discourses he never looked in the faces of his audience, not even opened his eyes. He rebuked the evildoer with great severity, and his words were seldom without effect. Yet in his sermons he was mild and gentle, rarely giving offence to individuals. When he met seculars in society (which, indeed, was very seldom) he conversed in an agreeable and pleasant manner. He had such an intimate knowledge of the writings of St Augustine, especially of his smaller works on devout subjects, that his whole doctrine seemed sometimes founded upon the doctrine and made up of the sayings of that great saint, as if he had consulted no other author. At the conclusion of each sermon, even of the longest, he was in the habit of reciting elegant verses in the Irish language, which contained the pith of what he had said. These verses were so fruitful of good that they appear to have been inspired less by the spirit of poetry than by the unction of the Holy Ghost.[67]

In this description the various elements which contributed to the friars' success as preachers and moral authorities converge. The combination of personal holiness and austerity, the citation of authorities, the use of vernacular verse — all these contributed to the reputation of the Franciscans and to their pastoral effectiveness. The reverence of the Gaelic Irish for the friars and the influence the friars had over them was remarked on by contemporaries. As the Imperial ambassador, Eustace Chapuys, observed in 1534

> among the wild Irish the Cordeliers are feared, obeyed, and almost adored, not only by the peasants but by the lords, who held them in such reverence as to endure from them blows with a stick.[68]

Perhaps, when all else failed, the friars were not beyond making their point more forcefully.

---

[67] Jennings (ed.), 'Donatus Moneyus: De Provincia Hiberniae S. Francisci', pp 49-50. Translation in *The Franciscan tertiary* v (1894), pp 196-7.   [68] *Calendar of letters, despatches, and state papers relating to negotiations between England and Spain, preserved in the archives of Simancas and elsewhere* (13 vols, London, 1862-1954), ii, p. 570.

The vocacyon of Johan Bale (1553): a retrospective sermon from Ireland

J.-A. George

It is difficult to imagine a sixteenth-century text more relevant to the topic of the early history of preaching in Ireland than *The vocacyon of Johan Bale to the bishoprick of Ossorie in Irelande.*[1] John Bale, erstwhile Carmelite friar and, ultimately, 'arch-Protestant propagandist and historian of the English Reformation,'[2] published this 'curious and interesting little pamphlet'[3] late in 1553 to make known the trials and tribulations he suffered whilst attempting to preach in the see of Ossory. As a result, one of *The vocacyon*'s primary functions is to act, in the opinion of Peter Happé and John N. King, as 'a consolatory text' to English Protestants.[4] This is verified by the self-contained preface to the treatise for it is addressed, in the manner of a sermon, to 'the folowers of Christes Gospell'[5] and opens with the words 'For thre consyderacyons chefely (dere bretherne) have I put fourth thys treatyse of my vocacyon to the churche of Ossorye in Irelande / of my harde chaunces therin / and of my fynall deliveraunce by the great goodnesse of God.'[6] Bale also makes his target audience (as well as his identification with them) explicitly apparent towards the close of the preface:

> I write not this rude treatise / for that I woulde receyve praise therof / but that I wolde God to have all the prayse / which hath bene a moste wonderfull wurker therin ... Moreover I have done it / for that my persecuted bretherne might in lyke maner have their rejoyce in that heavenly Lorde / which mightelye hath wrought in them their salvacion / by his graciouse callinge of them from wicked Papisme to true christianyte / and now tryeth their paciences by contynuall afflictions / and finally will delyver them / eyther from tyrannouse molestacions / as he hath done me / eyther els into martirdome for his truthes sake.[7]

---

1 Hereafter referred to as *The vocacyon*. All references from this text are taken from Peter Happé and John N. King (eds), *The vocacyon of Johan Bale* (Medieval & Renaissance Texts & Studies, Binghamton, New York, 1990). 2 Leslie P. Fairfield, *John Bale, mythmaker for the English Reformation*, (West Lafayette, Indiana, 1976), p. 1. 3 Fairfield, *John Bale*, p. 136. 4 *The vocacyon*, p. 7. 5 *The vocacyon*, p. 31. 6 *The vocacyon*, p. 31. 7 *The vocacyon*, pp 37-8.

Apart from offering consolation to his persecuted brethren, *The vocacyon* was also a way for Bale to vent 'his spleen against Irishmen, Flemish pirates, and papists in general.'[8] Not untypical is the description of the Irish, for example, as 'the ruffianes of that wilde nacyon.'[9] The woodcut on the title page (fig. 3) supports this view of the Irish papist 'other' for it depicts 'The English Christia[n],' hands meekly clasped to his bosom, confronted by the 'Irishe Papist' holding a sword menacingly in his hand.[10] The contrast between the two figures is enhanced by the fact that a sheep cowers behind the legs of the Englishman whilst a wolf, teeth bared, lunges by the side of the Irishman. Underneath this scene two passages from the Bible are quoted. The first is Psalm 91:3, 'God hath delivered me from the snare of the hunter / & fro[m] the noysome pestile[n]ce,' the second II Corinthians 11:30, 'If I must nedes reioyce / I wil reioyce of myne infirmytees.' The woodcut functions, in effect, as a visual sermon which supports pictorially the message Bale preaches via the actual text of *The vocacyon*. Propagandistic picture and words work successfully in tandem here and illustrate why, in the words of John C. Coldewey, 'John Bale cast an enormous shadow over the second quarter of the sixteenth century as a playwright and polemicist.'[11]

I

Bale's reasons for journeying to Ireland in 1552 have been recounted by numerous critics and historians. Of particular note, however, is Leslie P. Fairfield's wry account of them:

> Bale had been promoted (more likely deported) in August 1552 to the see of Ossory – the Tudor equivalent of a Siberian salt-mine, and a

---

8 Fairfield, *John Bale*, p. 137.   9 *The vocacyon*, p. 58.   10 Happé and King's note on the text of *The vocacyon* includes the following information: '*The Vocacyon* (STC 1307), according to the colophon, was printed in 1553, very shortly after the adventures described in it were over. The place of printing is allegedly Rome, though this is an impudent joke ... The woodcut on the title page was in the possession of Joos Lambrecht, who was at work in Wesel from the second half of 1553 until 1556, and it may demonstrate a joint enterprise with [Hugh] Singleton [owner of the printer's device on G8ᵛ].' (p. 17) Thora Balslev Blatt, in *The plays of John Bale: a study of ideas, technique and style* (Copenhagen, 1968) provides an interesting description of the costuming of the figures in the woodcut: 'In *The vocacyon of Johan Bale* the title page shows "The English Christian" versus "The Irish Papist." On the left is seen a man with folded hands and sober countenance, with head on one side, dressed in a knee-length coat and round cap; the lamb sheltering behind him proclaims his nature. He is attacked by a short-coated hefty fellow of fierce countenance under a narrow-brimmed hat; the man is drawing his sword, and a wolf by his side is about to jump for the lamb. The picture may give us a hint at the apparelling of good and evil characters' (p. 136, n. 22).   11 John C. Coldewey, 'The non-cycle plays and the East-Anglian tradition' in Richard Beadle (ed.), *The Cambridge companion to medieval English theatre* (Cambridge, 1994; rept 1996), p. 194.

The vocacyon
of Johā Bale to the
bishopzick of Ossozie in Ireladē his persecuciōs in y̆ same, z̃ finall delyueraunce.

The English Christiā / The Irishe Papist.

¶ God hath deliuered me from the snare of the hunter, z̃ frō y̆ noysome pestilēce. Psal.xcj.
¶ If I must nedes reioyce, I wil reioyce of myne infirmytees. ij. Cor.xj.

Figure 3: Title page from *The vocacyon of Johan Bale* ([Wesel], 1553).

post which Edward VI had been having difficulty filling. Bale and his wife Dorothy landed at Waterford in January 1553 and reached Kilkenny in time to preach in the cathedral there every Sunday and holy day in Lent. Bale's radical views did not sit well with most of the townspeople and the diocesan clergy. And after Edward VI had died in July and Queen Mary had been proclaimed at Kilkenny in August, Bale found his cathedral quite unsafe. Unfortunately his episcopal estate in the country was no more secure.[12]

Bale's own version of his summoning to Ossory has rather more of the miraculous about it :

> Upon the .15. daye of August / in the yeare from Christes incarnacion 1552 beynge the first daye of my deliveraunce / as God wolde / from a mortall ague / which had holde me long afore. In rejoyce that hys Majestie was come in progresse to Southampton / whiche was .5. myle from my personage of Byshoppes Stoke / within the same countye, I toke my horse about .10 of the clocke / for very weaknesse scant able to sytt hym / & so came thydre. Betwixt .2. & .3. of the clocke the same daye / I drewe towardes the place where as his Majestie was / and stode in the open strete ryght against the gallerye... the Kynge havynge informacion that I was in the strete / he marveled therof / for so much as it had bene tolde hym a lytle afore / that I was both dead & buried. With that hys grace came to the wyndowe / and earnestly behelde me a poore weake creature / as though he had had upon me so symple a subject / an earnest regarde / or rather a fatherly care.
>
> In the same very instaunt / as I have bene sens that time credibly infourmed / his Grace called unto him / the lordes of his most honourable counsell / so manie as were than present / willinge them to appoint me to the bishoprick of Ossorie in Irelande. Wherunto they all agreably consentinge / commaunded the letters of my first callinge therunto / by and by to be written and sent me.[13]

Demonstrating an awareness of many of the staple elements of hagiography, the subject (Bale) initially experiences 'deliveraunce' after a seemingly 'mortall ague'. He even undergoes, in fact, a type of resurrection, the king having been previously told 'that I was both dead & buried'. The 'poore weak

---

12 Fairfield, *John Bale*, p. 136. Andrew Hadfield, *Literature, politics and national identity: Reformation to Renaissance* (Cambridge, 1994), describes Bale's summoning to the see of Ossory in equally joyless terms: 'In 1552 Bale was awarded the dubious honour of the bishopric of Ossory by Edward who came to Southampton in person to grant him the see. Bale reluctantly set off for Ireland in December' (p. 55).   13 *The vocacyon*, pp 49-50.

creature,' once 'behelde' alive, then becomes 'In the same very instaunt' elevated 'to the bishoprick of Ossorie in Irelande'. The instantaneous nature of this elevation (apotheosis, even), especially because it has been verified in retrospect by Bale ('as I have bene sens that time credibly infourmed'), contributes to the miraculous quality of the event. It seems, then, that *The vocacyon* is more than just a consolatory sermon – it is a saint's life as well.

The hagiographical dimension of the text has been touched upon by at least two critics. We have, firstly, Fairfield's comment that 'the book lay squarely within the tradition of hagiography which Bale had already exploited for Protestant purposes'.[14] There is also Happé and King's more extended analysis of the subject:

> Bale's *Vocacyon* represents a precursor of the spiritual autobiographies that became fashionable within Puritan circles during the seventeenth century ... Literary antecedents include the visions of Juliana [*sic*] of Norwich (*c*.1343–*c*.1413) and *The book of Margery Kempe* (*c*.1436), the earliest autobiographical narrative extant in the English language. Unlike these illiterate medieval mystics, who had to rely upon amanuenses, Bale wrote his *Vocacyon* on his own, and presumably arranged for its publication ... *The vocacyon* lacks the degree of self-reflection found in *The book of Margery Kempe*, and the intense analysis of individual consciousness found in later autobiographies, but it shares the tendency of late sixteenth- and seventeenth-century Puritan diaries and confessional works to examine the experience of the self for marks of divine intervention and the operation of grace.[15]

It must needs be said that the parallels between *The vocacyon* and *The book of Margery Kempe* (and, hence, between Bale's text and late mediaeval hagiography) are far more striking than are allowed for in the passage above. In the same way that *The vocacyon* is meant to instruct and comfort a very specific readership, Kempe's *Book* is introduced as:

> ... a schort tretys and a comfortabyl for synful wrecchys, wher-in þei may haue gret solas and comfort to hem and vnderstondyn þe hy & vnspecabyl mercy of ower souereyn Sauyowr Cryst Ihesu ...[16]

There are also many similarities in the self-conscious way in which Bale and Kempe present themselves to their respective audiences. Bale stylises himself, as we have seen, as a 'poore weake creature' and Kempe's consistent

---

14 Fairfield, *John Bale*, p. 138.   15 *The vocacyon*, p. 9.   16 S.B. Meech (ed.), *The book of Margery Kempe* (Early English Text Society, 212, London, 1940; rept 1961, 1993), p. 2. All future references to this text are taken from this edition.

descriptions of herself as 'this creature', the phrase often punctuated by various adjectives which signal her humility, are too numerous to set down here.

The theatricality often noted in Bale's writing is, in turn, apparent in Kempe's *Book* as well; both are ever mindful of enemies and recount moments of opposition and struggle in highly dramatic ways. We see this in *The vocacyon* when Bale launches into one of his many tirades against clerical celibacy – a condition Bale preached strenuously against in several of his sermons and plays. The passage is composed in dialogic form and the 'stage directions' are easy to imagine:

> Muche were the prestes offended also / for that I had in my preachinges / willed them to have wives of their owne / & to leave the unshamefast occupienge / of other mennes wyves / doughters / and servauntes. But heare what answere they made me alwayes / yea the most viciouse men among them. What shulde we marrie (sayd they) for halfe a yeare / & so loose our livynges. Think ye not that these men were ghostly inspired? eyther yet had knowledge of some secrete mischefe wurkinge in Englande? I for my part have not a little sens that time marveled / whan it hath fallen to my remembraunce. Well the truthe is / I coulde never yet by any Godly or honest persuasion / bringe any of them to mariage / neither yet cause them whiche were knowne for unshamfast whorekeepers / to leave that fylthye & abhomynable occupyenge what though I most earnestly laboured it. But sens that tyme I have consydered by the jugement of the scriptures / that the impenytent ydolatour must therwith be also a filthie adulterer or most detestable sodomite. It is his just plage (Rom. I). We can not stoppe it.[17]

In *The book of Margery Kempe* the subject (Kempe) makes many enemies whilst on pilgrimage, her excessive tears, roaring and devotion (highly theatrical in themselves) alienating her from her fellow travellers. Like Bale, however, she has God on her side:

> ... And, whan owyr Lord had browt hem a-geyn to Venyce in safte, hir cuntre-men forsokyn hir & went a-way fro hir, leuyng hir a-lone. & summe of hem seyden þat þey wold not go wyth hir for an hundryd pownd. And, whan þei wer gon a-wey fro hir, þan owyr Lord Ihesu Crist, þat euyr helpyth at nede & neuyr forsakyth hys seruaw[nt þat] trewly trostith to hys mercy, seyd to hys creature, 'D[rede] þe not,

---

[17] *The vocacyon*, p. 55.

dowty*r*, for I xal ordeyn for þe ryth wel & br[yng þe] in safte to Rome & hom a-geyn in-to Inglond w*yth*-owtyn ony velany of þi body yf thow wilt be clad in white clothys & weryn hem as I seyd to þe whil þu wer in Inglond.'[18]

What also unites Bale and Kempe, of course, is the fact that they are both preachers. Kempe comes under fire regularly by the Church for ignoring the Pauline injunction which forbids women from preaching. As Clarissa W. Atkinson points out, however, Kempe was usually able to find novel ways round this:

> There are ancient and effective sanctions against women who preach and teach men. The archbishop of York tried to make Margery promise not to teach in his diocese, but she refused and dared to back up her refusal with Scripture ... Not surprisingly, the clerks said she must be possessed to speak of Scripture, calling upon their natural ally, Saint Paul, for reinforcement. Margery made a quick distinction between preaching and 'speaking of God'.[19]

Whilst Saint Paul's teaching played an adverse role in the 'preaching' career of Kempe, his life provided a strong role model for Bale in *The vocacyon*. 'Bale,' as Thora Balslev Blatt notes, 'treats his readers to a long enumeration of points [in this treatise] which show similarity between his fate and St Paul.'[20] She continues, 'With St Paul he [Bale] was exposed to tribulation for the sake of the Gospel.'[21] Indeed, Bale defines his main role as a Protestant bishop in the following manner: '... men shulde wele knowe / that the office of a Chrysten byshop / is not to loyter in blasphemouse papistrie / but purely to preache the Gospell of God / to his christened flocke.'[22] On another occasion he states: 'I preached the Gospell of the knowledge & right invocacion of God / I mayntened the politicall ordre by doctrine / & moved the commens alwayes to obeye their magistrates.'[23] In keeping with these sentiments, Bale later sternly sermonises to the Irish 'prestes' that '... their office by Christes strayght commaundement / was chiefly to preache / and instruct the people in the doctryne and wayes of God / and not to occupie so muche of the tyme in chauntynge / pypynge / and syngynge.'[24] Clearly, the vibrant musical tradition of the Catholic Church held no fascination for Bale and his ilk.

Though Bale, as we have already seen, suffered persecution in Ireland for his particular brand of preaching,[25] he also experienced a miracle in the

---

[18] *The book of Margery Kempe*, pp 75-6. [19] Clarissa W. Atkinson, *Mystic and pilgrim: the Book and the world of Margery Kempe* (London, 1983), p. 108. [20] Blatt, *The plays of John Bale*, p. 43. [21] Blatt, *The plays of John Bale*, p. 43. [22] *The vocacyon*, p. 31. [23] *The vocacyon*, p. 54. [24] *The vocacyon*, pp 54-5. [25] Bale was not alone in the persecutions he

pulpit whilst there. His rendering of this event begins in a very similar way to the first 'miracle' recounted in *The vocacyon*, the description of his summoning to the see of Ossory: once again, Bale succumbs to ill health but is unexpectedly restored:

> Within .ii. dayes after was I sycke agayn / so egerly / that noman thought I shulde have lyved / which malladie helde me till after Eastre. Yet in the meane tyme / I founde a waye to be brought to Kylkennie / where as I preached every sondaye & holy daye in lent / tyll the sondaye after Eastre was fully past / never felinge any maner of grefe of my sycknesse / for the tyme I was in the pulpet. Wherat many men / and my selfe also greatly mervaled.[26]

This account of the 'merval in the pulpet' is a fine instance of Bale's attempt in *The vocacyon* to create a native hagiographical tradition for his 'dere bretherne.' A comment made by Andrew Hadfield, in his book *Literature, politics and national identity: Reformation to Renaissance*, also comes to mind here. Hadfield, in comparing Bale with another equally polemical and 'bilious' writer, John Skelton, concludes:

> But most strikingly, one could say that it is as if Bale and Skelton face each other in the mirror of the Reformation, offering opposed and complementary images of Englishness from either side of the historical divide. Bale, no less than Skelton, sought to define a native identity throughout his long writing career.[27]

The nationalist, monarchist tendencies of *The vocacyon* are apparent as well in a particularly tense moment when Bale 'Upon the purificacion daye of Our Ladye' is about to be 'invested or consecrated / as they call it.'[28] All goes well until:

> ... Thomas Lockwode (Blockheade he myght wel be called) the deane of the cathedrall churche there / desired the lord chauncellor very instantly / that he wolde in no wise permyt that observacion to be done after that boke of consecratinge bishoppes / which was last set fourth in Englande by acte of parlement / alleginge that it wolde be both an occasion of tumulte / and also that it was not as yet consented to by acte of their parlement in Irelande.[29]

---

suffered whilst attempting to preach his faith in Ireland, as the following account from *The vocacyon* attests: 'In the meane time came sorowfull news unto me that M. Hugh Goodacker the Archebishop of Armach / was poysened at Dubline / by procurement of certen prestes of his diocese / for preachinge Gods verite & rebukinge their commen vices.' (p. 56)   **26** *The vocacyon*, p. 53.   **27** Hadfield, *Literature, politics and national identity*, p. 57.   **28** *The vocacyon*, p. 52.   **29** *The vocacyon*, p. 52.

As we might predict, Bale's response is unequivocal: 'Whan I see none other waye / I stepped fourth / and sayde, If Englande and Irelande be undre one kinge / they are both bounde to the obedience of one lawe undre him. And as for us / we came hyther as true subjectes of his / sworne to obeye that ordinaunce'.[30] It also illustrates Hadfield's remark that 'One of his [Bale's] fundamental beliefs was an absolute faith in the duty of subjects to obey the monarch'.[31]

But Bale was not, of course, the first to turn miracle stories to nationalistic ends. Bede shows us Pope Gregory writing to Augustine and expounding a not dissimilar philosophy: 'And whatever power of working miracles you have received or shall receive, consider that these gifts have been conferred not on you, but on those for whose salvation they have been granted you.'[32] The parallels established here between Bale's *Vocacyon* and Kempe's *Book*, as well as between Catholic and Protestant policy concerning the use and purpose of miracles, may go some way to supporting Patrick Collinson's proposition that:

> First Protestantism embraced the cultural forms which already existed and employed them for its own purposes, both instructively and as polemical weapons against its opponents ... [English Protestantism] produced no culture of its own but made an iconoclastic holocaust of the culture which already existed.[33]

II

In the third stanza of Bale's play *A Tragedye or Enterlude Manyfestyng the Chefe Promyses of God unto Man by All Ages in the Olde Lawe, From the Fall of Adam to the Incarnacyon of the Lorde Jesus Christ* (1538), his own character, Baleus Prolocutor, addresses the audience with these words:

> Yow therfor, good fryndes, I lovyngely exhorte
> To waye soche matters as wyll be uttered here,
> Of whome ye maye loke to have no tryfelinge sporte
> In fantasyes fayned, nor soche gaudysh gere;
> But the thynges that shall your inwarde stomake stere
> To rejoyce in God for your justyfycacyon,
> And alone in Christ to hope for your salvacyon.[34]

---

30 *The vocacyon*, p. 53. 31 Hadfield, *Literature, politics and national identity*, p. 51. 32 Bertram Colgrave and R.A.B. Mynors (eds), *Bede's ecclesiastical history of the English people* (Oxford, 1969), p. 111. The Latin text for this passage from I. 31 reads: 'Et quicquid de faciendis signis acceperis, uel accepisti, haec non tibi sed illis deputes donata, pro quorum tibi salute collata sunt.' (p. 110) 33 Patrick Collinson, *The birthpangs of Protestant England: religious and cultural changes in the sixteenth and seventeenth centuries* (London, 1988; rept 1991), pp 98, 94. 34 Peter Happé (ed.), *The complete plays of John Bale* (2 vols, Cambridge, 1986), ii, p. 2.

It is clear, even from these few lines, why Thora Balslev Blatt reached the conclusion that '... in all the prolocutor speeches Bale establishes the authoritative relationship of the preacher to his congregation'.[35] And what the dramatic preacher exhorts at the beginning of *The Chefe Promyses of God* is quite specific: a rejection of the 'tryfelinge sporte,' 'fantasyes fayned,' and 'gaudysh gere,' of the 'false' religion, Roman Catholicism. The vocabulary of the feigned and fantastical is typically used by Bale in this way and is often, as it is here, juxtaposed to the plain speaking of Protestant doctrine. To quote Blatt again:

> Though Bale cannot be called an innovator of the drama, he adapted the existing theatrical tradition to represent his view of the world and the forces which governed it. He modified the genres of mystery and morality so that they became serviceable means in the campaign of the 'new learning'; scorning the spectacular and amusing incidents which often enlivened the cycle plays, he concentrated on dramatic representations of the message of the Bible with nothing to distract attention from the spoken word. If we may judge from the titles of his lost series of plays on the life of Christ, he was also concerned to show Christ's conflict with Jewish authorities as a background to the struggle of reformers in the sixteenth century.[36]

Bale's concentration on preaching 'the message of the Bible' is also remarked upon by Happé and King, who state that 'The Bible provides the outstanding literary model for Bale's writings.'[37] As has already been mentioned, the life of Saint Paul is one of the key biographical models for *The vocacyon*. In its preface, Bale also urges his audience to 'marke the laboriouse procedinges of Abraham / Joseph / & Moyses / of David / Helyas / and Daniel / with the other olde fathers and prophetes' and 'discretely search the doynges of Peter / James and Johan / with the other of the Apostles and dysciples.'[38] All in all, Bale incorporates more than one hundred and ten biblical references into the 2059 lines of the text of *The vocacyon*.[39] The centrality of the Bible to Bale's work serves as a good illustration of a related argument formulated by Collinson:

> 'The Bible, the Bible only I say is the religion of Protestants'. So wrote William Chillingworth in 1638. And since for Protestants re-

---

35 Blatt, *The plays of John Bale*, p. 149. 36 Blatt, *The plays of John Bale*, p. 233. 37 *The vocacyon*, p. 10. 38 *The vocacyon*, p. 32. 39 See Happé and King's index of Biblical texts on pages 139-43 of their edition of *The vocacyon*. They introduce the index with the following remarks on Bale's translations of the Bible: 'When Bale writes "saith he," "saith the Lord," "saith St. Paul," and the like, he translates a Vulgate text. Sometimes his translations are rough, possibly indicating reliance upon memory.' (p. 139)

ligion was not one compartment of a segmented life but all-enveloping, this must also mean that the Bible only is the *culture* of Protestants.[40]

Bale's use of the Bible is his most powerful preaching weapon in *The vocacyon*, adding as it does an uncontestable authority to his 'sermon'. It is important to discover, however, the other ways in which Bale in this work lends authority to his words and causes his audience's collective 'inwarde stomake [to] stere / To rejoyce in God'. One thing he establishes immediately, for example, is the exalted lineage of the role of the preacher by reminding us that Christ himself was one:

> First / as concernynge the examples of holye scripture. Jesus the eternall sonne of the everlastynge father / in the Godhede preached to Adam in paradyse terrestre / and constytute hym so wele an instructour as a father over hys posteryte. He proved him also after he had sinned / by dyverse afflyctyons / and fynally promysed both to hym and to hys / deliveraunce in the sede of the woman / which at the lattre in hys owne persone he lovingly perfourmed. Christe the seyde sonne of God contynually still taught / by the mouthes of the fathers and the prophetes / tyll such tyme as he hymselfe came in the fleshe. Than was he above all others / of hys heavenly father appoynted / a universall doctor over all the worlde / and commaunded to be hearde / (Matth. iii).[41]

And Christ, like Bale, also had a 'vocacyon' and was persecuted by an alien clergy because of it: 'He folowed hys vocacyon in most ample wyse / very cruelly was he of the clergie than persecuted / and gloriously delyvered in hys resurrectyon from deathe.'[42] Similarly, Bale himself is eventually 'delyvered' as the full title of the work attests: *The vocacyon of Johan Bale to the byshoprycke of Ossorye in Irelande his harde chaunces therin / and finall delyveraunce.*

The actual style of *The vocacyon* also marks it out as a sermon. This is seen, as has been already suggested, in the opening of the preface where there is an address to the 'dere bretherne'. This is equivalent to Bale's use of 'good fryndes' in *The chefe promyses of God* discussed above. Bale makes extensive use as well of the preacher's tendency towards the rhetorical device of anaphora, a repetition that would have hammered home his message to

---

[40] Collinson, *The birthpangs of Protestant England*, p. 95. [41] *The vocacyon*, p. 32. [42] *The vocacyon*, p. 32. Of the title of Bale's work, Happé and King write: 'The title of Bale's book reflects the urgency of his concern to define his clerical vocation, and by extension that of any "true" minister, as a direct "calling" by God to preach biblical truth and administer what Protestants regard as the two sacraments of communion and baptism' (p. 14).

even the most sleepy of congregations. A particularly effective example of this technique is found in one of Bale's numerous narrations of his persecutions. 'Sainte Paul boasted muche of his persecucions', we are told, and Bale does the same in relation to his Irish troubles: 'The truthe of it is / that sense I toke that wayghtie office in hande / I have bene sycke to the very deathe / I have bene greved with the untowardnesse of ministers'.[43] The 'I have bene' is then repeated to thunderous anaphoric effect and is eventually expanded by the clause 'in parell':

> I have bene in journayes and labours / in injuryes and losses / in peines and in penuries.
> I have bene in strifes and contencions / in rebukynges and slaunderynges / and in great daunger of poyseninges and killinges.
> I have bene in parell of the heathen / in parell of wicked prestes / in parell of false justyces / in parell of trayterouse tenauntes / in parell of cursed tyrauntes / in parell of cruell kearnes and galloglasses.
> I have bene in parell of the sea / in parell of shypwrack / in parell of throwynge over the boorde / in parell of false bretherne / in parell of curiouse searchers / in parell of pirates / robbers and murtherers / and a great sort more.[44]

Bale makes a powerful and affecting case for his need for 'delyveruance' here. Indeed, if his own account is anything to go by, Bale must, in general, have been a convincing preacher for he tells us later in *The vocacyon* that as he is setting out for Ireland '... I toke my journeye from Byshops Stoke with my bokes and stuffe towardes Bristowe / where as I tarryed .xxvi. dayes for passage / *and diverse times preached in that worshipfull cytie at the instaunt desyre of the cytiezens*' [italics mine].[45]

The humility topos is also adopted in *The vocacyon* where Bale uses the language of the abject sinner to speak of himself and his own fallen nature: 'For I am but a clodde of coruption / felinge in my self as of my self / nothinge els but sinne and wickednesse.'[46] Such self abnegation is a common device in preaching and helps to create an identification between speaker and congregation. We see a similar vocabulary being used, for example, in *The book of Margery Kempe*. At the very opening of her treatise Kempe speaks of her relationship with God in the following terms:

> ... And *per*for, be þe leue of ower *mer*cyful Lord Cryst Ih*es*u, to þe magnyfying of hys holy name, Ih*es*u, þis lytyl tretys schal tretyn

---

43 *The vocacyon*, p. 34.   44 *The vocacyon*, p. 34. Bale also makes use of a rather effective extended simile on p. 35 of *The vocacyon* where he compares his circumstances at length, from lines 162-217 in fact, to those of Saint Paul.   45 *The vocacyon*, p. 51.   46 *The vocacyon*, p. 37.

sumdeel in parcel of hys wonderful werkys, how mercyfully, how benyngly, & how charytefully he meued & stered a synful catyf vnto hys love ...[47]

In the conclusion to *The vocacyon*, Bale emphasises the need for every individual to be humble in the face of God's goodness. His conscious use of 'congregacion' is also noteworthy here, returning us as it does to the image of Bale as a preacher and *The vocacyon* as a variety of sermon:

> A perpetuall and unplacable enemye is Sathan / and evermore hath bene / to that poore congregacion / sekinge not only to disfigure her / but also to spoyle her and destroye her utterly. Like as is saied (Gen. 3) that he shulde treade Christe on hele. This excedinge great benefight of the goodnesse of God / ought to be remembred / that he after the sinne of our first parentes / not only received this church to grace / but also hath ever sens / both preserved & defended it.[48]

III

One of the most oft quoted passages from *The vocacyon* is that concerning the performance of two of Bale's plays, 'a Tragedye of Gods promises' and 'a Commedie of sanct Johan Baptistes preachinges,' at the 'market crosse' in Kilkenny.[49] The moments leading up to the mention of the plays are, however, even more dramatic than the content of the dramas themselves for Bale has 'a do' with the 'prebendaryes and prestes' on the tense day when 'Ladye Marye with us at Kylkennye proclaimed Quene of Englande / Fraunce and Irelande':[50]

> I tolde them earnestly / whan they wolde have compelled me therunto / that I was not Moyses minister but Christes / I desyred them that they wolde not compell me to his denyall / which is (S. Paul sayth) in the repetinge of Moyses sacrementes & ceremoniall s[c]haddowes (Gal. v). With that I toke Christes testament in my hande / & went to the market crosse / the people in great nombre folowinge. There toke I the .xiii. chap. of S. Paule to the Roma. Declaringe to them brevely / what the autoritie was of the worldly powers & magistrates, what reverence & obedience were due to the same.[51]

Bale carries in his hand the only true prop of his 'vocacyon', 'Christes testament.' Followed by 'people in great nombre', who form his congregation

---

[47] Meech, *The book of Margery Kempe*, p. 1. [48] *The vocacyon*, p. 87. [49] *The vocacyon*, p. 59. [50] *The vocacyon*, p. 58. [51] *The vocacyon*, p. 59.

and, simultaneously, his audience (rather like the mobile audiences who followed the mediaeval mystery pageants from station to station), he reads from his script, Chapter 13 of the Epistle of Paul to the Romans, which begins: 'Let every soul be subject unto the higher powers. For there is no power but of God: the powers that be are ordained of God.'[52] In this scene, the image of Bale as preacher merges with, and eventually eclipses, that of Bale as playwright-prolocutor. It has been said that John Bale 'was after all not merely a hagiographer, antiquary, dramatist, and historical thinker – in the very core of his being he was a preacher too.'[53] Judging by *The vocacyon*, however, we might wish to modify the final part of this statement to read 'in the very core of his being he was a preacher first and foremost.'

---

52 Vulgate Ad Romanos 13: 1 reads: 'Omnis anima potestatibus sublimioribus sit: non est enim potestas nisi a Deo: quae autem sunt, a Deo ordinatae sunt.' For a discussion of how Bale's sermon can be read against the plays performed that day at the Market Crosse see Hadfield, *Literature, politics and national identity*, pp 74-6. He develops the argument here that Bale's 'sermon demanded loyalty to the new queen, but his plays told them that her rule was godless.' (p. 75)   53 Fairfield, *John Bale*, p. 140.

'Zeal for God and for souls': Counter-Reformation preaching in early seventeenth-century Ireland

Bernadette Cunningham

I

A talent for preaching was one of the attributes most frequently noted in contemporary biographical descriptions of many Catholic clergy in seventeenth-century Ireland. The short eulogistic biographies assembled by the Cistercian Malachy Hartry in 1649 concerning 'some holy and famous Irish Cistercian monks'[1] illustrate the importance contemporaries attached to the skill of preaching. The description of Paul Ragget, an eminent Kilkenny-born Cistercian, educated in Spain, was typical of the genre. 'After the usual course of philosophy and theology he was sent by his superior to his native country for the comfort of the Catholics. In his sermons he showed zeal for God and for souls, and his work bore fruit'.[2] More enthusiastic was the description of a Waterford priest named Thomas Lombard. Having studied in Ireland, England and Spain he joined the Cistercians. According to Hartry's account he returned to Ireland

> for the consolation of the Catholics groaning under continual persecution, and also for the conversion of their enemies. The advent of the Rev. Thomas was welcome to the Catholics, especially as he was the first preacher in his native city and of his Order since the suppression. Very soon his religious life, his wonderful learning, his frequent, almost daily, sermons, and his other kindly deeds, not to speak of his angelic appearance, were the wonder of all, even of the Protestants. He came to Ireland in 1601 and there he converted many to the true faith and gave proofs of his holiness.[3]

---

1 Denis Murphy (ed.), *Triumphalia chronologicae Monasterii Sanctae Crucis in Hibernia; de Cisterciensium Hibernorum viris illustribus* (Dublin, 1891), p. 225. 2 Murphy (ed.), *Triumphalia*, p. 269. 3 Murphy (ed.), *Triumphalia*, p. 261.

This eulogy epitomised the attributes of the good preacher, whose combination of exceptional learning with high moral standards was perceived as an example for the whole Christian community. One Dublin-based Franciscan, Thomas Strong, impressed his contemporaries with his skill in 'instructing, delighting and captivating the ear of his auditor with his variety and multiplicity of doctrinal matter'. He was of 'prodigious memory'.[4] Evidence of the respect earned by exceptional preachers through their virtue and learning was also documented in relation to members of the Society of Jesus. Richard Daton was highly regarded for his work in Limerick, where he was 'a most popular preacher', and consequently 'in the highest favour and esteem with the people of Limerick for his virtue and learning'.[5] Daton was among the exceptionally learned, however, and such eulogies would not have been merited by all who took to the pulpit.[6]

An exemplary lifestyle was necessary if the preacher was to have the necessary moral authority to win the respect of his listeners. The surviving contemporary biographical vignettes suggest that the clergy's status was determined by the fact of their ordination and by attributes such as learning and moral standing rather than wealth or social relationships.

Rev. John O'Heyne's late seventeenth-century biographical accounts of individual Irish Dominicans placed a particular emphasis on the preaching skills of his subjects.[7] It was this talent that ensured that Henry Burgatt was particularly highly regarded by those that knew him:

> His gifts showed themselves in Ireland, where he expounded the truths of the Gospel for many years with such learning, unction and elegance, that learned men marvelled how so small a man could be the possessor and eloquent exponent of so much knowledge. He distinguished himself not only by knowledge of spiritual things but by a most exemplary life, believing that an apostle should be not merely a light but a burning light and should preserve the salt of good works. This eminent man was well versed in dogmatic theology, canon law and controversy; strengthened by the study of the ancients, he was able to crush the enemies of religion in argument and converted many of them to the faith, the more learned among them fearing to meet him in controversy lest they should be confounded.[8]

4 Nicholas Archbold, 'Evangelicall fruict of the Seraphicall Franciscan Order, 1628' (British Library, London, Harley MS 3888, f. 110), cited in Raymond Gillespie, 'Catholic religious cultures in the diocese of Dublin, 1614-97' in James Kelly and Dáire Keogh (eds) *History of the Catholic diocese of Dublin* (Dublin, 2000), p. 141.   5 William Carrigan, *The history and antiquities of the diocese of Ossory* (4 vols, Dublin, 1905), iii, p. 261.   6 Daton received special mention in the introductory material published in Barnabas Kearney's Latin sermons, *Heliotrophium sive conciones tam de festis quam de dominicis quae in solari totius anni circulo occurrunt* (Lyons, 1622).   7 John O'Heyne, *The Irish Dominicans of the seventeenth century*, transl. Ambrose Coleman (Dundalk, 1902), pp 9-11.   8 O'Heyne, *Irish Dominicans*, pp 95-7.

Equally talented was Richard O'Madden (d. 1691) of Portumna, of whom O'Heyne noted: 'I often heard him preach and I never heard a more energetic preacher, neither in our own language nor in any other language I was acquainted with. He was very well versed in the science of the saints, and was also very meek and affable'.[9]

There is an implied contrast in O'Heyne's account between such accomplished public performers and more retiring clergy such as Thomas Fitzgerald whom he described as 'a simple pious and zealous man, [who] ministered to the spiritual needs of the citizens of Cork ... when he went about in the garb of a farm labourer'.[10] Whereas men like Fitzgerald may have pursued a lifestyle closer to the norm of clerical ministry in seventeenth-century Ireland, most of the extant evidence concerning Irish Counter-Reformation preachers and their sermons relates to those who were in some way exceptional.

II

These biographical accounts, despite their eulogistic nature, highlight the central objectives of those Catholic clergy engaged in preaching in seventeenth-century Ireland. The primary objective was to save souls. This was to be achieved through catechesis to counter ignorance and, where necessary, through defence of Catholic doctrine against heresy. By the 1630s, if not before, it is evident that the concern to counter heresy had abated, and Catholic preachers were predominantly concerned with the education and moral reform of their Catholic listeners.[11] The number of Catholic clergy active in early seventeenth-century Ireland is unclear. The best estimates suggest that there were perhaps 800 secular clergy and 300 members of religious orders working in Ireland by 1623, and that perhaps one-third of these had been educated in Continental Europe in seminaries formed under Counter-Reformation influence.[12] The decrees issued at the synod held at Kilkenny in 1614 expressed concerns about the inadequacies of some clergy, and measures were taken to exercise episcopal control over the activities of those who were so poorly educated that they were regarded as a danger to the spiritual well-being of the laity.[13] A 1677 synodal decree which instructed clergy in the diocese of Ossory to preach for at least fifteen minutes at every Mass is probably an indication that many clergy had previously failed to do so. In these circumstances, there was still a role for the mission preacher,

---

9 O'Heyne, *Irish Dominicans*, p. 211.   10 O'Heyne, *Irish Dominicans*, pp 65-7.   11 Patrick J. Corish, *The Catholic community in the seventeenth and eighteenth centuries* (Dublin, 1981), pp 29-30.   12 Corish, *Catholic community*, p. 26.   13 P. F. Moran, *History of the Catholic archbishops of Dublin since the Reformation* (Dublin, 1864), p. 456.

specially trained in the art of rhetoric, to supplement the probably rather mundane performances of the average parish priest. Much of the surviving evidence of Catholic preaching in seventeenth-century Ireland relates to the work of professional preachers, most of whom were Continentally-trained members of religious orders.

Aside from the problems posed by an uneducated clergy, there were other difficulties to be surmounted by the proponents of Counter-Reformation reform in Ireland. Their work was carried out in defiance of government policy. Most pre-Reformation churches were in Protestant hands by the early seventeenth century and Catholic clergy had little choice but to use the houses of the gentry and other secular places as venues for religious ceremonies. Gradually, new chapels were constructed where Mass could be celebrated,[14] but in the meantime the description of his ministry given by David Kearney, archbishop of Cashel, in 1609 was probably not unusual:

> We go around from one city to another, dressed in secular clothes ... we do not stop for any time in one place, but pass from one house to another, even in the cities and towns ... It is at night that we perform all the sacred functions ... celebrate Mass, give exhortations to the faithful.[15]

It is evident that the ecclesiastical structures within which these clergy worked were less than ideal, though there was clear progress towards the re-creation of a parish system in the course of the early seventeenth century. Under the guidelines issued at the Kilkenny synod in 1614, designed to cope with an inadequate parochial structure, individual clergy might have responsibility for more than one parish. As well as celebrating Mass and administering the sacraments, their responsibilities included instructing the faithful on some points of Christian doctrine each Sunday and holy day. When travelling through their parishes, spending the night at the houses of parishioners, priests were also obliged to avail of appropriate opportunities to teach prayers such as the Lord's Prayer and the Apostle's Creed to those in need of basic catechetical instruction.[16]

In addition to the activities of these parochial clergy, it was also stipulated at the 1614 Kilkenny synod that each deanery and town, or at the very least each diocese and city, should have one priest whose responsibility it was to act as preacher for that district. This measure was probably intended to compensate for the lack of learning and skill of some of the local clergy which left them less than adequate as preachers. In most instances these

---

14 Corish, *Catholic community*, pp 33-4.   15 Moran, *History of the Catholic archbishops of Dublin*, p. 236.   16 M. Comerford, *Collections relating to the dioceses of Kildare and Leighlin* (3 vols, Dublin, 1883), i, p. 246.

travelling preachers were likely to be members of religious orders, approved by the local bishop, and the laity whom they visited were expected to provide for their support and maintenance.[17]

III

Implicit in many of the accounts of sermons actually delivered by Jesuits, Dominicans, and others, is the impressive quality of the performance and the depth of the impact on the audience of sermons delivered by experienced preachers. To achieve such effects, preachers needed to be skilled in the art of rhetoric. Counter-Reformation clergy studied rhetoric as part of their seminary training, and the Jesuits in particular placed special emphasis on the practical elements of the art of preaching. Jesuit training in rhetoric was usually on the model recommended by Cypriano Soarez, whose manual of rhetoric, published at Paris in 1573, was widely used.[18] This recommended a tri-partite structure for sermons, comprising 'inventio', 'dispositio' and 'elocutio'. To communicate with and persuade an audience, Soarez advised the use of definition, etymology, syllogism, the description of causes and effects, the use of contrast. He advocated the heaping up of arguments so that they would overwhelm the hearer, and above all he advised that the orator should be well-stocked with examples. A store of anecdotes and proverbs was advocated as a particularly useful aid to the memory of the preacher.[19] To sustain the interest of the audience and to ensure that they understood the message Soarez advised that the preacher should endeavour to be dramatic and interesting and to use visual imagery. While it was appreciated that the more simple and pleasing the speech, the more likely it was to be believed, nevertheless the skilled preacher was also encouraged to be adventurous with language. Soarez gave advice on how to deal with new and unusual words, how to invent words by analogy, onomatopoeia, derivation and the invention of compounds. The use of word ornamentation and repetition was advocated to increase the attractiveness of the performance to the hearer.[20] It was widely accepted that the art of verbal persuasion was a skill

---

17 Comerford, *Collections relating to the dioceses of Kildare and Leighlin*, i, p. 246.   **18** C. Soarez, *De arte rhetorica libri tres ex Aristotele, Cicerone, et Quintilino praecipui deprompti* (Paris, 1573); see Peter Bayley, *French pulpit oratory, 1598-1650* (Cambridge, 1980), pp 21-5. For the books available to students at the Irish Franciscan college in Paris in 1621 see Brendan Jennings, 'Miscellaneous documents, I, 1588-1634' in *Archivium Hibernicum* xii (1946), pp 88-9.   **19** Bayley, *French pulpit oratory*, pp 25-9.   **20** Bayley, *French pulpit oratory*, pp 25-7. These rhetorical features were characteristic also of the prose writing of Geoffrey Keating, whose most substantial theological tract, *Trí bior-ghaoithe an bháis*, was strongly influenced by European sermon literature. Geoffrey Keating [Séathrún Kéitinn] *Trí bior-ghaoithe an bháis: the three shafts of death*, ed. Osborn Bergin (Dublin, 1931).

that could be acquired through study and practice. Thus the theory was put into practice in the universities and seminaries of early modern France, Italy, Spain and Spanish Flanders and Irish Counter-Reformation clergy educated there would have received a thorough grounding in the art of rhetoric.[21]

It appears, however, from the descriptions which John O'Heyne provides of Dominican preachers, that good-quality preaching was a skill that not all clergy could aspire to in practice. The practicalities of the task of public performance were such that a preacher needed a strong constitution to withstand the hardships of frequent travel, together with a clear voice and a commanding presence to ensure that his sermon could be heard. Thus among the friars at Coleraine was Rev. Thomas Mac Mahon (d. 1681) who was 'a learned man, but not effective as a preacher owing to a weak chest'. He was, nevertheless, 'a great catechist [and] a prudent and indefatigable confessor'.[22] Other practicalities included a thorough command of the language of the people. Depending on the part of the country in which the preacher found himself, a thorough knowledge of either Irish or English was necessary for effective communication with the laity. While preachers in the east coast towns of Dublin and Drogheda by the seventeenth century might normally use the English vernacular, in most other parts, and particularly in rural areas, fluency in Irish continued to be a prerequisite for effective communication. The necessary linguistic skills could be improved with practice, as in the case of O'Hegarty, a Dominican preacher in Drogheda who, although English was his native tongue, 'by constant practice became a very perfect preacher in both Irish and English'.[23] Similarly in the increasingly bilingual society that was seventeenth-century Ireland, William Barry 'preached in Irish and English with great distinction' and held the post of preacher general 'on account of his rhetorical powers'.[24] Among Jesuits, it was reported in 1608 that Christopher Holywood rarely worked outside Dublin, not just because of age and infirmity, but because he was ignorant of the Irish language. The Jesuits were conscious of the fact that 'some of our fathers, though learned and prudent and holy, cannot preach in Irish, and hence can work only in these one or two counties'. The problem was minor, however, as most Irish Jesuits could speak Irish and could therefore preach not just throughout Ireland but also in the highlands and isles of Scotland.[25] Some were bilingual, and regularly preached in both languages. Thus, most Catholic clergy could take for granted their own competence in the Irish language, whereas difficulties in training preachers competent in Irish had

---

21 It is clear from the carefully crafted theological writings of Barnabas Kearney, SJ, Aodh Mac Aingil, OFM, and Geoffrey Keating that they had a sophisticated understanding of the art of rhetoric. 22 O'Heyne, *Irish Dominicans*, p. 9. 23 O'Heyne, *Irish Dominicans*, p. 11. 24 O'Heyne, *Irish Dominicans*, pp 69-71. 25 Edmond Hogan, *Distinguished Irishmen of the sixteenth cenutry* (London, 1894), p. 462.

proved one of the most serious obstacles to the progress of the Protestant Reformation in seventeenth-century Ireland.[26]

IV

There is relatively little direct evidence, even in the case of the most renowned Irish preachers, concerning the precise circumstances in which sermons were delivered. Sermons were not normally integrated into the Eucharistic liturgy, but took place after Mass on Sundays and holy days. An Irish Franciscan catechism by Anthony Gearnon published in Louvain in 1645 offered instructions on how to listen to a sermon and illustrated this in a woodcut (fig. 4) which showed the pious gathered around the preacher while the dissolute lurked in an inn in the background. The laity were advised to attend with the intention of obtaining spiritual benefit, to listen to the words of the preacher with humility as though it was God speaking and to be attentive for points which they could apply to themselves. They should avoid jumping to conclusions about anything which displeased them since this was a ploy of the devil to distract them. The listeners were encouraged to recall the main points of the sermon afterwards in order to commit them to memory and thereby follow the path of virtue.[27] Gearnon was writing in the context of the regular Sunday sermon, and apparently in the light of experience of sometimes inappropriate responses to the efforts of the preacher.

In addition to sermons preached on Sundays and holy days some clergy took advantage of secular occasions at which large numbers of people were assembled by preaching sermons on fair days as the Munster Jesuit Barnabas Kearney did in 1605.[28] Kearney also conducted missions during Lent and Advent, the traditional times for preaching, and it was reported in one such instance that 'immense crowds' went to hear him.[29]

Jesuit letters reporting on the Society's activities in the early seventeenth century include some descriptions of the response of the laity to their efforts. One such letter reported that:

> So much attention is paid to preaching and exhortation that one man has preached twice on one and the same day, now in Irish and now in English, amidst the copious tears and abundant weeping of his hearers, both gentlemen of the highest rank and others even obstinate evil-doers'.[30]

[26] Toby Barnard, 'Protestants and the Irish language, c.1675-1725' in *Journal of Ecclesiastical History* xliv (1993), pp 243-72. [27] Anthony Gearnon, *Parrthas an anma* ed. Anselm Ó Fachtna (Dublin, 1953), pp 141-2. Gearnon's catechism was particularly popular in Munster. [28] Henry Fitzsimon, *Words of comfort to persecuted Catholics*, ed. Edmund Hogan (Dublin, 1881), p. 120. [29] Hogan, *Distinguished Irishmen*, p. 434. [30] Archives of the Irish Jesuit Province, Documents (translations), 1:107, cited in Samantha Meigs, *The Reformations in*

An Anma

An 5. Caibidil.

Don mhódh ar ar cóir an tShenmóir dhéirdhéis maille re tqba.

C. Cionas ar cóir don chrióchnóghdhe an tShenmóir dhéirdhéis?

F. Ó thús triallach cryce, maille re deighintin, to chum leighis dfaghail do chnéuchdaibh a anma, 7 to chum cnúasaigh spioradalta do dhéunamh fa a comhg.

Figure 4: The Counter-Reformation preacher (from Anthony Gearnon, *Parrathas an anma* [Louvain, 1645], p. 335).

The work of another Jesuit, Rev. Wale, in the neighbourhood of Carrick-on-Suir also attracted attention. When he celebrated Mass and preached a sermon on Sundays and festivals, the chapel in which he performed was filled to capacity, with many swarming about the doors and windows because there was no room inside. 'And when Father Wale, who is a man of great eloquence, preached on the Passion, he was interrupted so often by the sobs and cries of the faithful that he had to give up preaching, as his voice could not be heard.'[31] A Dublin Capuchin, Luke Bathe, had a similar reputation. It was recorded that his talent for persuasion was such that 'he never preached but tears rolled down continually from his auditor's eye. Some said that the Holy Ghost himself spake by that man.'[32]

Some preachers were concerned with the practical social implications of moral reform. The information that has survived about the activities of the Jesuit Barnabas Kearney in Munster makes clear that the preacher's social and political influence was not solely channelled through the pulpit.[33] Kearney used the pulpit to influence how people lived both their spiritual and their secular lives. As he travelled around the country the community regarded him not just as a person who would offer moral guidance but also as someone who was an appropriate arbitrator in civil disputes. In one recorded story, Kearney travelled into a county famous for its robberies

> and in his first discourse to the people and gentlemen, he preached vehemently against those robbers and the lords under whose wings they were sheltered. Then turning to the viscount and his three brothers who were present, he so set forth the enormity of their crimes that they were thunderstruck, and after the discourse sent for the preacher, got reconciled to God and their neighbours, and, wonderful to say, by their example moved all their subjects to true repentance in the space of six weeks during which the Jesuits remained with them.[34]

Following another sermon by Kearney in Munster it was reported that 'five men famous for cattle-lifting and the wildness of their careers were frightened by a sermon on the eternity of the pains of Hell; they went immediately to the Father to be reconciled to God, and promised to give up their sinful way of life'. The sermon must have been a considerable performance because the priest was 'so tired and sick after the sermon', that he postponed hearing their

---

Ireland (London, 1997), pp 110-11.   31 Hogan, *Distinguished Irishmen*, pp 430-1.   32 Nicholas Archbold, 'Evangelicall fruict of the Seraphicall Franciscan Order, 1628' (British Library, London, Harley MS 3888, ff. 105-105v).   33 Barnabas Kearney, a relative of David Kearney, archbishop of Cashel, was author of two substantial theological volumes in Latin, *Heliotrophium sive conciones tam de festis quam de dominicis quae in solari totius anni circulo occurrunt* (Lyons, 1622); *Heliotrophium sive conciones de mysteriis redemptionis humnae quae in dominica passione continentur* (Lyons, 1633).   34 Hogan, *Distinguished Irishmen*, p. 432.

confessions, but relented later because of their anxiety to repent and be reconciled to God.[35] After the adventures and exertions of such mission activity, Kearney was wont to return to Cashel for a rest 'if it be rest to preach twice every Sunday and holiday, and to settle disputes every day, and to promote the interests of peace and charity among those who are at variance.'[36]

V

Two volumes of theological writings in Latin, compiled by Barnabas Kearney, were published in France in the 1620s and 1630s. The first of these consisted of a series of sermons for Sundays and feastdays.[37] In each instance the theme of the sermon is a Scriptural quotation. There is an introductory section, then the Ave Maria, then three or occasionally four main points of exposition followed by a closing *exemplum*. The *exempla* are predominantly taken from Classical authors and the Church Fathers, including Cicero, Socrates, Eusebius, and Gregory of Nyssa. Each sermon quotes extensively from Scripture and the Church Fathers. In the printed text, references to these sources are highlighted in the margins of each page, and there is a detailed index of Scriptural quotations, arranged in the order of the books of the Bible. The volume also contains a thematic index of topics which is arranged in alphabetic order. These elements of the printed text were designed to facilitate the use of the compilation by other preachers as a handbook of homiletic sources and themes.

The sermons themselves are written so as to recreate as fully as possible the impact of the oral performance, with many rhetorical questions to entice the reader to engage with the text. Sequences of biblical and patristic citations in succession are followed by short explications. Analogies are used to illustrate particular points.[38] The sermons in Kearney's compilation range in length from approximately 6,000 to 12,000 words, which if delivered orally would perhaps have taken from 50 to 100 minutes to perform. In reality, however, the printed text of the sermons of this renowned Munster preacher gives relatively little away about the precise nature of the oral performance of such sermons. Reading the printed text of a sermon would have been a very different experience from attending the live performance. Kearney's printed Latin texts, published in France, had a different purpose and were aimed at a different audience from that to be found at a Munster fair - nonetheless, his oral performances would have drawn on the same

35 Hogan, *Distinguished Irishmen*, p. 433. 36 FitzSimon, *Words of comfort*, p. 120. 37 Kearney, *Heliotrophium sive conciones tam de festis quam de dominicis* (1622); the later volume (1633) is not presented in the form of sermons. 38 These are frequently noted as 'simile' in the printed marginal annotations.

corpus of learning, the same mastery of rhetoric, and the same set of religious convictions. The preacher's authority derived from his role as the interpreter of the Word of God. In so far as we can ascertain the probable content of sermons from the theological writings of seventeenth-century Irish clergy, the interpretation of Scripture was a key element in the structure. The published versions of Barnabas Kearney's sermons and likewise Geoffrey Keating's theological tract, *Trí bior-ghaoithe an bháis*, largely consisted of sequences of Scriptural quotations tersely elucidated in occasional explanatory sentences.[39] This style of preaching has been categorized by Philip Bayley, in his study of French preaching, as 'thesaurus sermons', because they consisted of long sequences of linked quotations, anecdotes and analogies. The ability of the preacher to provide extensive citations of sources, especially from the Scriptures and the Church Fathers, and then to draw analogies from nature or everyday life to elucidate a point, made them appear especially learned.[40] Preachers like Kearney and Keating constructed their sermons on the premise that references to Scripture were of themselves adequate and did not require much discussion. Just a very brief elucidation was offered of the meaning of passages quoted. The authority of Scripture was accepted as fundamental. Equally regarded as reliable guides to spiritual well-being were the writings of the Church Fathers. The view of life and death constructed by Augustine, Thomas Aquinas, and their followers, in particular, had a formative influence on the theological perspective of Keating's writings.[41]

The available evidence suggests that in a multitude of ways the sermons preached by Irish Counter-Reformation clergy in the seventeenth century were derivative of other homiletic sources. Indeed, in the case of Keating's theological discussion of sin and death, there are direct parallels with the contemporary French sermons of Pierre de Besse in terms of both style and content.[42] A renowned French preacher, de Besse was active in the early

---

39 Although Keating's text was not presented to the reader in ready-made sermon format, it is nonetheless a useful proxy for the likely content of the sermons for which he was renowned. It was evidently used by other clergy as the basis of sermons well into the eighteenth century. A 1752 colophon in one manuscript copy of the text, added by a priest of the diocese of Killala, noted that Keating's work was being copied (from a text owned by another priest) 'for the good of his soul and for the public ... who will read or hear it' (National Library of Ireland, Dublin, MS G333, f. [3]). For further discussion see Bernadette Cunningham, *The world of Geoffrey Keating: history, myth and religion in seventeenth-century Ireland* (Dublin, 2000), pp 43-58. **40** Bayley, *French public oratory*, pp 77-85. **41** Cunningham, *World of Geoffrey Keating*, pp 47-57. Those clergy who later used Keating's tract valued it because it 'followed the track of scripture, and the apostles, and the religious authors', National Library of Ireland, Dublin, MS G333, f [3]. **42** Tadhg Ó Dúshláine, *An Eoraip agus litríocht na Gaeilge, 1600-1650* (Baile Átha Cliath, 1987), pp 50-60; Bernadette Cunningham, 'The sources of *Trí bior-ghaoithe an bháis*: another French sermon' in *Éigse* xxxi (1999), pp 73-8.

decades of the seventeenth century when Keating would have been in France. He published several large volumes of sermons for the Sundays and festivals of the year, and also issued collections of Lent and Advent sermons.[43] Once published, these would have been used by other preachers in France as models for their own performances, and it may well be that Keating heard rather than read the material found in the sermons of Besse that also feature in *Trí bior-ghaoithe an bháis*.[44]

Although modelled on the work of his French contemporaries, Keating's theological writings were nonetheless innovative in an Irish context. His work was an amalgam of old and new, and by virtue of being written in the Irish vernacular rather than in Latin, his texts reached new audiences. His two theological prose works, *Eochair-sgiath an Aifrinn* and *Trí bior-ghaoithe an bháis*, made available to Irish readers, in accessible language, material that had hitherto only been available in Latin to the educated men of the Church. In this he had much in common with late-medieval English preachers, who were essentially popularizers rather than innovators. They tended to be 'backward-looking in their choice of sources', relying on established 'classics' rather than the latest theological ideas of their contemporaries in the universities.[45] Keating also connected to a tradition which had roots in the middle ages in the way in which he organised his sermons around an opening Scriptural theme, developing it in diverse ways, and dividing the discussion into headings.[46]

There is clear evidence of his training in rhetoric throughout Keating's work, not least in the manner in which he was drawn again and again to the discussion of opposites. Virtues featured as the opposites of particular vices, death was contrasted with life, but above all heavenly glory was contrasted with eternal damnation. The audience was left in no doubt that if they did not repent and live a moral life, then damnation was a very real alternative to salvation.[47]

Keating frequently grouped his examples into threes, or sevens. Thus, for instance, in a discussion on purgatory and the communion of saints, he explained that there were seven categories of the dead. Three of these groups, atheists, believers who were wrongdoers, and unbaptised children, were beyond the help of the prayers of the living. The next three groups,

---

[43] Pierre de Besse, *Conceptions theologiques sur les quatres fin de l'homme, preschées en un Advant l'an 1605* (Paris, 1606); *Conceptions theologiques sur toutes les festes des saincts autres solemnelles de l'annee, preschees en divers lieux* (3 vols, Paris, 1618); *Conceptions theologiques sur tous les dimanches de l'annee*, (2 vols, Paris, 1624).   [44] Ó Dúshláine, *An Eoraip agus litríocht na Gaeilge*, pp 50-60; Cunningham, 'The sources of *Trí bior-ghaoithe an bháis*', pp 73-8.   [45] H. Leith Spencer, *English preaching in the late middle ages* (Oxford, 1993), p. 17.   [46] Essentially, the 'modern' form of preaching; see p. 74 and n. 56 above and Spencer, *English preaching*, pp 228-68; see Keating, *Trí bior-ghaoithe an bháis*, passim.   [47] For example, Keating *Trí bior-ghaoithe an bháis*, ll 6955-72; 10990-95.

baptised children, martyrs, and the righteous who were always devout and honest, did not need help as they were already saved. Finally, there were the believers who were moderately devout and honest. These were in purgatory for three reasons: venial sin, sin forgotten in confession, or sin confessed but for which reparation had not been made.[48] This kind of categorization was probably engaged in both to assist the preacher in remembering the sermon for oral delivery without recourse to notes and also to enable the listener to remember what had been heard. On occasion, Keating ended his discussion of a moral or theological topic by reciting a stanza of poetry. Such verses, usually ascribed to unnamed Irish poets,[49] or an even more vague 'somebody',[50] were evidently not cited because of the reputation of their authors. Rather, they had an important mnemonic effect for both preacher and listener, summarizing the argument of the sermon in a few brief lines. Such verses would also have helped the listener to relate to the classical and Scriptural ideas contained in the text by summarizing the material in a style that appeared both familiar and easy to remember. The Louvain Franciscan Bonaventure Ó hEodhasa, whose printed Irish catechism (1611) was designed for use among Irish speakers, likewise used poetry as a means of presenting Catholic doctrine in a form that could easily be committed to memory.[51]

Geoffrey Keating's theological writings contain many other devices designed to make the ideas he discussed more easily intelligible to general lay audiences. In particular he made extensive use of *exempla*, as his medieval predecessors (discussed by Alan Fletcher and Colmán Ó Clabaigh above) had done. Keating's *exempla* were drawn from a new compendium published in 1603 under the title *Magnum speculum exemplorum*.[52] This substantial volume was itself a reworking of a fourteenth-century compilation, the *Scala coeli*, the first printed edition of which was issued in 1480.[53] There is evidence that copies of *Magnum speculum exemplorum* were available in Ireland in the 1650s since one of the scribes who made a copy of Keating's tract on the Mass in 1657 inserted the original Latin of some of the *exempla* which Keating had cited in Irish.[54] Another Louvain-based Irish Franciscan Aodh Mac Aingil (Hugh MacCaughwell) also used stories from these sources.

---

48 Keating, *Trí bior-ghaoithe an bháis*, book 3, ch. 3. **49** 'mar adeir an file Gaoidhealach', Keating, *Trí bior-ghaoithe an bháis*, ll 7432-6; 7738-43. **50** Keating, *Trí bior-ghaoithe an bháis*, ll 7870-1. **51** Bonabhentura Ó hEodhasa, *An teagasc Críosdaithe* (Antwerp, 1611), ed. F. Mac Raghnaill (Dublin, 1976). **52** *Magnum speculum exemplorum* (Douai, 1603, rept 1605). Later editions from 1607 onwards are organised in a different format, and Keating's citations are from the 1603/1605 version. **53** Johannes Gobius, *Scala coeli* (Ulm, 1480). For a modern edition see Marie-Anne Polo de Beaulieu (ed.), *La scala coeli de Jean Gobi* (Paris, 1991). **54** National Library of Ireland, Dublin MS G 49 transcribed by Seán mac Torna Uí Mhaoilchonaire in 1657; see Pádraig Ó Fiannachta, 'Seán mac Torna Í Mhaoilchonaire agus *Eochair-sciath an Aifrinn*' in *Éigse* x (1961-3), pp 198-207; Pádraig Ó Fiannachta, 'Scéalta ón *Magnum speculum exemplorum*' in *Irish Ecclesiastical Record*, 5th ser. xcix no. 3 (1963), pp 177-84.

They were incorporated into his treatise on penance first published in Irish in 1618 under the title *Scathán Shacramuinte na haithridhe*.[55] These Latin compilations were preachers' handbooks comprising a vast range of vivid vignettes recounting tales of misfortune and punishment resulting from moral laxity.[56] The various seventeenth-century editions of the *Magnum speculum exemplorum* were arranged by theme (or occasionally by source), with extensive indexes to facilitate the speedy construction of a sermon on a wide choice of topics. They did not provide ready-made sermons, but provided illustrative material that certainly greatly eased the preachers' task of communicating difficult theological concepts to general lay audiences.[57]

One such *exemplum* told the story of a woman who had concealed a sin of incest for eleven years, because she was too ashamed to confess it to any clergy known to her. Eventually when two preachers whom she did not know arrived in the castle where she lived she confessed her sin to one of them. As she did so, the second preacher saw long snakes coming from her mouth and going out the door. At the end of the confession he saw a large dragon sticking his head out of her mouth and going back inside, and subsequently the other snakes returned. Her most serious sin had remained unconfessed. The two clerics departed, and on their journey one told the other what he had seen. The confessor realized that the woman had concealed a sin and they decided to return to the castle. They found the woman dead. The clergy prayed that God would reveal to them what had happened to the woman. After three days they saw the woman riding a dragon with snakes around her neck and dogs chewing at her hands and she told them that because of her concealed sin she faced eternal damnation. The story continued by giving the woman's explanations for the symbolism of the dragons and other demons that were tormenting her in terms of punishment for the sins she had committed. She explained that the shame that discouraged people from confessing their sins was the cause of many people going to hell. Having listed the most common sins that led to damnation, she was suddenly swept off to hell by the dragon, and the clergy could no longer speak to her.

This story was recounted by Geoffrey Keating in the eleventh chapter of his tract on the Mass, *Eochair sgiath an Aifrinn*.[58] The chapter was devoted to

---

55 Aodh Mac Aingil, *Scáthán shacramuinte na haithridhe*, ed. Cainneach Ó Maonaigh (Baile Átha Cliath, 1952), pp 83-5; For a discussion of Mac Aingil's use of *exempla* see Ó Dúshláine, *An Eoraip agus litríocht na Gaeilge*, pp 85-96. See also Mícheál Mac Craith, '*Scáthán shacramuinte na haithridhe*: scáthán na sacraiminte céanna' in *Léachtaí Cholm Cille* xxx (2000), pp 28-64. 56 F.C. Tubach, *Index exemplorum: a handbook of medieval religious tales* (FF Communications, no. 204, Helsinki, 1969) provides a detailed index to the themes of stories narrated in medieval moral tales, covering material published in *Scala coeli*, *Magnum speculum exemplorum* among other sources. 57 For an overview of the use of moral tales in the Irish preaching tradition see Tadhg Ó Dúshláine, '"Ag so scéal uafásach eile ...": scéalaíocht na seanmóire' in *Léachtaí Cholm Cille* xxx (2000), pp 75-97. 58 Geoffrey Keating [Seathrún Céitinn], *Eochair-sgiath an Aifrinn: an explanatory defence of the mass*, ed. Patrick

illustrating that confession to a priest was compulsory. Writing in the opening decades of the seventeenth century, Keating cited the medieval *Scala coeli* as the source of the story, though it is more likely that he derived it from the later *Magnum speculum exemplorum* where it is the twenty-second *exemplum* given under the heading 'Confessio', with *Scala coeli* again acknowledged as the source.[59] The same story, with *Scala coeli* still cited as its source, formed part of an Irish sermon on confession which was the work of a Franciscan preacher in the early eighteenth century.[60] In this instance, however, it appears that it was a manuscript of Keating's *Eochair-sgiath an Aifrinn* rather than the *Scala coeli* that was consulted. Nevertheless, the older Latin source was still mentioned by name by the preacher, probably to enhance the aura of learning of his discourse. By pausing to explain that the Latin words *scala coeli* meant 'the ladder of the kingdom of God',[61] the preacher may have been more concerned to assert his learning than to edify his listeners.

The eighteenth-century Franciscan preacher who recited this *exemplum* in his sermon on confession, an elucidation of the theme of Luke 11:14 which he quoted as 'Jesus was driving out a demon which was dumb',[62] made some changes to the story as compared with Keating's version. In particular, the Franciscan omitted to mention that the sin was one of incest. He also changed the woman's list of the sins that most commonly caused people to go to hell. Where Keating's version emphasized sexual sins and superstition, the Franciscan retelling of the story simply listed pride, greed and envy (three of the Seven Deadly Sins). Thus Keating's version was far more faithful to the medieval source.[63]

The story was highly visual, with a strong sense of the dramatic. It was bound to enliven the sermon performance, and it was an effective means of ensuring the hearer was left in no doubt about the dire consequences of failure to confess sin. It was also particularly appropriate for use by travelling mission preachers since the clergy in the story were visitors not personally known to the woman sinner. The universality of such moral tales together with their flexibility - each preacher could retell them in his own words and with their own particular emphases - explains their extraordinary longevity in the repertoire of professional preachers.

Not every preacher had to rely on ready-made compilations of *exempla* for his repertoire of moral tales. The life of Daniel Nolan (d. 1677), a

O'Brien (Dublin, 1898), pp 80-1.   **59** For further discussion of Keating's use of *Magnum speculum exemplorum* see Cunningham, *The world of Geoffrey Keating*, pp 35-7, 50-2.   **60** Cainneach Ó Maonaigh (ed.), *Seanmónta chúige Uladh* (Baile Átha Cliath, 1965), pp xv, 14-15.   **61** 'dreimire fhlaitheas Dé', Ó Maonaigh (ed.), *Seanmónta chúige Uladh*, p. 14.   **62** *Erat Jesus ejiciens daemonium, et illud erat mutum*. 'Bhí Iosa a teilgint diabhail amach agas bhí se balbh, agan an tan do dhí se amach é, labuair an balbhan'. The quotation is that found in the Vulgate except that the preacher inserted the name of Jesus for the sake of clarity.   **63** Keating, *Eochair sgiath an Aifrinn*, pp 80-1.

Dominican preacher from Athenry in County Galway, was sufficiently colourful to ensure he had his own personal selection of stories of temptation, sin and repentance. Returning as a prodigal son after an affair with an English widow that lasted for a year and a half, 'in a spirit of the most profound humility he implored mercy with tears, and begged to be received again amongst the brethren'.[64] The General of the order, 'like the Father in the Gospel', welcomed him back. Having studied philosophy and theology, Nolan was sent back to Ireland as a preacher in 1665, where

> he preached like a sounding trumpet, confirming the Catholics in the faith and confuting the Protestants in all patience and sound doctrine. He was most fluent in English as well as in his own tongue. He was a sound theologian very much given to study; he was a finished controversialist, and efficaciously convinced several Protestants.[65]

Just as Daniel O'Houlahan 'used modestly and to the great edification of his hearers to tell the story of his fall, not indeed from the faith but from his vows',[66] other preachers may well have told stories from their own personal experience to edify their congregations. However, the evidence from those selected sermons that have survived in written form appears to suggest that it was more usual for preachers to rely on stories of others to illustrate their sermons.

Preachers with experience of their congregations' relatively unsophisticated understanding of theological matters were likely to rely on time-honoured concepts familiar to their listeners rather than attempt too much innovation. Most preachers were concerned to be communicators and teachers rather than innovators, and would not usually have entered into debate on the latest theological controversies. The preacher's duty, according to the medieval Franciscan Rule, was 'to preach of the vices and virtues, the penalties of hell and the glory of heaven', and it is clear that many a preacher tried to do so in an interesting and effective manner.[67] While audiences liked some originality in the treatment of traditional themes, they felt reassured by familiarity. It is unsurprising, therefore, that the understanding of good and evil which underpinned Keating's arguments about the nature of sin was a medieval one. The concept of the Seven Deadly Sins rather than the Ten Commandments formed the basis of his moral framework. In an Irish context, where the Seven Deadly Sins would have formed the core of traditional moral teaching, the use of the Ten Commandments, on the model of the Catechism of the Council of Trent, might have been too innovative. Keating

---

64 O'Heyne, *Irish Dominicans*, p. 141.　65 O'Heyne, *Irish Dominicans*, p. 141.　66 O'Heyne, *Irish Dominicans*, p. 143.　67 Spencer, *English preaching*, p. 93, citing S. Wenzel, *Verses in sermons, Fasciculus Morum and its Middle English poems* (Cambridge, Mass, 1978), pp 9-10.

could be confident, however, that his audiences would be familiar with the moral framework shaped around the Seven Deadly Sins.[68] All seven, pride, covetousness, lust, envy, gluttony, anger and sloth, had a strong social aspect, and conveyed an understanding of sin as offence against the community as well as being a turning away from God. A familiarity with the Seven Deadly Sins so permeated medieval and early modern thinking, teaching and literature (in the writings of Geoffrey Chaucer or Dante Alighieri for example) that it was unthinkable that they would not have featured in Irish theological writings in the seventeenth century. This traditional approach contrasted with the catechetical model adopted by at least some of the Irish Franciscan catechists active in Louvain in the early seventeenth century. Aodh Mac Aingil used the Ten Commandments as the framework for his examination of conscience in his *Scáthán Shacramuinte na haithridhe*.[69] Although produced on the Continent, there is evidence that this work was accessible in Ireland, and it is likely that it too provided the basis for much sermon material.[70] However, it cannot necessarily be implied that the theological context of Mac Aingil's text immediately became the norm for Irish Franciscan preachers. Indeed, the example cited above, of an eighteenth-century preacher, presumed to be a Franciscan, deriving his material from Keating, shows no diminution in the use of the Seven Deadly Sins as the basis of a moral framework.[71]

VI

The immediacy of the sermon experience, and the affinity between preacher and congregation arising from their being drawn together for the event which included the sermon performance, would have been conducive to the preacher drawing directly on the concerns and circumstances of the congregation to illustrate his argument. Thus there was both a social and a political element to the ideas expressed by a preacher like Geoffrey Keating in early seventeenth-century Munster. In emphasizing sins against the social order that were a particular problem in an Irish context, Keating mentioned adultery, the oppression of the Church, and the treacherous spilling of blood. Keating interpreted these major problems in Irish society as God's revenge on the Irish for the sins of their forefathers.[72] He argued that many of the houses of the Irish nobility had been destroyed or were now occupied

---

[68] For discussion of these contrasting traditions see John Bossy, 'Moral arithmetic: seven sins into ten commandments' in Edmund Leites (ed.), *Conscience and casuistry in early modern Europe* (Cambridge, 1988), pp 213-34. [69] Mac Aingil, *Scáthán Shacramuinte na haithridhe*, ed. Canice Mooney, pp 94-104. [70] See Ó Fiannachta, 'Seán Ó Maolchonaire agus *Eochair-sciath an Aifrinn*'. [71] Ó Maonaigh (ed.), *Seanmónta chúige Uladh*, p. 15. [72] Keating, *Trí bior-ghaoithe an bháis*, ll 5384-476.

by foreigners, and that the Irish nobility were living in slavery or poverty as a consequence of the pride and injustice of their own ancestors.[73] Such arguments were presented as illustrations of the need for repentance, for living moral lives, and particularly for giving priority to spiritual well-being even if it involved risking loss of worldly wealth. Keating criticized those dissolute Irish who for reasons of greed were acquiring wealth and land for themselves or their families in an unjust manner that was against the will of God.[74] He particularly criticized those who were renouncing or hiding their Catholic faith for fear of displaying disobedience to secular authority. Keating warned them not to make an enemy of God for the sake of transient friendship on earth.[75] He went further, arguing that just as Jonas had been prepared to die, so the Irish should be prepared to die rather than allow their Catholic faith to be destroyed.[76] He insisted that the fate God had allowed the Israelites to suffer would also be suffered by the people of Ireland, and that they would have drawn God's wrath on themselves.[77]

Keating's awareness of the political and social circumstances of his audience, as revealed in his theological writings, would have been derived from his everyday experience of living as part of the Catholic community of Munster in the early seventeenth century.[78] It is likely that his sermons to that community, like his prose writings, would have interpreted the teachings of the Gospel in the light of the immediate social and political concerns of his congregations. He was not concerned with the doings of heretics, he argued, but was concerned with the salvation of the souls of his own Catholic congregation.[79] Keating's writings provide an example of the work of one of the more highly educated secular clergy which may well be untypical. Nevertheless, the popularity of his theological works, as evidenced by their circulation in manuscript well into the nineteenth century, is evidence that his work and his outlook still had appeal for the clergy and their flocks for many generations after he had himself worked as a preacher in the diocese of Lismore.

The records of the English administration in seventeenth-century Ireland occasionally draw attention to the activities of Catholic preachers, and particularly their role in encouraging the laity to disobey secular authority. The activities of such preachers were monitored, and in consequence some descriptions of the circumstances in which sermons were delivered have

---

73 Keating, *Trí bior-ghaoithe an bháis*, ll 5356-61.   74 Keating, *Trí bior-ghaoithe an bháis*, ll 3546-7.   75 Keating, *Trí bior-ghaoithe an bháis*, ll 3549-56.   76 Keating, *Trí bior-ghaoithe an bháis*, ll 6056-76.   77 Keating, *Trí bior-ghaoithe an bháis*, ll 6097-118.   78 For an examination of the contemporary political circumstances within which Keating's comments may be interpreted see David Edwards, 'The poisoned chalice: the Ormond inheritance, sectarian division and the emergence of James Butler, 1614-1642', in Toby Barnard and Jane Fenlon (eds), *The dukes of Ormonde, 1610-1745* (Woodbridge, 2000), pp 55-82.   79 Keating, *Trí bior-ghaoithe an bháis*, ll 3549-50.

survived. On 11 October 1613, a Franciscan friar named Turlogh McCrodyn delivered a sermon at a venue in the woods in County Londonderry to an assembled gathering of 1,000 people including fourteen other priests. This preacher was described as being about thirty years of age and had been sent by the pope along with two other friars on a mission to preach to the people of Ulster. On the occasion of the sermon described, the preacher had stayed in the area for four days during which time he said Mass each day, but only preached once. The eyewitness account records that the preacher exhorted the congregation to reform their wicked lives. He criticized their drunkenness, fornication, and lack of devotion and zeal. He warned them not to be tempted by fear or desire for gain to attend the Protestant service, telling them 'those were the devil's words, which the English ministers spake, and all should be damned that heard them'.[80] He advocated that they should go into rebellion rather than attend the Protestant church, and should suffer death rather than submit. This preacher, like Keating, told the audience that God was punishing them for their own sins by allowing their lands to be given to strangers and heretics. However, the Franciscan went further by exhorting them to fast and pray and to be reassured that it would not be long before they were restored to their former prosperity.[81] Whereas Keating's comments to a Munster audience consistently focused on the ultimate objective of eternal salvation, even when he drew on the local political context for illustrative material, it appears clear that this Franciscan preacher in Ulster in 1613 delivered a highly charged political speech in the course of his religious sermon. The available evidence for the political and social context within which sermons were delivered suggests that preachers were acutely conscious of the expectations of their listeners, and tailored their performances accordingly. The direct communication between clergy and congregation engaged in on the occasion of a sermon was a primary mechanism through which the ideas of Counter-Reformation Catholicism could be conveyed to the Irish laity. The impact of that communication was constrained not just by the limits on the talents and learning of the clergy, and the inherently traditional nature of preacher's handbooks, but also by the circumstances, expectations and prior knowledge of the audience. In so far as the sermon was to be a major channel for reform, the Catholic Reformation in Ireland was likely to be a conservative affair.

---

80 *Calendar of state papers, Ireland, 1611–14*, pp 429–31. 81 See above, n. 73; *Calendar of state papers, Ireland, 1611–14*, pp 429–31.

The reformed preacher: Irish Protestant preaching 1660-1700

Raymond Gillespie

I

If the Protestant Reformation began with the principle of *Scriptura sola*, it soon became clear that in Ireland this was in need of qualification. Language differences, low literacy levels and problems with the distribution of texts were only part of the challenge. More important was the fact that the Bible was a difficult and potentially subversive text which could not be allowed to circulate in an unmediated form. It needed to be read within the communities of believers who established the parameters for understanding and interpreting the text.[1] The way in which these parameters were established and conveyed was through the sermon which remained the most effective way of communicating religious messages in seventeenth-century Ireland. As the Presbyterian minister of Derry, Robert Craghead, put it starkly in the 1690s, 'God saveth by preaching'.[2] However, preaching involved a great deal more than simply conveying a religious message. It also established a set of social relationships between the preacher and his audience. This was not just the relationship of speaker and listener. Preachers taught their hearers not only the language and symbols of religious discourse but also what bound them together as a social group and what separated them from other groups, both Protestant and Catholic. The religious sociability which surrounded the sermon was an important element in the social and cultural cement of the various groups that made up late seventeenth-century Irish society. As a result, social bonds almost always complemented congregational ones. When the Kilkenny Baptist Ann Fowke recorded that her grandfather had moved to the town 'for the sake of being near the means of grace' it was as much to do with meeting other members of the congregation as with listening to sermons.[3] Concrete benefits might flow from such sociability. Through meetings

[1] Raymond Gillespie, 'Reading the Bible in seventeenth-century Ireland' in Bernadette Cunningham and Máire Kennedy (eds), *The experience of reading: Irish historical perspectives* (Dublin, 1999), pp 39-59. [2] Robert Craghead, *An answer to a late book entitled a discourse concerning the inventions of men in the worship of God* (Edinburgh, 1694), pp 65, 67, 88. [3] *A memoir of Mistress Ann Fowke nee Geale* (Dublin, 1892), p. 9.

of the congregation, for instance, it was possible to make commercial contacts or to recruit apprentices. Thus the Independent minister at Limerick, John Bailey urged his congregation to 'be stirring up one another, be glad to see each other and be useful to one another both to body and soul as there is occasion'.[4] Such religious sociability resulted in a cohesion between church and community, creating powerful bonds which proved difficult to break.

There were different techniques in the construction of community which reflected themselves in different preaching styles. In the Church of Ireland its established status and the hierarchical nature of religious authority led preachers to take their lead in the choice of subjects and manner of preaching from their bishops. The bishops with their fear of enthusiasm emphasized moderation and sober preaching. When Narcissus Marsh, archbishop of Dublin, addressed his clergy at the metropolitan visitation in 1694 he urged them to make their sermons 'plain and practical'. He advised that they should be methodical 'for method doth much help the memory of the illiterate'. They were not to preach on mysteries such as the Incarnation or the Trinity and were not to raise passions but to inform judgement.[5] The clergy of the established church, not dependent on the consumerism of voluntary religion, seem to have followed his injunctions. Sermons in the Church of Ireland tradition became rather arid and formalized affairs. One Quaker, William Mathews, was disappointed in 1675 when being persuaded to attend a Church of Ireland service

> where he expected to hear something of satisfaction but found none, only saying that the people were to mind family duties and pray to God for, saith he, he told us nothing of note but that God was in the heaven said he. If asked how a man should come to Him, they then told him by minding family duties.[6]

On more spectacular occasions sermons came to have a ritualized form with the same sentiments, whether relevant or not, repeatedly trotted out. As one of the barons of the Exchequer noted of Archbishop William King's thanksgiving sermon after the victory at Blemheim in 1704, 'in short he said all the things that a man could wish a good bishop to say and make no doubt that either the intelligence I formerly had written to your grace [the duke of

---

4 T.C. Barnard, 'Identities, ethnicity and tradition in Irish dissent' in Kevin Herlihy (ed.), *The Irish dissenting tradition* (Dublin, 1995), pp 45-8; Raymond Gillespie, 'The Presbyterian revolution in Ulster, 1660-1700' in W.J. Sheils and Diana Wood (eds), *The churches, Ireland and the Irish: studies in church history xxv* (Oxford, 1989), pp 161-4; John Bailey, 'To may loving friends at Limerick' in John Bailey, *Man's chief end to glorify God* (Boston, 1989), p. 34.
5 *A charge given by Narcissus, lord archbishop of Dublin to his clergy of the province of Leinster at his primary triennial visitation, 1694* (Dublin, 1694), pp 7-9. 6 Society of Friends Historical Library, Dublin, MM II F1, p. 23.

Ormond] an account of was mistaken or else that some people have one body of divinity for private conversation and another for public preaching'.[7] Sermons could be and were repeated, even to the same congregations within a short space of time. One sermon diary kept by a preacher in the Newry area for the 1690s suggests that some sermons could be repeated twice to the same congregation within a few weeks.[8] Hardly surprisingly, Church of Ireland clergy reported a lack of enthusiasm from among their listeners. In the diocese of Derry during the 1690s a common reason for non attendance at church was the poor quality of preaching. Bishop Wetenhall of Cork complained in 1683 that during lessons the congregation whispered and observed strangers or their neighbours and the sermon had barely begun before 'some have plainly and designedly composed themselves for sleep', while others censured the preacher or were engaged in 'mutual caresses'.[9] Archbishop Marsh likewise complained of those who spent the sermon 'whispering, sleeping or gazing about on everyone that comes in' and when challenged about lack of attention during sermons the Dublin Presbyterian minister Joseph Boyse tartly replied 'nor do I find that a man can sleep more securely and quietly in the meeting than in the parish church'.[10]

If the late seventeenth-century Church of Ireland preacher had little to recommend him to the community of the parish, the dissenting preacher was a much more interesting figure. The voluntary nature of dissenting meetings meant that the relationship between minister and people was much more developed than in the context of the parish church. It was the clergy who acted as a focus for worship and as such gave meaning to the symbols of dissent. Ministers also served as a fixed point for religious sociability. To be without a minister was to leave a congregation with an uncertain future.[11] For this reason there were strong links between the person of the minister, the theological stance of the congregation and the members of that congregation. Thus, for example, the gaoler at Youghal in the 1650s told one of his prisoners that he could not be good because he did not approve of James Wood, the Independent minister at Youghal, to whose congregation the gaoler belonged.[12] Congregations looked up to their minister as a leader

---

7 Historical Manuscripts Commission, *Calendar of the manuscripts of the marquis of Ormonde* (new series, 8 vols, London, 1902-20), viii, p. 113. For a study of one class of public sermons, T.C. Barnard, 'The uses of 23 October 1641 and Irish Protestant celebrations' in *English Historical Review* cvi (1991), pp 889-920.   8 Marsh's Library, Dublin, MS Z4. 5. 19.   9 Trinity College, Dublin, MS 1995-2008/359; Edward Wetenhall, *A practical and plain discourse of the form of godliness visible in the present age* (Dublin, 1683), pp 111-12.   10 *A charge given by Narcissus*, p. 25, Joseph Boyse, *Remarks on a late discourse of William, lord bishop of Derry, concerning the inventions of men in the worship of God* (Dublin, 1694), p. 128.   11 See the examples in Kevin Herlihy, 'The faithful remnant: Irish Baptists, 1650-1750' in Kevin Herlihy (ed.), *The Irish dissenting tradition* (Dublin, 1995), pp 73-4, 76-80.   12 Walter Gostellow, *Charles Stuart and Oliver Cromwell united* (London, 1654), p. 120.

in difficult times and regarded him as a continuing source of guidance. The elderly minister of Cook Street Presbyterian church in Dublin, John Pinney, who fled Ireland in 1688, being 'old and unfit to raise a congreg[ation] for others to succeed in', was memorialized by that congregation in February 1692 to return so that they might

> again to enjoy your presence and labours among us which is the great desire and longing of your poor people ... the Lord having so endeared our affection to you by that good we have received by your labours through the blessing of God and that comfortable society we have had with you while amongst us which we being deprived of this long time hath been a great grief to us.[13]

Even when a minister finally left a congregation he was often consulted by congregations about a variety of issues. When the Covenanter John Crookshank left his Raphoe congregation in 1660, for instance, they wrote to him hoping 'your way be cleared to come again' and in the interim he 'would mind us in all your approaches to God and that the Lord will enable us to stand out all storms'. In return Crookshank urged them to adhere to 'fundamental truths'.[14] The remainder of this essay will concentrate on the dissenting preacher and the social and religious bonds he created which shaped and were shaped by his preaching skills.

II

While it is easy to recognise the importance of the preacher and his sermon as a way of constructing voluntary religious communities in the later seventeenth century, it is more difficult to describe how that worked in practice. This is partly because of the enormous variation in the styles of ministry within Irish dissent which, in part, reflected the relative importance of the community and institutional structures. At one end of the spectrum there were Quakers who, having no sacramental or public preaching tradition, saw little need for a formal ordained ministry and abandoned it. They retained only a group of licensed 'public friends' speaking by the aid of the Spirit. At the other end of the spectrum lay Presbyterians from a Scottish tradition who paid particular attention to organisational frameworks.[15] As the

---

[13] Geoffrey Nuttall (ed.), *The letters of John Pinney* (Oxford, 1939), pp 57, 84-7. [14] Bodleian Library Oxford, Rawlinson MS D830, ff 463, 464-5, 469-70, 471, 472-8v. Similarly John Bailey in exile told his Limerick congregation that they would meet 'at the throne of Grace' by praying for one another (Bailey, 'To my loving friends at Limerick' in John Bailey, *Man's chief end to glorify God* (Boston, 1689), p. 12). [15] This model is more fully developed in Raymond Gillespie, 'Dissenters and nonconformists' in Herlihy (ed.), *The Irish dissenting*

structures of Presbyterianism in Ulster consolidated themselves in the late seventeenth century the minister became a broker between the local congregation and the centralizing structures. Each congregation was required to support its own minister, at a level of income determined by the presbytery. The minister's orthodoxy and educational qualifications were centrally approved. While ministers became the guarantors of orthodoxy within their own communities they also became foci of the tensions which existed between local realities and centralist aspirations and which led to local outbursts of anti-clericalism.[16] Between these two poles there was a wide variety of ministerial activity and experience.

In the rural dissenting communities of southern Ireland most congregations could not support their own ministers, unless a wealthy patron stepped into the breach. Travelling preachers sometimes emerged, supported by local families in their work. Ann Fowke, for instance, recorded how her grandfather 'kept two or three rooms furnished for the conveniency of travelling' ministers'.[17] The Dublin Presbyterian, John Cook, spent most of 1698 on a preaching tour of Carlow, Clonmel, Waterford, Cork, Kinsale and Limerick before being established with a congregation supported by a patron at Tipperary.[18] On the more radical wing of dissent Zephany Smith of Multyfarnham in Westmeath, who had come to Ireland from New England in the 1650s, began a preaching tour on 17 March 1663, moving from Cloyne to Bandon, Kinsale, Cork 'and other places'. By 29 May he was near Clonmel in the house of Thomas Batty 'where he preached and read a psalm to Mrs Batty and her family and two men of Clonmel and intended to make known to them hereupon what God had made known to him'. He was arrested by soldiers but hoped to preach again 'in God's good time'.[19]

Despite the difficulties presented by these varying styles of dissenting preaching ministry it is possible to hazard some form of generalization about the relationships between ministers and their flock. A useful starting point is provided by some comments by Robert Chambers, a Dublin Presbyterian minister who had previously been both a clergyman of the Church of Ireland and an Independent preacher. In his catechism of 1679 Chambers used his commentary on the sixty-fourth question in the Westminster Shorter Catechism (on the fifth commandment) to set out what he saw as a contract between ministers and people. The people's responsibilities to their minister were

> To hold them in honour and bear true love for their work.
> Diligently to attend their ministry, receiving their doctrine with gladness of heart.

tradition, pp 11-28.   16 Gillespie, 'The Presbyterian revolution in Ulster, 1660-1700', pp 165-8, 169-70.   17 *A memoir of Mistress Ann Fowke nee Geale*, p. 9.   18 Presbyterian Historical Society, Belfast, Diary of John Cook.   19 Bodleian Library, Oxford, Carte MS 32, f. 530; St John D. Seymour, *The puritans in Ireland, 1647-61* (Oxford, 1912), p. 221.

> To do what they are able to maintain them comfortably.
> Willingly to submit to reproofs and censures.
> Praying for the blessing of God on them and their labours.
> Not endeavouring their reproach but vindicating and defending them against the lies and slanders of ungodly men.

In return the ministers' role was

> In private to give up themselves to reading, meditation and prayer.
> To be diligent in the public preaching of the word and the dispensation of all other ordinances.
> To labour so as to keep the holy things of God from contempt.
> Watching over their flock that they may be not corrupted by false doctrines or evil conversation.
> In being examples to their flock in holy life and good works.
> Expressing their fatherly love to the souls of the people by being much in prayer to God for them night and day.
> Rejoicing in their profiting and owning their thanksgiving to God for it.[20]

In this sort of model the minister appears as a professionally spiritual person whose primary role was not as an ecclesiastical administrator or a solver of the problems of the community but as a preacher, teacher, interpreter of the Bible and pastor. For this reason the laity were urged to support them. As Claudius Gilbert, a Limerick preacher sympathetic to Presbyterianism, put it in the 1650s, 'Christ's sheep must attend their shepherds who are deputed by that great shepherd of their souls', or as Chambers expressed it, 'keep close to your pastors whom Christ has set over you to explain and apply the word of life to you'.[21] These were sentiments echoed by both ministers and laity. The 1692 memorial from the Cook Street congregation to John Pinney, for instance, spoke of the need for ministers to 'break the bread of life to them'.[22] One of the ways in which this piety was manifested in the lay experience was in ministerial learning. Congregations expected their ministers to be learned and to display that learning in their preaching. The London bookseller, John Dunton, visiting Dublin in the 1690s recorded that the dissenters there

> are supplied with sober and pious teachers, among whom the reverend Mr Boyse may justly be named the chief; one who by continual

20 Union Theological College, Belfast, Robert Chambers, MS 'Explanation of the shorter catechism', pp 369-70. 21 Claudius Gilbert, *A sovereign antidote against sinful errors* (London, 1658), pp 18, 80; Union Theological College, Belfast, Robert Chambers, MS 'Explanation of the shorter catechism', sig B1. 22 Nuttall, *Letters of John Pinney*, p. 86.

and hard study every day fits himself with new acquisitions towards the happy discharging of his pastoral care which he expresses with so much meekness and force of persuasion as makes him at once mightily beloved and followed.[23]

By the end of the century even those sects, such as the Baptists, who had begun their ministry in Ireland by relying on untrained lay preachers were forced to take note of the lay demand for learning. In response to this the Baptists established an education fund for the training of their ministry.

The nonconformist ministerial image of themselves as a group of professionally learned and pious men reflects many of the lay perceptions of them. Joseph Boyse, the minister of Wood Street Presbyterian church in Dublin, preaching at the funeral of Rev. Elias Travers of Cook Street in 1705, characterized him as a man with 'a rich stock of divine and human knowledge' which he applied to his flock.[24] Lack of learning could, in the eyes of some, have dire consequences. Thus the Ulster Presbyterian minister Patrick Adair blamed the disruptive actions of Andrew McCormick, who promoted the Covenanter cause in the 1660s, on his lack of education.[25] In the case of Presbyterians the standard of learning was enforced through the requirements of the presbyteries for ordination and of the eighty-nine ministers who were active in Ireland between 1660 and 1690, twenty-eight were graduates of the University of Edinburgh, thirty-nine of Glasgow University and ten of other Scottish universities. In only twelve cases are university qualifications not recorded.[26]

However, learning was not sufficient by itself; it had to be applied in a pastoral context. In addition to describing Elias Travers as learned, in his funeral sermon, Joseph Boyse recorded his 'copious fluency of suitable scriptural expressions' for prayer and the 'solidity [and] the unaffected seriousness and gravity and the flowing plainness and perspicuity wherewith he was wont to deliver the oracles of God'. Even more important was the 'admirable seriousness of his unblemished holy conversation to the dignity of his profession as a minister' and he carried 'his honourable character as a minister without the least observable stain upon it'. His ministry was characterised by 'the glory of God, the reputation of his holy profession, the deification of the church and the salvation of those precious 'souls that are committed to our charge'.[27] Nor was this mere rhetoric over a coffin since other ministers recorded the same sentiments when alive. The Dublin Presbyterian John Cook noted in his diary of ordination that

23 John Dunton, *The Dublin scuffle* (London, 1699, new edition, Dublin, 2000), p. 175. 24 Joseph Boyse, *The works of the reverend and learned Mr Joseph Boyse of Dublin* (2 vols, London 1728), i, pp 430-2. 25 Patrick Adair, *A true narrative of the rise and progress of the Presbyterian church in Ireland* ed. W. D. Killen (Belfast, 1866), pp 284-5. 26 Based on James Mc Connell, S.G. Mc Connell, *Fasti of the Irish presbyterian church, 1613-1840* (Belfast, n.d.). 27 Boyse, *Works*, i, pp 430-2.

> it is aweful to consider that ministers of Jesus Christ are either for the rise or downfall of others, according as they themselves are exemplary for piety or profaneness – they are the salt and light of the world and need to be clear of darkness and corruption.[28]

It was clear in the minds of at least some ministers and laity that pastors were a rather special group of professionals in spirituality.

Like most relationships between professionals and lay men and women the relationship was asymmetrical. This lack of symmetry revolved around the issue of the role and status of the ministerial office. Did the minister draw his authority from the congregation who called him, or did he derive it from membership of a sacred order conferred by ordination? Increasingly in the later seventeenth century the answer to this question by many ministers stressed ordination as their distinctive quality. The Killileagh Presbyterian James Trail, reflecting on denominational divisions in the early eighteenth century, drew the distinction between the 'form and manner of worship that divides the laity' and 'the admission of entrants into the ministry that divides the clergy of both [Church of Ireland and Presbyterian] churches'.[29] Such was the importance of ordination to the dissenting clergy that recognition of orders became one of the most contentious issues between them and the Church of Ireland in the late seventeenth century. The Dublin Presbyterian Joseph Boyse argued violently with William King, the bishop of Derry, that the congregation's right of calling a minister was scriptural but that they did not owe him 'blind obedience' and that the power of pastor was 'for edification'. Boyse was equally clear, however, that ordination was a process separate from a call.[30] The form of that ordination might vary. Presbyterians of Scottish extraction in Ulster held that it should be performed by the presbytery.[31] In Dublin there seems to have been a similar arrangement which also embraced the Independents. At the Dublin ordination of the Presbyterian Gideon Jacque in 1681, the Laggan presbytery noted that 'the English brethren that are of our judgement' might take part and 'such ministers of the congregational way as have been ordained by a consistory of presbyters.'[32] The ministerial concern with ordination undoubtedly helped to give the dissenting churches an institutional shape for it emphasized the importance of the presbytery or group of clergy. As Patrick Adair, writing about the difficulties of the Church at the Restoration, warned his readers, ministers were

---

28 Presbyterian Historical Society, Belfast, Diary of John Cook, 20 March 1697. The biblical allusion is to Matt 5: 13-14.   29 Public Record Office of Northern Ireland, D1460/1, f. 11.   30 Phil Kilroy, *Protestant dissent and controversy in Ireland, 1660-1715* (Cork, 1994), pp 50-2, 173-4; Boyse, *Remarks*, pp 178.   31 For the Ulster practice, Richard Greaves, *God's other children: Protestant nonconformists and the emergence of denominational churches in Ireland, 1660-1700* (Stanford, 1997), pp 176-83.   32 Public Record Office of Northern Ireland, D1759/1E/2, p. 94.

embodied with a society of godly ministers, and by their solemn engagements at their ordination obliged to walk in subordination to their brethren, that they take not singular courses on their own ... though sometimes it may look like zeal; nor walk in a separate way, especially where they may have the advice of their brethren. For a society of godly ministers may expect more assistance than a single person.[33]

The questions of ordination and of institutional development were tightly bound together.

If the institution of ordination was becoming more clearly defined among Presbyterians and Independents in the later seventeenth century, so too was its theology. The ministry was held to be a divine institution which could not be exercised by individual congregations. The Scottish Presbyterian minister of Derry, Robert Craghead, described the Church as 'having a ministry and gospel ordinances according to Christ's institution and our ministers gifted by Him with some measure of competent qualifications for all ministerial work, diligent in their work and of godly conversation'. In the same vein Robert Chambers declared, if ministers did not have those gifts of the Spirit manifested in the ability to pray and preach they should be silenced.[34] The Church of Ireland might explain these gifts in terms of apostolic succession, but dissenters had to invent their own alternative explanation. That explanation was most clearly articulated in an ordination hymn composed by Joseph Boyse in the 1690s which stressed that the spiritual gifts given to the apostles and evangelists were now given to pastors and teachers for their great charge and ministry to edify the Church.[35]

Other dissenting groups adopted different ideas. The Irish Baptists, for instance, urged that there be 'a stablished ministry' in churches and State support in the 1650s made that possible.[36] However, that does not mean that they advocated a formal ordination procedure with a theology of apostolic succession. In the later seventeenth century Baptist preachers such as Jerome Sankey seem not to have been formally ordained and when the Cork landlord Edward Riggs set up a congregation in the late seventeenth century, a later tradition recorded that 'it was his custom to collect his Protestant neighbours and preach to them in his own house on the Lord's day'.[37] Authority in this

33 Adair, *A true narrative*, p. 261. 34 Craghead, *An answer to a late book*, pp 140; Union Theological College, Belfast, Robert Chambers, MS 'Explanation of the shorter catechism', pp 585, 587-8. 35 Raymond Gillespie, '"A good and godly exercise": singing the word in Irish dissent, 1660-1700' in Kevin Herlihy (ed.), *Propagating the word in Irish dissent* (Dublin, 1998), p. 36. 36 B.G. Owens (ed.), *The Ilston book: earliest register of Welsh Baptists* (Aberystwyth, 1996), p. 76; H.D. Gribbon, 'Some lesser known sources of Irish Baptist history' in *Journal of the Irish Baptist Historical Society* vi (1973-4), p. 62. 37 Cork Baptist Church, Cork Church Book, p. 3.

context was derived from the meeting rather than from some ordination ritual. Such a view left Baptists open to the charge from the Church of Ireland of being ill educated and unlettered, and therefore not able to interpret the complexities of Scripture in a way that would be edifying to their congregations.

This spiritually charged and professionally pious ministry, separated from the laity by ordination, might meet their congregations in a range of ways and situations. They visited the sick, especially the dying, to exhort them to repent, they counselled those with troubled consciences and before communion services they attempted to patch up disputes within the congregation for fear that disagreements would interfere with the social miracle of the communion. Many people might never have cause to consult their clergy in this way. Others might see them in a much more generalized way as articulators, through preaching, of the position of the dissenting community. When Joseph Boyse and Nathaniel Weld preached in Dublin on the death of Queen Mary in 1695, one of the congregation, Duncan Cummings, rushed their sermons into print, using a group of Dublin Presbyterian printers, because:

> I judge the publication of 'em may tend to promote more of that good understanding and hearty affection among Protestants which has long been the desire of all good men. And this end I hope they will be serviceable to attain by removing some of the prejudices against dissenters which have so much contributed to alienate the minds of their fellow Protestants from them.[38]

There were also more intimate occasions when ministers and people might come into contact and their relationship develop. The most popular activity around which clergy and people met was preaching. Preaching was seen by ministers as a central part of their work and the sermon formed a focal point of almost every act of dissenting worship from the normal Sunday service to special occasions, such as fasts. At least one sermon was preached every Sunday and, in the case of Burt in Donegal and in some congregations in Dublin, two or three sermons were the norm.[39] These varied in length from half an hour in the case of some Ulster congregations to much longer sermons elsewhere. Dublin dissenting meetings in the 1660s, for instance, could last between three and four hours with most of that time being taken up with the sermon.[40] Indeed this emphasis on preaching became one of the

---

38 [Joseph Boyse, Nathaniel Weld], *Two sermons preached on a day of fasting and humiliation kept by the Protestant dissenters in Dublin on the sad occasion of the death of the late gracious queen* (Dublin, 1695), sig. A1.   39 Union Theological College, Belfast, Burt Session book; Bodleian Library, Oxford, Carte MS 45, f. 437.   40 Boyse, *Remarks*, p. 93; Bodleian Library, Oxford, Carte MS 45, f. 437. It was claimed that the Church of Ireland offered two sermons every week, each an hour long, Edward Wetenhall, *The gifts and offices in the public worship of*

grounds on which the dissenters were both criticized and satirized. Edward Wetenhall, the precentor of Christ Church cathedral, wrote in the 1670s of dissenting preaching which was the 'whole business of the ministry and hearing all the religion of the people as if ... [one] were only to be ever learning and never come to a knowledge of the truth, to have itching ears and an unstable heart'.[41]

Such preaching was a genuinely popular activity and it is difficult to overestimate the demand for sermons by the laity. As the Larne session noted in 1701 'it is considered that unless there be a sermon they will hardly meet'. Edward Synge, the rector of Summerhill in County Meath where the landlord was a convinced Presbyterian, saw the possibilities of this. He wrote to his bishop in 1683 noting the poor attendance at afternoon catechesis and evening prayer, but the inclusion of a sermon in the proceedings 'brought so great a congregation after as before noon' who would then proceed to listen to another sermon by the Presbyterian minister later.[42] It was by the standard of this preaching that people judged their ministers and a powerful preacher was an important draw to worship. John Dunton, sermon tasting in the Dublin of the 1690s, repeatedly stressed this. Nathaniel Weld, Independent minister of New Row, was 'a person of sobriety, learning and solid judgement and much admired and followed for his preaching', he being 'a pious and excellent preacher', while Alexander Sinclare, a Scottish Presbyterian minister preaching in Bull Alley, was 'a most affectionate preacher'.[43]

III

It is difficult to explain fully why preaching should have been such a popular activity because very few dissenting sermons have survived either in manuscript or print and the immediate context of their delivery has been lost. However, we can approach this problem by considering what these dissenting sermons were not. They were neither moral lectures nor philosophical discourses. By contrast, such dissenting sermons as survive are concerned with the immediacy of religious experience and intended, in the words of the preface to Joseph Boyse's published sermons, to promote 'true piety and holiness'. These were sermons preached to a gathered church concerned with practical divinity. As Boyse had explained of his published works, 'how they may suit the palate of curious readers I am not very anxious to know having designed them for the use of such as have a true relish for the plain

God (Dublin, 1678), p. 681. 41 Wetenhall, *The gifts and offices in the public worship of God*, p. 578. 42 Presbyterian Historical Society, Belfast, Larne Session Book, 30 April, 1701; Armagh Public Library, Dopping correspondence, no. 36. The sermons preached at Summerhill are in Trinity College, Dublin, MS 2467, ff 6-42. 43 Dunton, *The Dublin scuffle*, pp 176, 194.

and unadulterated truth of the word of God'. To listen to a dissenting sermon was to come close to 'the plain and unadulterated truth of the word of God' and hence the sermon was often seen as one of main means of salvation.[44]

The immediacy of the message was complemented by an immediacy of delivery. The ministerial presence conveyed the authority of the preacher in gesture and tone as much as in content. While many dissenting clergy preached from notes they did not read sermons from prepared texts.[45] Dissenting commentators were scathing about those of the Church of Ireland who adopted this practice. In 1681, for instance, it was reported from the diocese of Derry that tradesmen would read either shorthand notes or printed sermons to their families and then 'laugh at the bishop and boast that they have done as much as the bishop himself'.[46] Dissenting preaching, by contrast, was more about performance than reading. The difference was emphasized by Robert Chambers who claimed that 'there is much difference between hearing and reading, between a lively voice and breathless lines as much as is between cold meat and hot'.[47] Of course, there were rules for the performance of the sermon. In 1697 the Synod of Ulster declared that preachers must 'use a sound form of words in preaching, abstaining from all romantic expressions and hard words which the vulgar do not understand and also from all sordid words and phrases'. Individual ministers might also give advice along these lines.[48] As a result there developed a particular vocabulary and intonation associated with dissenting pulpit oratory. This was the sort of rhetoric satirized mercilessly by Ben Jonson in the speeches of Zeal-of-the-land Busy in his *Bartholomew Fair*. The criticism was certainly taken in Dublin when the play was performed there in 1670, since Busy was transformed from a layman in the original text to 'the poor shadow of a nonconformist minister'. Honour was only satisfied when the gallery of the theatre collapsed during the performance, leading the Presbyterian minister Patrick Adair to conclude that this was a punishment from God for such impiety.[49]

Even within these rules preaching could be a dramatic experience. John Leslie, the bishop of Down and Connor, probably chose his words carefully when, preaching the visitation sermon in 1638, he observed of the

---

44 J[oseph] B[oyse], *Sermons preached on various subjects* (2 vols, Dublin, 1708), i; sig A2-A2v. **45** For example, *Calendar of State Papers, Ireland, 1660-2*, pp 41-3, 115-6. **46** Charles McNeill (ed.), *Tanner letters* (Dublin, 1943), pp 452-3. **47** Union Theological College, Belfast, Robert Chambers, MS 'Explanation of the shorter catechism', sig A2. **48** *Records of the general synod of Ulster* (3 vols, Belfast, 1890-8), i, p. 25; Thomas Houston (ed.), *A brief historical account of the life of Mr John Livingston* (Edinburgh, 1848), pp 229-30. **49** For the language, Jonas Barish, *Ben Jonson and the language of prose comedy* (Cambridge, MA, 1960), pp 197-204; Adair, *True narrative*, pp 303-4. For the events surrounding this, W.S. Clark, *The early Irish stage* (Oxford, 1955), pp 69-70.

Presbyterians in his diocese, 'while divine service is reading they walk in the churchyard and when prayer is ended they come rushing into the church, as it were to the play house, to hear a sermon'.[50] Later in the century John Dunton witnessed such a performance when he saw Joseph Boyse preaching on the four last things in 1698: 'his subject was heaven when ... I heard him, and he preached in such an extraordinary manner on that subject, as if (with St Paul) he had been in the third heaven himself and was returned to relate what he had seen'.[51] Such performance may have been exceptional, but the importance of such performances were appreciated by others. Edward Wetenhall, later bishop of Cork, preaching in Christ Church, Dublin, in 1672, pilloried the 'inward titillations of griefs, hopes or joys' which formed the core of the dissenting conversion experience and was stimulated by the sermon. He observed:

> and because novelty had this effect especially if it set up (as was the custom) with some mimic gestures and tones [they] therefore could hear sermons and long winded prayers all their days. Nor were they concerned to understand or remember them, much less to practice them. It was enough if they were moved and wrought upon by the present hearing of them ... I am far from censuring all non conformists of this weakness but the event shows it to have been a good many who will say they have wondrously profited by such a sermon of which they are not able to tell you two words ... they mean their affections were tickled and stirred by it.[52]

The importance of gesture was also highlighted in a satirical account of the highwayman Redmond O'Hanlon who, it was claimed, was recruited by Presbyterians in Armagh because of his ability to make 'wry faces' and to imitate the minister's 'pulpit postures'.[53] The sense of the importance of the dramatic performance is conveyed in an attack on dissenting preaching by William Sheridan, bishop of Kilmore, in 1685. Sheridan held that dissenters felt they had worshipped God if they had travelled to the preacher and 'if they commend the preacher for bawling loud and making faces and thumping the pulpit and holding forth for two of three hours and preaching off [the] Book such stuff as it is impossible for a considering person to write'.[54] Congregations clearly expected their ministers to be capable of

50 John Leslie, *A speech delivered at the visitation of Down and Connor held at Lisnegarvey the 26th of September 1638* (London, 1639), p. 4.   51 Dunton, *Dublin scuffle*, p. 194.   52 Edward Wetenhall, *Collyrium: a sermon of destructive ignorance and saving knowledge preached in Christ Church, Dublin, August 4, 1672* (London, 1672), pp 14-15, 22.   53 *Life and death of the incomparable and indefatigable Tory, Redmond O Hanlyn, commonly called Count Hanlyn in a letter to Mr R.A. in Dublin* (Dublin, 1682), pp 7-8.   54 William Sheridan, *St Paul's confession of faith or a brief account of his religion in a sermon preached at St Warboroughs church, Dublin,*

dramatic pulpit oratory. John Cooke, for instance, failed to be chosen as Boyse's assistant at Wood Street in 1703 because of 'the lameness of my voice' and Boyse himself felt he had to defend Elias Travers in his funeral sermon, claiming that he compensated in other ways for 'want of elevation of voice and earnestness of expression'.[55] Failure to convey the Word in an appropriately dramatic way had important repercussions. Some of the congregation might sleep, not turn up, or in the long run gravitate to a more dramatic preacher elsewhere.[56]

If preaching was a ministerial performance, the listening by the congregation was also an active task. Minister and people co-operated in the sermon. In Boyse's published sermons, for instance, he rarely addressed the congregation in the second person, always preferring 'we' or 'us' as a form of address, implying a communal effort in interpreting the message. Active listening was seen as an important part of congregational support for the minister. As Joseph Boyse put it in his funeral sermon for Elias Travers, 'and O my brethren with what ardour or zeal and affection should we speak to you or you hear the great things of God ... And may we so speak and you so hear that our mutual account may be joyful'.[57] Such listening involved more than simply paying attention. The sermon was to be listened to only after diligent preparation and prayer and was to be received with faith.[58] The dissenting style of preaching was to expand and apply the biblical text and in that sense reading of Scripture and preaching were closely interlinked. In practical terms this involved not the focusing on a single text but rather on the interpretation of that text by comparing it with texts from other parts of the Scriptures which might help elucidate it. Chambers, for instance, urged his catechumens to 'be very diligent in comparing one Scripture with another' and ministers, according to Joseph Boyse, were not sparing in their use of concordances. This Scriptural paper chase was an activity sermon listeners were encouraged to participate in and many brought their own Bibles to church. Thus 'a great part of the time [of the sermon] is spent by the people consulting and comparing various parts of the word of God'.[59]

Congregational activity would not stop with consulting their Bibles, for some people at least wished to keep a more permanent record of what they heard. Some took notes which varied from jottings to full transcripts of the text, probably made from shorthand notes.[60] Some of these were certainly

March 22 1684/5 (Dublin, 1685), p. 11. For similar comments by Dudley Loftus, Marsh's Library, Dublin, MS Z4. 5. 14, p. 105. **55** Presbyterian Historical Society, Belfast, Diary of John Cooke, March 1703; Boyse, *Works*, i, p. 431. **56** Raymond Gillespie, *Devoted people: belief and religion in early modern Ireland* (Manchester, 1997), pp 21-3. **57** Boyse, *Works*, i, p. 433. **58** Union Theological College, Belfast, Robert Chambers, MS 'Explanation of the Shorter Catechism', p. 482, 487-8. **59** Boyse, *Remarks*, pp 93, 98 145; Chambers, MS 'Explanation of the Shorter catechism', p. 28. **60** For example, National Library of Ireland, Dublin, MS 4201 (Independent); Public Record Office of Northern Ireland, D1759/2B/2

kept, but in other cases, according to Robert Chambers, notes were discarded after the service. Note taking was encouraged by ministers and it was accommodated in their craft of sermon construction. Joseph Boyse's sermons, for instance, are arranged under headings and subheadings so that their structure was easily recorded either by memorization or on paper in notes. In other cases ministers were urged to publish their sermons for future reference. Boyse's funeral sermon for Elias Travers, for instance, was 'printed at request of the congregation' according to the title page of one printing of the text and his sermons published in 1705 were 'most of them preached on particular occasions [and] are now in compliance with the request of many that heard them collected into one volume'. These seem to have been printed privately 'for the use of the author', as the imprint expressed it, which suggests that Boyse either gave them away or sold them himself.[61] In moving from the oral world to that of writing or print these texts changed their function and meaning, and hence the nature of the relationship between minister and people. 'Writing', noted Robert Chambers, 'is of singular use to keep things on record which else would be forgotten'.[62] However, writing allowed the sort of detailed analysis of content which the performance of a sermon would not. As a result the minister moved from being a focal point for rallying the congregation to the provider of texts around which a cohesive 'textual community', which excluded the merely interested, might develop.[63] As Boyse in the preface to the second volume of his published sermons explained:

> the sermons contained in this volume were formerly preached to you; so to render them of more lasting use and service to the good of your souls is my chief design in their present publication. They may when leisurely read make a more deep and durable impression than they could when transiently heard.[64]

The difference between hearing and reading was highlighted in the typography of the text. Sermons by Boyse printed as single items retained something of the congregational reaction to the text in the numerous scriptural references given in the margin to be followed up. In the collected sermons the marginal notes were removed, suggesting that a less active and more meditative role was envisioned for the reader.

(Presbyterian); Trinity College, Dublin, MS 151 (Baptist). 61 Boyse, *Sermons preached on various subjects*, i, sig A2. The first volume was printed by Samuel Powell and the second later the same year by E. Waters. 62 Union Theological College, Belfast, Robert Chambers, MS 'Explanation of the shorter catechism', sig A2. 63 For the same process of using a text as a focus of the community, Gillespie, "'A good and godly exercise'", pp 24-45. 64 Boyse, *Sermons preached on various subjects*, ii, sig A2.

Boyse was not the only person to appreciate the importance of the written word in shaping the nature of the dissenting community. The Independent minister John Bailey from Limerick, leaving Ireland in 1689, urged his congregation to get copies of his sermons and to use their sermon notes and study them in his absence as a way of providing a focus for the community. Bailey saw the notes as being read out in the meeting so that those who could not read would also benefit.[65]

In this way the text moved back into the oral world of performance. The Limerick congregation were not alone. Ann Fowke remembered how one member of a Baptist congregation 'took short hand most of the sermon every Lord's day which he afterwards read to his family and then prayed with them' and William Sheridan, bishop of Kilmore, claimed that dissenters repeated the sermon they heard in the morning to their families in the evening.[66] Speech, manuscript and print were not distinct ways of ministerial communication but were complementary to each other. In this way coherence was achieved among a wide range of illiterate and literate people around texts which moved easily from oral to written forms and back into oral transmission again, all of which were centred on the minister.

Understanding the full impact of the interaction of attentive listening with performance preaching is difficult. Only one piece of congregational reaction has survived in the form of the testimonies from John Roger's Independent congregation at Christ Church in the 1650s. These portray a range of experiences but one might serve to highlight the main features of links between ministers and people. Elizabeth Chambers, the widow of an army officer, moved around a number of Dublin churches in 1649-50 tasting sermons and judging their preachers. She first went to St Catherine's 'but I could not well hear the minister', and she did not approve of what she heard. Another preacher she frequented 'moved' her, but she found no 'satisfaction' in his sermons. Hearing Rogers, however, it seemed that 'the ablest preachers speak from inward revealing, Christ revealed in them'. Roger's initial message depressed her but she read over her sermon notes and taking her Bible 'looked out and turned to the proofs that Master Rogers mentioned and examined them'. Listening to Rogers preach again she received some comfort and 'I was much raised up and went home with joy' and eventually became a member of the church.[67] In such ways dramatic preaching and the written word served to interact in forming the binding forces between ministers and people and ensuring the survival of the dissenting community.

---

65 Bailey, 'To may loving friends at Limerick' in Bailey, *Man's chief end*, pp 13, 21 32. **66** *Memoir of Ann Fowke*, p. 33; Sheridan, *St Paul's confession*, p. 11. **67** John Rogers, *Ohel or Beth Shemesh* (London, 1653), pp 407-8.

IV

There was little doubt in Ireland after 1660 that the Church of Ireland would be maintained. The result was that the preaching tradition in that denomination waned. What is more surprising is the survival of dissenting congregations despite sporadic pressure from central government for conformity to the Church established by law, the financial commitment involved in supporting dissenting clergy as well as paying tithes, and the social disadvantages of belonging to a dissenting congregation. Part of the explanation of that survival was the creation of what may be described as a culture of dissent bound together by symbols which expressed something of what it meant to be a dissenter. These symbols included the dissenting communion service, styles of prayer, practices of singing and forms of reading (especially the Bible) and hearing.[68] Such symbols were not uniform across Irish dissent, or even within denominational traditions. Modes of singing, for instance, varied between Presbyterians of a Scottish tradition in Ulster and those of southern Ireland who were of English extraction. Central to this was the evolution of a dissenting preaching style which proved to be genuinely popular and through the performance of preaching created a series of social bonds which proved impossible to fracture. The survival of voluntary religion and effective preaching were inseparable.

---

[68] These are examined in Gillespie, *Devoted people*, pp 99-101; Gillespie, '"A good and godly exercise"', pp 24-45; Gillespie. 'Reading the Bible in seventeenth-century Ireland'.

Index

Aachen 33
'Abbot of Gloucester's feast' 91
Abbreviatio Statutorum 82
Abraham 47
Acts of Peter (and Paul) 50
Adair, Patrick 133-4, 138
Adare 84
Ad Cenam Domini, see under sermons
Admonitio generalis, see under Charlemagne, Emperor
Admont, Godfrey of 48
Adomnán (St) 44
ad populum, see under sermons
ad status, see under sermons
Alcuin 33
Alighieri, Dante 124
Alphabetum narracionum 75, 75n60
Ambrose (St) 86, 89
Annals of the Four Masters 91
Annals of Ulster 84, 92
Anne (St), Guild of 73, 73n52
Antichrist 44
Antiphonary of Bangor 33
Apocalypse of Peter 50, 50n31
'Apostles' Creed 34, 53, 111
Aquevilla, Nicholas de 74, 74n55, 76; *Sermones de sanctis et festis* 74; *Sermones dominicales* 74
Aquinas, Thomas 89-90, 118
Ardee 72
Arianism, 22
Aristotle 51n35, 89
Arles, Caesarius of 24
Arley 57n2
Armagh 66n28, 71, 139
ars predicandi 41, 83, 85
Astley 57n2
Athboy 72
Athenry 123
Athy 84
Atkinson, Clarissa W. 100
Atkinson, Robert 53n39
Aue, Hartmann von 47n25; *Der arme Heinrich* 47n25
Augustine (St) 22, 35n75, 54, 65, 65n25, 86, 89-90, 93, 102, 118; *Enarrationes in Psalmos* 22; *Confessions* 65, 65n25; Rule of 60
Augustine (St), Rule of, see under Augustine (St)
Augustodunensis, Honorius 41n4, 48; *Elucidarium* 50n30; *Speculum Ecclesie* 41n4, 48

Bailey, John 128, 130n14, 142
Balbus, John, of Genoa 88; *Catholicon* 88
Bale, Dorothy 97
Bale, John, bishop of Ossory 15-16, 16n7, 94-7, 97n12, 98-100, 100n25, 101-4, 104n42, 105-7; *The vocacyon of Johan Bale to the bishoprick of Ossorie in Irelande* 15, 94, 94n1, 95, 98-101, 101n25, 102-7; *A Commedie of sanct Johan Baptistes preachinges* 106; *A Tragedye or Enterlude Manyfestyng the Chefe Promyses of God unto Man* 102-4, 106; plays of 15-16, 102-4, 106
Bandon 131
Baptists 127, 133, 135-6, 141-2
Barcelona 82
Barry, William 113
Bartholomaeus Anglicus 88; *De proprietatibus rerum* 88
Bartholomew Fair, see under Jonson, Ben
Bathe, Luke 116
Batty, Thomas 131
Batty, wife of Batty, Thomas 131
Bayley, Philip 118
Becket, Thomas (St) 62n18
Bede 48-9, 89-90, 102
Benedictines 92
Benskin, Michael 71n41
Bernard (St) 48, 86, 89; *Sermones per annum* 86; *Sermones super cantica canticorum* 86
Besse, Pierre de 118-19
Bible, exegesis of, in sermons 16, 25, 30-1, 127
Bischoff, Bernhard 26, 28, 31, 31n61

Bishopstoke 97, 105
Bitonto, Luke of 86; *Sermones dominicales* 86
Blatt, Thora Balslev 100, 103
Blenheim 128
Boethius 89
Bologna 83
Bonaventure (St) 48, 48n27, 86, 89-90; *Soliloquium* 89
Boyse, Joseph 129, 132-7, 139-42
Bretha Nemed toísech 12, 12n4
Bristol 105
Bruce, Robert 57n4
Bryn, R.F.M. 86n30
Bull Alley 137
Burgatt, Henry 109
Burnell family, of Drogheda 75
Burnell, Robert 75
Burt 136
Butler, James, duke of Ormond 128-9

Cambrai Homily, *see under* sermons
Cambridge 83
canons regular, of St Augustine 60, 73-4
Capistran, John 88
Capuchins, *see under* friars
Carlow 84, 131
Carmelites, *see under* friars
carols 91
Carrick-on-Suir 116
Cashel 117
Cassiodorus 89
catalogue, of Youghal library 85, 85n26, 86
Catherine (St), church of, Dublin 142
Catholicon, *see under* Balbus, John, of Genoa
Chambers, Elizabeth 142
Chambers, Robert 131-2, 135, 138, 141
Chapuys, Eustace 93
Charlemagne, Emperor 33, 41; *Admonitio generalis* 41
Chaucer, Geoffrey 124
Chillingworth, William 103
Christ Church Cathedral, Dublin 73-4, 137, 139, 142
Chrysostom, John 89
Church of Ireland 128-9, 131, 134-6, 136n40, 138, 143
Ciarán (St), of Clonmacnoise 47-8
Cicero, Marcus Tullius 117
Cigman, Gloria 55
Cistercians 92, 108

Clairvaux 86
Clare, County 58, 90
Clogher 84, 92
Cloghran 66-7
Clonfert 56
Clonmacnoise 56n1
Clonmel 131
Cloyne 131
Cluny, Peter of 90
Coccia, Edmundo 26
Coldewey, John C. 95
Coleraine 73, 113
Colinson, Patrick 103
Collectanea, *see under* Pseudo-Bede
Collinson, Patrick 102
Colmar 42
Cologne 83, 87-8
Colum Cille (St) 47, 47n24
Columbanus (St), abbot of Bobbio 13, 20-2, 38, 42; *Instructiones* 20-1, 21n20, 22, 38, 42
A Commedie of sanct Johan Baptistes preachinges, *see under* Bale, John, bishop of Ossory
confession 65, 65n26, 70n39, 77, 89, 91, 117, 120-2
Connacht 56, 56n1, 81-3
Constance, Council of 87
Constantine, Emperor 44
Constantinople, Council of 33
Cook Street, Dublin, *see under* Dublin
Cooke, John 131, 133, 140
Cork 110, 131, 135
Cork, County 84
Córus Béscnai 12, 12n4
Counter Reformation 16, 111-13, 118, 126
Covenanters 130, 133
Craghead, Robert 127, 135
Cranley, Thomas, archbishop of Dublin 61, 61n14, 62, 65, 73
Creevelea 84, 84n19
Crookshank, John 130
Cross, James E. 39, 39n90
crusades 80n75, 91
culdees 43n11
Cummings, Duncan 136
Cunningham, Bernadette 16, 80nn75-6
Cyprian (St) 54

d'Avray, David 88
Dá Brón Flatha Nime 44
Damian, Peter 90

dancing 67-70
Dante, see Alighieri
Daton, Richard 109, 109n6
David, P. 26-7, 27n46, 30
'Death's Duel', see under Donne, John, dean of St Paul's, London
De duodecim abusivis seculi 14, 54
De modo confitendi 62n17
De principibus et populis, see under sermons
De proprietatibus rerum, see under Bartholomaeus Anglicus
Der arme Heinrich; see under Aue, Hartmann von
Derry 127, 129, 135, 138
de sanctis, see under sermons
de tempore, see under sermons
Dialogues, see under Gregory the Great (St)
Dies Dominica 19
Distinctiones, see under Gilbert the Minorite
Docking, Thomas 74n55; *Super Deuteronomium* 74n55
Dominicans, see under friars
Donation of Constantine 45
Donegal, County 84, 136
Donne, John, dean of St Paul's 11; 'Death's Duel' 11
Drogheda 56, 72, 72n47, 75, 75n58, 76, 76n61, 76n67, 80, 92, 113; see also land-gavel
Dromiskin 72
Dronke, Peter 20
Dublin 60, 67, 73-4, 101n25, 109, 113, 116, 129-34, 136-9, 142; Cook Street 130, 132-3; High Street, 73; Wood Street 133, 140
Dudley, Louise 35-6
Dumville, David 50
Dundalk 72
Dunton, John 132, 137, 139

Edinburgh, University of 133
Edward III, king of England 72n44
Edward VI, king of England 97, 97n12
Elijah 44-5
Elucidarium, see under Augustodunensis, Honorius
Enarrationes in Psalmos; see under Augustine (St)
Ennis 84
Enoch 44

Eochair-sgiath an Aifrinn, see under Keating, Geoffrey
Eriugena, John Scottus 13, 20, 20n14, 21; *Homily on the prologue to the Gospel of John* 20, 20n14, 21
Eusebius 117
evil clerics 70
executors 70
exegesis, see Bible
exemplum and *exempla* 15, 41, 48, 65, 69-70, 70n37, 70n39, 72, 74-5, 75n60, 77, 79, 85, 88, 90, 90n49, 91, 117, 120-2

Fairfield, Leslie P. 95, 98
Fall and Passion 66n30
Festial, see under Mirk, John
Fifteen Signs before Judgement 66n30, 71
Fís Adomnán 44-5
Fitzgerald, Thomas 110
FitzRalph, Richard, archbishop of Armagh 58, 67, 71-2, 72n44, 72n47, 73, 76, 76n67, 78, 80, 80n75
Flemyng, Richard, bishop of Lincoln 86-7
Fletcher, Alan J. 13-14, 42n6, 71n41, 83, 85, 87, 89-91, 120
Flower, Robin 90
Fourth Lateran Council, 83
Fowke, Ann 127, 131, 142
Francis (St) 48, 82, 84; Rule of 83, 123
Franciscan Rule, see under Francis (St)
friars 14, 56-7, 61-2, 62n17, 63, 63n21, 64n23, 64n24, 67, 70-1, 74, 77-8, 80n75, 81-94; Capuchins 116; Carmelites 94; Dominicans 83, 86-7, 109, 112-13, 123; Franciscans 14, 56-7, 57n4, 58, 60n10, 62-3, 66n28, 67, 70-1, 74, 74n55, 77n69, 81-93, 109, 112n18, 114, 120, 122, 124, 126; Third Order 82

Gall (St) 42
Galway, County 123
Gearnon, Anthony 114, 114n27
George, J.-A. 15
Gerson, Jean 86
Gesta Romanorum 88
Gilbert the Minorite 67; *Distinctiones* 67
Gilbert, Claudius 132
Gillespie, Raymond 16-17
Glasgow, University of 133

Goodacre, Hugh, archbishop of
    Armagh 101n25
Gospel-Book, see under Weissenburg,
    Otfrid of
Graeculus 86
Green, D.H. 55
Greenock 72
Grégoire, Réginald 36
Gregory the Great (St) 23, 49, 51, 86,
    89-90, 102; *Dialogues* 86; *Homilia in
    Evangelia* 49; *Letters* 86; *Moralia in
    Job* 51
Grosjean, Paul 43

Habe, Adam 83n14
Hadfield, Andrew 101-2
hand, moralized 77, 77n72, 79
Happé, Peter 94, 98, 103
Hartry, Malachy 16, 108
Hauck, Albert 20-1, 21n20
Hel, Patrick 87
Heliotrophium, see under Kearney,
    Barnabas
Henry III, king of England 80n75
Henry V, king of England 76n63,
    76n66
Herefordshire 62n16
Herolt, John 87-8
High Street, Dublin, *see under* Dublin
Himmel und Hölle 51, 51n34
Hogge, William 73
Holywood, Christopher 113
Homilia in Evangelia, see under Gregory
    the Great (St)
homiliaries, see under sermons
Homiliary of Toledo 36
homilies, see sermons
Homiliu-Bok 43
*Homily on the prologue to the Gospel of
    John, see under* Eriugena, John
    Scottus
Hothum, John 66-7

Ignorancia sacerdotum 65-6n28
improperia 63
Independents 127, 129, 131, 134-5, 137,
    140n60, 142
'In nomine Dei summi' 13, 30
Instructiones; see under Columbanus
    (St), abbot of Bobbio

Jacque, Gideon 134
James (St) 70n37

Jerome (St) 46, 89-90
Jesuits 111, 113-14, 116
Jonson, Ben 138; *Bartholomew Fair* 138

Kantwell, Nicholas 74n57
Katwell, Nicholas 74
Kearney, Barnabas 109n6, 113n21, 114,
    116, 116n33, 117-18; *Heliotrophium*
    109n6, 116n33
Kearney, David, archbishop of Cashel
    111, 116n33
Keating, Geoffrey 112n20, 113n21,
    118, 118n39, 119-20, 120n52, 121-
    2, 122n59, 123-5, 125n78, 126;
    Eochair-sgiath an Aifrinn, 119-22;
    Trí bior-ghaoithe an bháis 112n20,
    118-19
Kells 72
Kempe, Margery 98-100, 102, 105; *The
    book of Margery Kempe* 15, 98-9,
    102, 105
Kenney, J.F. 21, 38
Kilcrea 88
Kildare, Michael of 63
Kilkenny 15, 16n7, 74n57, 84, 92, 97,
    101, 106, 108, 110-11, 127
Killileagh 134
King, John N. 94, 98, 103
King, William, bishop of Derry and
    archbishop of Dublin 128, 134
Kinsale 131
Knock, John 66

Laggan 134
Laing, Margaret 61n16, 66n29
Laistner, M.L.W. 30-1
Lambeth, Council of 65, 65n28
Lambrecht, Joos 95
land-gavel, of Drogheda 75, 76n61
'Land of Cokaygne' 92
Lapidge, Michael 21
Larne 137
Lausanne, James of 86, 86n27;
    Sermones dominicales 86
lawyers 70
Lecce, Robert Carraciolo of 87; *opera
    varia* 87; *Sermones dominicales* 87;
    Sermones de laudibus sanctorum 87
Leclerq, J. 30
Ledrede, Richard, bishop of Ossory 92,
    92n60
Legenda aurea, see under Voragine,
    James of

Index

Leighlin 84
Leinster 84
Leitrim, County 84
Leo III, pope 33
Leslie, John, bishop of Down and Connor 138
Lete þe cukewald syte at hom 68
Letters, of St Gregory the Great, *see under* Gregory the Great (St)
Liber exemplorum 56-7, 60-1, 70-1, 78, 83
Life of Adam and Eve 47n25
Lilleshall Abbey, Shropshire 73
Limerick 58n6, 90, 109, 128, 130n14, 131-2, 142
Lismore 125
Little, A.G. 70
Lochmayr, Michael 87
Lockwode, Thomas 101
Loftus, Dudley 140n54
Lollards 55, 74
Lombard, Peter 89-90; *Sentences* 89
Lombard, Thomas 16, 108
Lombardy 21
London 132
Londonderry, County 126
Lord's Prayer 23; see also *Pater noster*
Louerd, þu clepedest me 64
Louth, County 72
Louvain 114, 120, 124

Mac Aingil, Aodh 113n21, 120, 121n55, 124; *Scathán Shacramuinte na haithridhe* 121, 124
McCormick, Andrew 133
McCrodyn, Turlogh 126
Mac Donncha, Frederic 40, 53, 54n40
Mac Eoin, Gearóid 40, 53
MacGrath, Bernard 92
MacGrath, Brian 84
Mac Mahon, Thomas 113
McNally, Robert 19, 19n5, 27, 30, 30n54, 31-5, 37-8
McNamara, Martin 25n40, 29n53, 36, 43n13, 50
McNulty, Angus 92
Magnum speculum exemplorum 120-1, 121n56, 122, 122n59
Maillard, Olivier 88
Man and wyman, loket to me 63
Mansfieldstown 72
Marsh, Narcissus, archbishop of Dublin 128-9

Marstrander, Carl 36
Martin (St) 42, 48
Martin, Lawrence 27-8
Martinsmünster, Colmar 42
martyrdom 18, 49, 49n29, 50, 55
Mary (St), Blessed Virgin 70, 70n37, 71, 77, 87, 89-92, 101
Mary, Queen [†1558] 97, 106
Mary, Queen [†1695] 136
Mathews, William 128
merchants 70, 72, 72n47
Meath, County 72, 137
Meyer, Kuno 50
Mirk, John 73-4; *Festial* 73-4
Mochua (St), of Balla 47
'modern' sermon form, *see under* sermons
Monahincha 85
Mooney, Donatus 84-5, 92
Moralia in Job, see under Gregory the Great (St)
Multyfarnham 67, 131
Munster 81, 114, 114n27, 116-17, 124-6
Murdoch, Brian 13-14, 57, 61
Muspilli 45n16

Nenagh 58n6, 84, 90
New Row 137
Newry 129
Nicaenoconstantinopolitan Creed 33
Nicene Creed 32
Nider, John 88
Nolan, Daniel 122-3
Normandy 76n63, 76n66
Norreys, Thomas 73, 73nn51-2, 74
Norwich, Julian of 98
Nyssa, Gregory of 117

O vos omnes qui transitis per viam 63, 64n23
O'Brien, family of 90
Ó Brolcháin, Máel Ísu, of Armagh 53
Ó Clabaigh, Colmán 14, 57, 60n10, 78, 120
Octavian, archbishop of Armagh 91
Ó Cuinn, Tomás 56, 56n1, 57, 60, 70n40, 83
O'Daly, Tadhg Camchosach 92
O'Donnell, J.J. 30n54, 35
O'Duffy, Eoghan 92-3
O'Fallon, Donal 84
O'Fallon, Donal, bishop of Derry 91-2
O'Feidhil, Patrick 84, 92
Of my husband giu I noht 68

O'Gallagher, Tuathal balbh 91
O'Hanlon, Redmond 139
O'Hegarty, Patrick 113
Ó hEodhasa, Bonaventure 120
O'Heyne, John 109-10, 113
O'Higgins, Philip bocht 92
O'Houlahan, Daniel 123
O'Loughlin, Thomas 13-14, 40n1, 43, 43n11, 55n44
O'Madden, Richard 110
O Maelechlan, Donald 78n74
O'Mahoney, Francis 92
Ó Maolchonaire, Seán mac Torna 120n54
Ó Néill, Pádraig 48n28, 49
On God þu sal aue in wrchepe 66
opera varia, of Robert Carraciolo of Lecce, *see under* Lecce, Robert Carraciolo of
Origen 89
Ormond, *see* Butler
Ossory 92, 94-5, 97-8, 101, 110
Oxford 61, 61n14, 83

Palude, Peter of 87
Paris 83, 86, 112, 112n18
Pater noster 33, 72; *see also* Lord's Prayer
Patrick (St) 43-4, 46, 48, 84, 92; *Vita tripartita* 43, 45-6, 46n21, 47
Paul (St) 44, 61, 100, 103, 103n39, 105, 105n44, 106-7, 139
Pecham, John, archbishop of Canterbury 66n28, 70n38
Peraldus, William 67; *Summa de vitiis* 67
Peter (St) 44
Pinney, John 130, 132
Poenitentiale Bigotianum 49
Portumna 110
preachers, exemplary lifestyle of, *see under* sermons
preaching, in early Ireland; in later medieval Ireland; in early modern Ireland; Protestant; as vector of social values; of dissenters; *see under* sermons
Prebiarium de Multorium Exemplaribus 49
Presbyterians 127, 129-39, 141, 141n60, 143
Pseudo-Augustine 54n41
Pseudo-Bede 19
Pseudo-Cyprian 54n41

Quakers 128, 130

Quatuor novissima, see under Vliederhoven, Gerard of

Ragget, Paul 108
Raphoe 130
Red Book of Ossory 92
Reformation 15, 101, 114, 127
Reimpredigt 42; *see also* verse sermons *under* sermons
Rennes, 88-90; sermons in 42n9
reportatio, see under sermons
Restoration 134
Riez, Faustus of 21n20
Ríagal Phátraic 12, 12n4
Riggs, Edward 135
Rittmueller, Jean 40, 42n9, 53
Robert, Friar 62
Rogers, John 142
Rome 95, 100
Roscrea 85
Rosserrilly 84
Rychmund 76n62

St Gall, Ermenrich of 42
saints, lives of 14, 41, 45, 52-4, 86, 88, 98
St Victor, Hugh of 89
Saltair na Rann 45, 45n18
Sankey, Jerome 135
Sardius 49
Sarmun 64n24, 66n30
Sarum Use 76n65
Scala coeli 121n56, 122
Scathán Shacramuinte na haithridhe, see under Mac Aingil, Aodh
Scéla Lái Brátha 44-5, 45n18, 51-2
Scéla na hEsérgi 44-5
Seebass, Otto 20, 21n20
Sentences, see under Lombard, Peter
sermo ad reges, see under sermons
sermon diary, *see under* sermons
Sermones aurei de sanctis, of Leonard of Udine, *see under* Udine, Leonard of
Sermones de laudibus sanctorum, of Robert Carraciolo of Lecce, *see under* Lecce, Robert Carraciolo of
Sermones de sanctis et festis, of Nicholas de Aquevilla, *see under* Aquevilla, Nicholas de
Sermones dominicales, of James of Lausanne, *see under* Lausanne, James of
Sermones dominicales, of Luke of Bitonto, *see under* Bitonto, Luke of

Index

Sermones dominicales, of Nicholas de Aquevilla, *see under* Aquevilla, Nicholas de
Sermones dominicales, of Robert Carraciolo of Lecce, *see under* Lecce, Robert Carraciolo of
Sermones per annum, of St Bernard, *see under* Bernard (St)
Sermones quondam Ricardi Flemeng 86
Sermones super cantica canticorum, of St Bernard, *see under* Bernard (St)
sermons, in early Ireland 12-13, 18-39; in later medieval Ireland 12, 14, 40-80; in early modern Ireland 12, 14, 16, 81-143; in English 14; in Irish 13-14; in Latin 13-14, 18; in verse 60, 63; ad *populum* 62, 72; ad *status* 14; *De principibus et populis* 54n42; *sermo ad reges* 14, 52, 54; *de sanctis*, 52, 54, 61, 67; *de tempore*, 52, 61, 67; definitions of 13, 19, 19n9; reasons for lack of manuscripts of 12-13; as performance 14-17, 122, 126, 138-40, 143; as vectors of social values 16-17, 127-43; construction of 14, 112, 119; 'modern' form of 72, 74, 76-8; *reportatio* 58-9; sermon diary 58, 72, 72n45, 129; of dissenting preachers 16-17, 136-8, 142-3; Protestant 16, 127-43; preacher's exemplary lifestyle 109; homiliaries 41, 52-3; *Ad Cenam Domini* 53; Cambrai Homily 18, 42, 48, 52, 55
Seven Deadly Sins 66n30, 71-2, 123-4, 127
Severus, Sulpicius 48
Sex aetates mundi 40
Seymour, St John D. 36, 50
Sharpe, Richard 21
Sheridan, William, bishop of Kilmore 139, 142
Shropshire 73
Silvester (St) 44
Sinclare, Alexander 137
Singleton, Hugh 95
Sir Eglamour of Artois 47n25
Skelton, John 101
Skreen 72, 80
Smith, Zephany 131
Soarez, Cypriano 112
Society of Jesus 109, 114
Socrates 117
Soliloquium, see under Bonaventure (St)

Southampton 97, 97n12
Speculum Ecclesie; *see under* Augustodunensis, Honorius
Stancliffe, Clare 21
Stokes, Whitley 40, 42-5, 53
Stowe Missal 18-19, 33, 33n74, 35
Strabo, Walahfrid 42
Strachan, John 50
Strasbourg 83
Strong, Thomas 109
Summa de vitiis, see under Peraldus, William
Summa vocabulorum cum expositione in lingau teutonica 88
Summerhill 137
Super Deuteronomium, see under Docking, Thomas
Synge, Edward 137

An Teanga Bithnua 44-5, 52
Ten Commandments 66n30, 71, 123-4
Termonfekin 72
The book of Margery Kempe, see under Kempe, Margery
The pride of life 60, 63
The vocacyon of Johan Bale to the bishoprick of Ossorie in Irelande; *see under* Bale, John, bishop of Ossory
Thesaurus novus 87
Third Order, *see under* friars
Timoleague 84, 92
Tipperary, County 131
'Tract on the Mass' 19, 35
A Tragedye or Enterlude Manyfestyng the Chefe Promyses of God unto Man, see under Bale, John, bishop of Ossory
Trail, James 134
Travers, Elias 133, 140-1
Trent, Council of 123
Trí bior-ghaoithe an bháis, see under Keating, Geoffrey
Trim 72
Tristram, Hildegard 40, 42-4, 50, 53

Udine, Leonard of 87; *Sermones aurei de sanctis* 87
Ulster 81-2, 83n14, 126, 131, 133-4, 134n31, 136, 143
Ulster, Synod of 138
Utrecht 88

Van, Paul 87
Venice 87, 99

verse sermons, *see under* sermons
Vita tripartita; *see under* Patrick (St)
Vitae Patrum 88
Vliederhoven, Gerard of 86; *Quatuor novissima* 86
Voragine, James of 86, 88-9; *Legenda aurea* 86, 88

Wack, Mary F. 30n54, 37
Wale 116
Walker, G.S.M. 21
Wanne Ich þenche þinges þre 62, 64
Warwickshire 56, 57n2
Waterford 57, 97, 108, 131
Watt, John 61, 78
Weissenburg, Otfrid of 52, 52n37, 53; *Gospel-Book* 52-3
Weld, Nathaniel 136-7
Wesel 95n10

West, Máire 40n1
Westmeath, County 67, 131
Westminster Shorter Catechism 131
Wetenhall, Edward, bishop of Cork 129, 137, 139
White, H.J. 29
Willard, Rudolph 35-6
Wilmart, André 22-3, 23n34-5, 25nn36, 25n38, 25n40, 43
Wood Street, Dublin, *see under* Dublin
Wood, James 129
Worcestershire 56, 57n2, 62n16
Wordsworth, J. 29
Wright, Charles D. 37, 39

Yonge, Henry 73
Youghal 60n10, 85, 87-8, 90, 129

Zachaeus 42

Index of Manuscripts

This Index lists all manuscripts cited in this book. (Page references, which follow immediately after the shelfmark, are enclosed in round brackets to avoid possible confusion with the shelfmark proper.)

Armagh, Armagh Public Library
Dopping correspondence, no. 36 (137n42)

Belfast, Presbyterian Historical Society
Diary of John Cooke (134n28, 140n55)
Larne Session Book (137n42)

Belfast, Public Record Office of Northern Ireland
D1460/1 (134n29)
D1759/2B/2 (140n60)
D1759/1E/2 (134n32)

Belfast, Union Theological College
Burt Session Book (136n39)
Robert Chambers, 'Explanation of the shorter catechism' (132nn20-1, 135n34, 138n47, 140nn58-9, 141n62)

Berlin, Staatsbibliotek Preussicher Kulturbesitz
MS Theologischen Lateinischen folio 703 (85)

Cambridge, Pembroke College
MS 25 (54)

Chatsworth, Chatsworth House Library
Book of Lismore (43, 46-7, 47n23, 53)

Cork, Cork Baptist Church
Cork Church Book (135n37)

Cracow, Cathedral Library
MS 140 Kp [43] (Catechesis Cracoviensis; 25-6, 25n40, 29n53, 30)

Dublin, Marsh's Library
MS Z4. 5. 14 (140n54)
MS Z4. 5. 19 (129n8)

Dublin, National Library of Ireland
MS 4201 (140n60)
MS 9596 (61n12, 73, 75, 75nn59-60, 76, 78)
MS G 49 (120n54)
MS G 333 (118n39, 118n41)

Dublin, Royal Irish Academy
MS 476 [Liber Flavus Fergusiorum] (36-7, 42)
MS 1229 [Lebor na hUidre] (42-4, 44n15, 45, 51-3)
MS 1230 [Leabhar Breac] (14, 36, 40, 40n2, 41n3, 42-3, 45n18, 46, 46n21, 47, 47n24, 48, 52-3, 53n39, 54)

Dublin, Trinity College
MS 52 [Book of Armagh] (31)
MS 59 [Book of Dimma] (33)
MS 151 (141n60)
MS 201 (73)
MS 204 (73-4, 74n55)
MS 347 (61, 63, 66-7, 71)
MS 667 (58, 70n37, 73, 77, 77nn69-71, 89-90, 90nn48-50, 91nn51-3)
MS 1318 [Yellow Book of Lecan] (45, 50)
MS 1995-2008/359 (129n9)

Durham, University Library
MS Cosin B.IV.19 (69, 71)

London, British Library
MS Egerton 93 (46)
MS Harley 913 (57, 58, 60, 61n15, 63-4, 64n24, 65-6, 67n31, 71, 91)
MS Harley 3888 (109n4, 116n32)

Oxford, Bodleian Library
MS Bodley 144 (72nn46-8, 76n67)
MS Carte 32 (131n19)
MS Carte 45 (136n39)
MS Rawlinson B 512 (45)
MS Rawlinson D 830 (130n14)

Oxford, New College
MS 88 (61, 61n12, 62, 62n16, 62n19, 63-4, 64n22, 65, 65n25, 66, 66n29, 67, 71)

153

Oxford, University College
MS Latin 61 (35)

Paris, Bibliothèque Nationale
MS Lat. 2628 (35-6)
MS Celt. 1 (89n39)

Rennes, Bibliothèque municipale
MS 598 [15,489] (89n39)

Rome, Biblioteca Apostolica Vaticana
MS Reg. lat. 49 (*Catechesis Celtica*; 22, 24n33, 25, 26n40, 43, 43n11)
MS Pal. lat. 220
MS Pal. lat. 212

Verona, Biblioteca Capitolare
MS LXVII (64) (*Catechesis Veronensis*; 25-7, 25n40, 29n53, 30)